CONSCIOUS SELF-LOVE

by Jill Blackwell, PhD

ISBN: 9781657653085

Published: January 30, 2020

Copyright © 2020

Except as provided by the Copy Right Act, no part of this publication may be reproduced, stored in a retrieval system or transmitted in any form or by any means without the prior written permission of the publisher.

drjillblackwell@gmail.com / consciousself-love.com

Dedication:

This book is dedicated to Kevin and Sean - I don't know if I picked you, or you picked me, but Thank God! In all my attempts to understand relationships and get them right I cannot thank you enough for ours! I am so grateful for each moment with you great guys and pray daily for our harmonious relations where I accept, honor, and am present with (in a state of joy) your beautiful souls. That the three of us are communing in this life is my most favorite gift from God. I am also grateful for all the family line karma we got to clear in this life and thankful to our helpers! Well done!

Intention:

May every sentence of this text provide helpful and useful information to each beautiful soul who comes in contact with it. May everyone who reads this book grow exponentially in Conscious Self-love. May those who read or interact with this text be blessed with helpful self-awareness and insights, undoing of trauma and challenges, and a redoing of love for themselves and others. May this gift to themselves and others impact our world in such a positive and profound way. Please ensure all complied words in this text cause only good to come.

Thank You To:

This book is only possible because in my journey I received love from the following guides to help me understand and become self-aware on my conscious self-love journey....

Master John Douglas, Thomas Gates, Michael Golzmane, Joel Groner, Artie Wu, KumariDevi/Paula Muran, Victoria Benoit, Hargopal, Danu Morigan, Michelle, and the Dear Mother Meera.

*And of course thank you to my dear friends and family: Gloria, Anna, Vicki, Katie, Glenn, Greg, Josephine, Jen, Kim, Marc, and Jack & Patty! Special thank you to my editors: Alyssa Myers for your help in the early stage and to the wonderful April Krivenski whom I simply adore!

Many thanks to Dr. George Michel who started the whole ball rolling.

** All directly quoted material is believed to be public domain information and available via Internet free to quote sites, or referenced in the Bibliography. All paraphrased and cited (author name) information is also considered public domain and on the Internet, see Bibliography to locate the references. The resources page contains public domain information on the Internet to help readers locate additional educational information by the wonderful authors who developed their helpful materials.

Table of Contents

Chapter One: The Case for Conscious Self-Love..................7

Chapter Two. Something Happened on the Way to Love Myself.....15

    What is Self-Love..................15

    What Self-Love is Not..................17

    Conscious Self-Love Defined..................19

    What Happened to Us?..................21

    Prerequisites and Effects of Conscious Self-Love..................24

    The Timing of Things..................26

    First Relationships and a Lack of Self-Love..................34

    There is Hope for Conscious Self-Love No Matter Where You Are.48

Chapter Three. Self-Awareness: Clearing the Past..................53

    The Family Unit..................54

    Moms..................58

    Dads..................85

    The Parental Unit Relationship Model..................91

    People Who Don't Love Themselves are Mean..................97

    How the External Imprints Affect Us..................102

    The Subconscious..................102

    The Subconscious Story..................104

Chapter Four. Practicing Conscious Self-Love: Daily BEs..................111

    The Lens of Protecting Your Peace..................118

Table of Contents (continued)

    The Lens of Self-Compassion..127

    The Lens of Forgiveness..133

    The Lens of Gratitude...145

    The Lens of Receiving Love..150

    The Lens of Kindness...152

Chapter Five. Practicing Conscious Self-Love: Daily DOs...........157

    DOING your Daily BE of Protecting Your Peace..........................160

    DOING your Daily BE of Self-Compassion, Love, & Kindness..189

    DOING your Daily BE of Gratitude...215

    DOING your Daily BE of Forgiveness....................................220

    The Daily Do of Self-Care..233

    To Do or Be that is the Question..244

    Do Get Help from Others...249

Chapter Six. Helping Others Develop Conscious Self-Love........263

    Life Purpose..263

    Helping Children Love Themselves.......................................270

    Helping Relationship Partners Love Themselves......................297

    Who Can we Trust in Consciousness Raising..........................319

Resources..323

Activities Index...327

Bibliography..329

Chapter One: The Case for Conscious Self-Love

"Your task is not to seek for love

But merely to seek and find all the barriers within yourself

that you have built against it"

Rumi

I am so glad you are in receipt of this book, *Conscious Self-Love*! I got the idea for the "conscious" part of the title because at first I thought we would be raising consciousness (the noun) through the lens of regular old self-love, as if that was the goal state we should strive toward. We can still do that, but now after months of important lessons about self-love, I feel like quite possibly we can use raised consciousness to grow our self-love, because maybe *conscious self-love* IS the goal state!

What if the whole purpose of our time on Earth right now is to learn to love ourselves, unconditionally, where we accept ourselves and take care of ourselves, regardless of the parental/societal conditioning we received? What if we are here to learn from the partnership choices we made (via our very own choices and attraction that grew out those very early experiences of feeling unworthy). What if we are all here to learn how to leave the conditional love behind and learn to love ourselves unconditionally no matter what? Maybe everyone's life purpose is to learn to master conscious (and unconditional) self-love. Sure there will be jobs you will have and tasks to accept if you choose, but most will be related to you learning the one big thing.....to love yourself - unconditionally.

You might even say, *"Oh, I already love myself!! I really do!"* Then you think for a second and it hits you. *But... Wait is that okay? Aren't I being selfish, what about the others?"* Even if you move forward saying, *yes, I want to love myself more-starting today!* you will start to see the ins and outs and ups and downs to get to a state where you feel mostly self-love for yourself.

You might've been working on yourself - shining up your outside parts (I call these your lotus petals). You have read books, maybe even taken classes. You are trying to be more kind, present, less judgmental, more forgiving. You are trying and trying, but there is always a little resentment slipping in, a bit of irritation. You think, gosh, *just how much work do I have to put in here to get peaceful?* I read all the books about the lotus leaves, but nothing about the heart-the juicy center-which I think is the most important part. The center, juicy part required to make all of the leaves healthy and vibrant is your very own self-love!

Conscious self-love, self-acceptance, self-care, self-kindness, self-compassion, and self-forgiveness toward your very own self/soul is not a luxury you can get around to when you have time. It is essential, requisite, vital, and crucial for you to be a good parent, relationship partner, human and behave in the world (for your sake as well as these other humans). I feel like no one ever told me that!!

That's where the conscious part of self-love comes in. Real self-love is complex. It requires you to be conscious and make healthy, loving choices toward yourself and for your well-being and happiness in the context of your momentary self-awareness and self-acceptance. Past discussion of regular self-love might've missed the point and became too muddled with self-care. People saw self-love as egocentric or selfish. *Conscious self-love* seems to be a more acceptable term than just regular self-love. Maybe this is because the misconceptions may be minimized, and maybe because it will remind people that to love yourself unconditionally truly requires some active awareness, acceptance, and engagement (consciousness). You can't be unconscious and truly love yourself (or I have yet to see it).

To love yourself unconditionally does require your consciousness most of the time. It requires you to be looking at fear, others, and your ego while choosing to love and accept yourself unconditionally in spite of these other things. It is a quieting of the ego, it's thoughts and emotions even, and a relaxed and present state of love for yourself. It's not a "now you have it, now you don't" kind of thing. Conscious self-love is a moment by moment conscious decision to relate to yourself (and then others!) in an unconditionally loving way. We try to get rid of, or at least quiet the ego, but in a moment by moment situation you can acknowledge your ego (or quiet it) and choose to love and accept yourself anyway. You can have a discussion with someone who is all ego and choose to relate to yourself and even them with self-love. Conscious self-love is all about you and no one else, or their ego.

I also chose the conscious part of this book title, *Conscious Self-Love* because "conscious" (the adjective) to me means actively engaging, being present, making choices, and relating to yourself and others in the context of whatever you are conscious of. This consciousness is always consistent with good outcomes. There is conscious parenting (Dr. Shefali Tsabary), conscious uncoupling (Gwyneth Paltrow), conscious relationships, and likely many more conscious things to come. I love all of these things!

Conscious self-love can be a noun as in a goal state today, and as a fulfilled state soon. When you do, you will have peace! Practicing conscious self-love (as a verb) is a way of being, which may quite possibly end your never-ending search for your "purpose," your never-ending participation in fix-it courses/book/classes, your unending search for answers, you accepting unhealthy relationships and treatment from others that you don't like-and then blaming it on them. Practicing conscious self-love will stop your confusion, answer your life questions, and bring you back to your true and beautiful and loveable authentic self.

Possessing conscious self-love (noun) and moving through life practicing self-love (verb) will have many personal benefits surrounding your family, friends, and your impact the world at large! Over time, you will see how practicing conscious self-love quiets your ego and it's frantic list of irrational needs. Some maintain you reach enlightenment when you are ruled from your soul instead of your ego. Practicing conscious self-love will get you there!

I added the conscious to this book title to help us get real about our idea of self-love. You will read later about doing and being. Lots of the time when we are in fix-it mode (doing) we will try and fix anyone and everyone (e.g., ourselves, kids, parents, people in the world). This is not self-love. It may look like that because we are helping. Maybe you are doing it on a bigger scale, you started a coaching business and think you are really really helping. You are doing your part and being a very good person! It can appear as though you are doing good for yourself and others; but the helping, fixing, and loving is ego motivated, to get stuff, to prove to yourself and others you are worthy (because deep down you may not believe that). You have been doing nice things to win other's approval, so you can prove you are doing good and are a good person. These actions are not self-love, AND they serve to take us away from this idea of conscious self-love. These actions even help us avoid truly loving ourselves. The difference between conscious parenting and regular old parenting is taking the ego out and parenting from a position of true love, from your heart, soul, and true self. My idea here is similar!

The fixers are reading this thinking *"oh this is my new purpose - to get everyone to have conscious self-love and I can teach them."* I love that and I am not making jokes about you, I am with you. I am/was a fixer!! I am a psychologist and licensed professional counselor. This is my fourth publication to help people. For Pete's sake I started this book in fix-it mode! I wanted to fix you/me. I wanted to do that because I felt like I was broken, so I was sure you were too. Fixers are constant judgers and projectors. *What is wrong with me/you? Hm, I know how to fix that?*, or *I need to find out how to fix that*; making lists of all the things to do to improve in me, you, the house.

When I am practicing conscious self-love, I see my unconditional beauty and I am able to see it in you. I relate to you in a much healthier and loving way. There is nothing to fix and no more lists because we are perfect. But even if we are not perfect, I wouldn't be able to see it anyway because I am not judging or listing all of your problems/things to improve on. All I see is my love for you.

Why do we need this unicorn of conscious self-love? All of our seeing of other's lack of perfection and then judging them, picking on them, and fixing them is a projection of our lack of self-love and acceptance. The harsher our internal self-talk (our inner critic) the harsher our outer talk to others (bitterness and meanness) and judgments.

The antidote for judgment is compassion. Particularly self-compassion. Still, you won't be able to muster self-compassion until you practice self-love. The world needs everyone to collect themselves and find their self-love.

If you were not taught (or shown by overt examples to you, or by watching your parent) how to relate to yourself with compassion, acceptance, and understanding/forgiveness (the very important third component of self-compassion), then I can guarantee you are not practicing conscious self-love. Because our parents were not conscious in their parenting behaviors we received projections of their inner workings and past negative experiences that did not help us develop our self-love, and most likely interfered with it. Practicing self-love is a task you will need to embark on alone and depending on your parental conditioning you might need to unpack a lot of things to get there.

All of your past experiences of others being unkind to you (because as Dr. Shefali noted most people are still unconscious) are obviously upsetting, but if we see the experiences as in the past and lessons for us to grow from, then we can move toward conscious self-love. The whole purpose of such experiences was to get you to see the glitch in your matrix and flip your conscious self-love switch to ON. Because, regardless of how anyone treated you, felt about you (in their actual behaviors OR your perceptions of their behaviors, or even just the vibe you got because of your exquisite sensitivity), you are here to love yourself anyway. Any time you don't love yourself, your ego is in charge and love and connection with your true self is not possible.

Given what has happened in your past, the trauma, abandonment, growing up with narcissists, just plain unconscious parents, picking bad partners (as a result of one of these problems), what you know about the world, and your remaining life questions, how on Earth can we get from point A to Conscious Self-Love? That is a good question! The conscious self-love journey may require fostering self-awareness, self-acceptance, understanding of other's behavior and your behavior, undoing, relearning. The un's and re's may require little tweaks, or big tweaks, depending on the conditions placed on the love you received all through this life (and maybe before!). Little or big tweaks depending on your personal experiences with the conditions and who delivered them to you (and even more important-your perceptions of those experiences). The tweaks can also depend on just how long you bought into the conditions before you saw the glitch in your matrix. Still, I encourage you and have hope and faith you can get to the place of conscious self-love!

What a hugely important and challenging quest to possess and practice conscious self-love. Thank you for picking up this book. By just finishing these few pages I think you have answered hopefully your last clarion call invitation to love yourself a bit more. Thank goodness! The calls get louder and louder and I hope I caught you at the molehill instead of the mountain. Still, it doesn't really matter when. All the calls/lessons we've encountered (stimulated by our feelings of lack of deservingness and lack of love for ourselves) were carried out by actors WE hired to trigger us, or remind us of something very important we need to know... **You are worthy of your very own unconditional love! You can start giving it to yourself now. Today. And let's help everyone practice conscious self-love and see the world change in amazing ways.**

We are all teachers and *way showers* for others. We take turns on *who is who* at any moment in a relationship. I know we think there are gurus and experts, but I want to tell you that the only expert on you is you. There are a lot of "experts" in the world right now, but unless they are practicing conscious self-love they will not be able to help you. We cannot give away what we don't have. I could never really help you have more love if I didn't have it myself. Just like we can't be kind to others (even though we desperately want to be) if we cannot be kind to ourselves. We cannot love another (even though we want to desperately) until we truly and consciously love ourselves.

What if you showed and taught someone how to love another person unconditionally? Just what if you showed/taught one person this monumental life purpose task! What if you showed/taught a small group, a bigger group? One by one we change the world. Doing this would require one and only one thing: that you loved yourself consciously and unconditionally and you were out in the world being you. You don't need to develop a master class to do this, just be in conscious self-love with you.

In reading this book you may ultimately help others, but the most important recipient of this gift will need to be you. Just you. There is nothing to do but love you - for real - and all the people you know (or who see you - out and about) will grow just by seeing YOU do this for you. You don't have to ditch anyone, or leave them behind (my personal beef with those "spiritual" messages about how we outgrow people in our lives - more on this later), because you are not defined by anyone or how they relate to you.

How other people relate to you is nothing more than a projection of how you are relating to yourself in 3D as a gift for you to see. Based on the notion that you cannot give away what you don't have, I think these things are true:

- People who practice conscious self-love are really the only people capable of unconditionally loving others.
- People who practice conscious self-love are kind to themselves and treat others with kindness.
- People who practice conscious self-love accept themselves and treat others with acceptance.
- People who practice conscious self-love forgive themselves and treat others with forgiveness.
- People who practice conscious self-love take care of their bodies and teach others to do the same.
- People who practice conscious self-love teach others to love themselves (especially their children).
- People who practice conscious self-love teach others to take care of themselves and the circle of love, acceptance, forgiveness, and care grows.
- People who don't practice conscious self-love can try to be loving and kind to others, but soon the lack of conscious self-love, manifesting as constant fixing/giving and seeking love from the outside, will cause inner and outer turmoil; creating a cycle of self-hate to be passed down generationally and spill out into our world.

Chapter Two: Something Happened on the Way to Love Myself

"Loving ourselves is not being egotistical;
it is absolutely vital to our optimal health and happiness.
The more we love ourselves and embrace our ego,
the easier it becomes for us to see ourselves beyond our ego
and to become aware of our infinite selves."
Anita Moorjani (from Instagram @anitamoorjani)

The road to love myself and to write this book was bumpy, windy, rather long, with numerous stops along the way. Sharing my story and the different things I have tried to arrive at my place of conscious self-love might be helpful on your journey. I suspect you are in receipt of this manuscript because that is the case.

What is Self-love

Self-love is different than other self-things (e.g., self-esteem, self-confidence, self-control), and I feel it is the most important self-thing to cultivate and possess. I believe self-love sits at your core, your center, making all other self-things possible! I think when you possess more self-love than self-hate then all the other self-things can grow. If you don't possess self-love, I don't believe the other self-things will be yours to embody authentically.

Self-love is different than self-esteem, which is holding yourself and your actions in high regard (faith, pride, and confidence). Self-love is different than self-efficacy, which is more about your belief in your ability to impact yourself and others and succeed (your effectiveness). Self-love is an unconditional positive regard for yourself. Self-love is not based on any conditions, any outcome, or any way you need to be. It is a kindness to yourself and an understanding for yourself, your emotions, and your behaviors. It is accepting yourself and all your parts, and it is self-judgment free. I just used the word "accepting" and I should also bring up "awareness" at this time, as it seems as these two things are very close to this self-love concept. I am actually not sure about the order of this triangle (which comes first, is one a prerequisite for another?). Just today I heard Deepak Chopra say, "real self-acceptance (without conditions) is needed for self-love." To me that suggests, self-acceptance is a prerequisite to self-love. Of course that makes sense. For me though, I found it easier to get to a place of love for myself first, and then I was able to accept things about me and my life. Self-acceptance for me was more a process of conscious and unconditional self-love. Still, it may be different for everyone, and a good note to bring up here, we are all our own personal experts. We interact with and rely on lovely people to guide us and help us learn. Still, the greatest guide is your inner self (also called higher self, soul, true self). Whatever she says goes!

When in a self-love state you are still self-aware and living in the now. When it comes to you, you love yourself and are actively responsible for your own well-being and happiness and making sure your environment (external and internal) is supporting this need. When there is a weakness, there is almost immediate forgiveness for yourself. However, there must be no self-abuse, because you love you. You don't want to increase difficulty or add to any suffering. It is just love for the reason of love, because you love you, and you relate to yourself in a loving way.

Holding yourself in high regard, feeling worthy, approving of yourself, and a belief in your ability to move through life effectively are all important, but as humans interacting with ourselves and others in the world, I believe the most important self-attribute to cultivate is self-love. I don't think it is an all or nothing concept, but if you lean more toward the side of self-dislike than self-love, your default will be self-dislike and all incoming information will be processed through that lens.

I don't believe it is the norm to be mostly in self-love, conscious self-love, or even the norm to be in self-like, unfortunately. Because of this, we must take active/conscious steps to grow our self-love and then we must remain conscious of this self-love to maintain it. Once you do, you, your loved ones, and the world will benefit!

What Self-love is Not

As the quote at the beginning of this chapter suggests, there are some misunderstandings about self-love. Self-love is not narcissistic. In fact, I believe narcissists are full to their brim with self-hate. Narcissists want love, but can't supply it on their own. They manipulate and try to control their environments and enter into relationships with others, especially empaths, givers, and people with low self-love to start (which depletes these nice partners even further). This action of the narcissist trying to replace their self-hate with stolen love doesn't work because self-love cannot come from others and we are just left with two people with no self-love.

Loving yourself is also not a self-absorbed "me, me, me" mentality. When you are feeling uncertain of yourself and in need of love from others, it is then we act very needy and everything is indeed about me, me, me. *See me. Fix me. Am I okay? Do you like me? I am doing good, right? Do you see my partner - he is not loving me enough, see? But wait, do you like me?* When you are in self-love there are no questions or needs of this nature. You are not striving for love coins from another. With true and conscious self-love you are far less self-absorbed and realize others' behaviors toward you are projections of how they are feeling about themselves. The same goes for you. If you are experiencing your partner not loving you enough it is because he/she is mirroring how YOU feel about yourself. When you say my partner is not good enough for me, you are really saying - I am not good enough for myself. This is not practicing conscious self-love.

Self-love is also not self-centered or self-focused. I feel like everyone in the world is already so focused on themselves. We move through our days unconsciously, riddled with our problems and anxiety, projecting the problems onto others. This was me too before I stepped into this self-love area. We are so self-focused and unconscious we would miss a gorilla walking across a game of catch (Google selective attention gorilla experiment). There is psychological research showing a person can have a conversation with someone, then a researcher manipulates the situation with a noise so the person turns their head and the target confederate is replaced with a new person, and the person doesn't even notice talking to a new person! Indeed the world of people we are sitting next to right now is self-centered and unconscious.

I believe the amount of self-focus, self-centeredness, and self-concern is directly and inversely proportional to your self-love! That is, I believe the more self-love you have, the less self-centered you are. The Dalai Lama wrote, "Being too self-centered can give rise to anxiety and depression. An effective antidote is to cultivate a sense of altruism, taking the whole of humanity into account." I love that and will add, an antidote may also be to raise your self-love consciously. The irony is a lack of self-love shows up as boastful, judgmental, superior, separate, selfish, and ego-based, and most people this these people are too into themselves.

The paradox of loving yourself consciously is that you actually are less self-absorbed and even less me, me, me. There are fewer relationship problems because you are loving yourself- your partner may notice this too! I am certain conscious self-love is a requisite for happy and normal functioning on Earth.

Because of the confusion related to self-love, I settled on the term Conscious Self-Love and thought it would alleviate the trouble we might have with the idea. Only after I thought of putting these great words together did I realize the qualitative differences between conscious self-love and regular ol' self-love. Regular ol' self-love and saying you love yourself and planning your self-care activities and boundaries because you love yourself are steps in the right direction! But, and this is a big but, I don't think it is enough.

Conscious Self-Love Defined

Conscious self-love is the practice of unconditional love for you. Conscious self-love is loving yourself - with the ego out (or at least acknowledged and soothed). You love yourself just because, and that is all. It is not even about accepting your weaknesses and loving yourself anyway (although that is true), it is more of a global being in a state of self-love. There is nothing you need to be doing or fixing (you or anyone else). Thinking that you need to be better to deserve love from others (or that you need a better partner, or you are a bad partner picker) are all little messages to help us remember our purpose to learn to love ourselves unconditionally. These difficult partnerships showed up as we ordained- to jog our memory back to the state of conscious self-love. The glitches in your matrix that suggest something is wrong are here for a reason. Let them work for you instead of against you. Be grateful for these messages (some people call them lessons). Developing gratitude for these messages will help you practice conscious self-love.

In conscious self-love, you love you - period. It is soul driven, not ego driven. You act like you love you. You behave toward yourself and others like you love you. Like how your best friend feels about you. Not for stuff, not to fulfill your "purpose," not to get reinforced so you feel worthy of love. Conscious self-love is loving yourself unconditionally for the reason that you are a beautiful soul-here learning to love yourself. You impact the world not by developing master classes, but by showing others how good that looks (which ultimately spreads it around although that is not incumbent upon you). Conscious self-love has no ego motivation. Could you imagine this world full of conscious self-loving humans?

With all the self-care strategies and other strategies to grow in regular ol' self-love there are things to do, boundaries to set, a laundry list of items to think about, and ultimately change. You may even get overwhelmed by all the things to do to develop your regular self-love. This is not the case with conscious self-love.

In **conscious self-love** there is nothing to do, there is just to BE, to be in love with you and your beautiful soul. You would think that just BEING should be easier than DOING, but it actually requires more consciousness, acceptance, and self-love. To get conscious we get to the present moment and be there as much as possible. Once present we need awareness of truths about our past story, our subconscious/ego patterns driving our behavior. Then with this awareness we make conscious loving choices instead of our default choices based on lack of love. In conscious self-love we are aware the past was more a series of lessons. We muster gratitude for them (we are no longer their victim). We are in the present and not worried or anxious about the future and the things that might happen. Instead we are hopeful and believe in our adaptive and happy future, and most of the time we are extracting all of the juicy parts of life in each moment. Living it up!

I know people love discussing boundaries these days and I help people set them when they ask, but I am not a fan of boundaries. Can you believe I just said that? When you are practicing conscious self-love you really don't even need a boundary because things other people do are not really problematic. For that reason I am more a fan of helping people practice conscious self-love, where they can exist without needing boundaries.

Boundaries to me are attempts to control others and set up a conditional environment where you won't be triggered. I don't see the use in that. We get great information about our inner selves from our relationships and the mirrors our partners hold up for us (so we can see important information about ourselves). Why do we want to control that? If we create a conditional environment for ourselves with these boundaries, we are interfering with our opportunity to grow in conscious self-love. Moreover, with boundaries we are giving these other people (the boundary recipient) power to dictate how we feel by their behaviors, the exact opposite of what will happen in conscious self-love. In conscious self-love there is a peace and a surrender because of a certainty that whatever is coming is going to be perfect for us in the moment it arrives. If someone tries to (or accidently) does or say something to upset you, it just doesn't upset you. Now that is powerful stuff (and a bit less time consuming than boundary setting too)!

What Happened to Us?

Because it is not the norm to possess this magical panacea and elixir, conscious self-love, I wondered why. It is not even the norm to come across any conscious people in a whole day. I think the parental conditioning we received (even well-meaning), the schooling, and just the mere interacting with other humans (who are also low in self-love and consciousness) causes self-love questions and doubts. Conditional love by unconscious parenting makes us feel unworthy of love. Then, there is so much misinformation about what we can do for ourselves without appearing boastful, selfish, or full of ourselves, that we overcorrect. There is also much misinformation on what it means to have a successful life (our school system, children's sports programs, etc.) that the main point to experience, enjoy, accept, and appreciate life is not considered.

I realized this misunderstanding about self-love in my own children when beginning my work on this manuscript. When I first had the idea to write the book I texted my sons the title and one texted back, "Oh self-love is selfish." I think that is a common reaction. You might've bought this book under a cloak and large sunglasses. You might have it squirreled away under something at home because you don't want to explain to someone that it is okay to love yourself. Some of us are raised to be of service to others (but please know you will be of greater service if you love yourself), and some are raised to be humble and put others needs/wants/desires first most of the time. You might not even believe it is okay to love yourself, or that you deserve love yet. Let's keep going anyway.

I texted my son back... "Loving yourself is the opposite of selfish. Narcissists hate themselves, that is why they hurt others and try to rob them of their love (to steal their love and light for themselves - because they have none!). If you love yourself, you take care of others and teach others to take care of themselves. If you love yourself, you accept yourself and you accept others. Loving yourself is really quite a gift to give to your family, friends, acquaintances, and the world." My son didn't write back right away. I hoped he was pondering my words. I had spent the first 20 years of his life being so devoted as his mother and putting my needs last that I am sure it appeared loving myself was the last on my list - and truthfully it was.

It was in that moment I realized that my valiant efforts to raise a whole person would be lost if the main message I modeled to him was: I myself am not worth my love. That would mean HE is not worth his love. What a devastating realization. His very response to me told me I did something wrong and I needed to do some undoing. How can my son think it is not okay to love himself? It sure looked like some of his behaviors toward himself were not loving, or even self-liking. And if I am being perfectly honest the way he treated himself and his body looked a lot like self-hate. I just sat with that painful realization.

I reflected and then answered my own question. My example to my son was- as a parent, spouse, teacher your needs come second, third (or maybe not even at all). It is true, as parents we take care of our children. It is a hierarchical relationship and we are not to expect our children to take care of us, or to deliver any self-love coins. We can also expect this mostly one-sided relationship will be time consuming and we need to follow more rules to get it right. Still, we can carry out this parenting mission and be of huge service to our children while still trying to love ourselves at the same time (without expecting our kids to fulfill us). In order to do that we would need to be conscious and practice self-love. That was the answer.

It was clear I was demonstrating my "parenting excellence" to the outside world. I was doing this though for some reason, likely an ego-driven reason; to prove my "momming" skills, show I was different than my bad mom, and get some love coins from my kids for my valiant and great efforts.

My non-conscious parenting behaviors, driven by the conditional and unconscious parenting I received likely impacted their feelings of responsibility to me; which I didn't really want to do. The message from the beginning should have been, in this family we ALL love ourselves. My service to my sons is now more of a reflection of me loving myself, my beautiful choices, and my life. Of course I love the stuffing out of them. I am concentrating less about parenting instructions (after reading 25+ books about getting parenting right) and failing; and focusing more on parenting from my place of conscious self-love. In this place I am relating to them in a much better way and even showing them a thing or two about healthy ways to relate to themselves.

Interestingly, both boys picked up on my transformation, and our relationships got even more harmonious (which I did not specifically intend for) when I started showing up differently, not for them, but for me! When I started practicing conscious self-love. They caught on and I saw them relate to me differently AND relate to themselves differently! It was like they now had permission to love, accept, and have compassion for themselves. Even after my years of fixing and controlling them.

It is my belief that being high in conscious self-love will take care most of life's possible insults and help you smoothly navigate the bumps. I think of all the turmoil our kids face with drug use, bullying, suicide, or abuse of self and others and think gosh if you really loved yourself, you'd have to take better care of you.

I couldn't give the self-love message (either modeling it, or speaking to it) from the beginning because I didn't know about self-love. I certainly was not in possession of it and sadly instead modeled quite a bit of self-dislike to my loved ones. I provided unhelpful messages of how to treat me and how I/they could ultimately expect to be treated by others (because of the abuse I encountered in my life, but even more so by **how I internalized the abuse** and made it significant in my life story). I had no one person in my life to provide context to the things that were happening to me in my youth to prevent the experiences being processed as trauma. I made the hard parts of my life story significant and kept them going with intention, regret, and resentment. But, that is not the only way to deal with the past.

Once I became aware of the layered situation, I tried many wonderful things to undo the conditioning from my mom. The conditioning turned into subconscious patterns I carried with me and ruled most of my days. My days were not about me. Once I became aware of that situation I was able to grow. Once my realization and path to the self-love panacea opened up, I couldn't help but grow. Some things I tried were so very helpful in leading me to self-love, and even the things I tried that stood in opposition to self-love were beautiful lessons of what was not to work for me. There is a duality about things in life (e.g., yin-yang, masculine-feminine, givers-takers). It might be the case you need to see both sides in order to understand the full picture and ultimately determine the best balance for you (in lots of different areas) to live a joyous life.

Prerequisites and Effects of Conscious Self-Love

The importance of conscious self-love for a happy life cannot be underestimated. Interestingly, the prerequisites for self-love are the very consequences of self-love. The relationship is complex. The more self-love you have, the more gratitude, compassion, forgiveness, and joy you'll experience, and then give out. Also the more gratitude, compassion, and forgiveness you have, the more self-love you'll have.

Holy Moly. My favorite thing about complex things is to make them simple. I do love science and analyzing things, but that's all about integrating and synthesizing information to arrive at one simple solution to understand something. As this relates to self-love and my personal life, that meant checking out a lot of information and boiling it down to what worked for me, letting go of the past and other crap, and just making things simple, graceful, and peaceful. For me this simplicity makes me happy. This state helps me see things clearly allows me to help others and myself in most any situation. I can write this book because I engaged with so many helpful resources of people I consider experts. Every time I needed some information it was like a helpful resource showed right up. Are you quiet enough to experience this magic of finding just what you need when you need it in your own life? The first and most helpful of resources were those of Louise Hay, founder of Hay House (the most important publisher/source for inspirational and transformational books and products).

Louise Hay (1984) offered a beautiful dedication in her incredible book, *You Can Heal Your Life*. She wrote, "May this offering help you find the place within where you know your own self-worth, the part that is pure love and self-acceptance." Dear reader, we must find this beautiful place of yours right now.

Louise Hay was really the pioneer of this important self-love work. She knew since the 1970s that self-love was the key to both physical and mental health. Her messages reached, helped, and saved many, but what happened, and why is there so much more to do? Didn't we all get Louise's important memo? Also, it seems like the self-harm we could do to ourselves in the past had lower stakes and/or less harmful consequences to the things happening these days, so the message of the salience of self-love needs to get to you and others *now*.

Think of all the beautiful and coveted attributes for moving through a healthy life: compassion, mercy, love, forgiveness, acceptance, kindness. Do you think it's possible to care for others over and over and not yourself (and not get resentful, bitter, irritated)? Do you think it is possible to be kind to others consistently and be mean to yourself in your thoughts and actions? Do you think it is possible to forgive or accept others for who they are if you don't forgive or accept yourself? Can you have compassion for another, if you don't have it for yourself? Do you think you can love another human if you don't love yourself? These are all rhetorical questions of course.

I heard a little about self-care and tried my monthly massage and bath, but if you don't love yourself, taking care of yourself can be challenging. When we mention self-care it is almost like a joke. We make jokes to test the waters about how this person we are talking to will judge us for taking some time for ourselves. We would never talk about self-love and self-care care unless we were in really safe company. This needs to stop.

The Timing of Things

The concept of perfect timing is really relative. I know we pray for things and usually want them to happen now, but there is a perfect order to things. Although I look back and think, "Wow, I wish I would've learned about self-love sooner, or had it as a youth because it would have prevented a bit of stress/bad feelings and I would've been a better mother." But, if I did, I would have missed out on all sorts of lessons important in my life (and my kids might've missed theirs)! It is too easy for me to see both sides now; understanding the challenge during the lesson but also the positive outgrowth from the lesson. I don't know if I would even trade the pain of the lesson for the growth. In retrospect it wasn't the lesson that was so offensive, it was the extra suffering I added to the lesson. By not recognizing the lesson was there to help me, this caused me to add self-abuse and meanness to myself and others. I added to it because I wasn't practicing conscious self-love. That was the main and really only problem. That is why I am writing this book - to help you avoid the "extra" we so easily add to ourselves when not practicing conscious self-love!

Part of my timing had to do with some lessons I still needed to come to grips with in romantic relationships. In romantic relationships, it is not how much someone loves you that makes you love yourself, or determines how great the relationship is. The success of a romantic relationship is really and completely about how much you love yourself. No matter how hard someone hugs you, they can't put your pieces back together for you (I see that message on Instagram a lot). If you don't love yourself it really won't matter if another person DOES love you - you won't see it, or believe it. There will always be doubt. Searching for clues/evidence/proof of their lack of love instead of their actual love will most likely result in some serious self-sabotage.

Knowing the value of the lesson, I am in an interesting spot as a psychologist. I think my role is not to take the pain away, but to help people see the lessons, and not add any suffering. While the lesson is happening I can assist by helping people recognize what makes them happy on a daily basis. That is really what life is all is about anyway, isn't it? I used to approach people's challenges as a problem solver. I still am, but in a bit of a different way. I help people suffer less, enjoy life more, and make sense of their life lessons, which are ultimately here to be helpful.

A little secret is that you don't even need me, you can do these things for yourself! Still, you might need assistance. If you are in a self-loathing place it is much harder to get up and out to get the assistance you really need. That's why it is good to have a few people around you who practice conscious self-love, so they can help you see even the slightest glimpse of your worthiness of your love. That is why self-love is so important. It is crucial you love and take care of yourself to make sure you see and experience the good parts of life; to recognize your role as your own helper for the inevitable challenges we all face, AND to shine this light for others to adopt as their own.

Relationships and self-love. When you show up in a relationship practicing conscious self-love, you are capable of loving and accepting the other person and being with them in the moment. It is in this place you can experience the fun and joy and even address challenging experiences. You are capable of both giving love AND receiving love. So many people say they want love, but refuse it at all turns. This lack of receiving behavior harms a person, and robs their partner of getting to give to them (and all the bonuses that come with giving).

In order for you to have self-love you must master the art of both giving and receiving. We will discuss more about how to do this in Chapter 4. There must be a balance to the giving and receiving (in all relationships - outside of the parent-child relationship, whereby the parent is mostly the giver and their child the taker). Giving is sacred and allows the giver to increase their vibration. You must receive to keep your energy fueled. Giving, but also being able to receive, are equally important in manifesting abundance and must be kept in balance. Think of giving as the masculine energy and receiving as the female energy; and strive to maintain both in your relationship. Stop denying compliments, offers of help, acknowledgement, gifts, "oh no you shouldn't haves," assistance, all of it. You do deserve to receive and it is most important that you do (so you don't get resentful later!, and so your nice friends can get their rewards for giving too).

Some people feel awkward receiving gifts, they may feel they might owe someone something, the other person is in control, didn't have a good example of a parent receiving gifts/love because of their unworthy feelings. Maybe they feel it might not be fair to receive, or they are so used to taking care of their own parents and family members, they just don't know how to do receive. The receiving is easy- smile, be grateful, tell the giver how their gift made you feel, show appreciation, offer thanks, let your heart open more and more with each lovely gift. Your gift giver (if they are practicing conscious self-love) doesn't want anything gifted back to them to even a score. They just want you to be happy and enjoy. If your gift giver does want something in return then that is their self-love problem, not your problem (you can give them a copy of this book for their next gift :) Start practicing receiving gifts and love today! Take it all in and just be grateful!

Practicing conscious self-love takes the responsibility off others to put your pieces back together, and fixing all the unlove you felt towards yourself throughout your life. You aren't looking for someone to complete you, fix you, or someone to love you - that is not going to work anyway if you don't love yourself and will most likely just be a burden for both of you. When you love yourself, both parties are free to enjoy the fruits and joy of the relationship and life's experiences with another soul, unencumbered. You don't need anyone to fix you. With you, all parts are already included and you are ready to reveal the 2.0 happy version. I promise.

Plus, if you love yourself, it won't even matter if someone else does - you can enjoy your experiences on your own without triggering any abandonment issues. Most importantly, if someone you love doesn't love you back, that's OKAY (and their loss!). You are practicing conscious self-love, so you are all good! Then, when you are single again and looking for a fun partner to add to your life, you can get on the road to finding a relationship for fun and enjoyment instead of for costly repairs.

I not only engaged in, but sought out relationships with narcissists, people who resented me, and takers. Picked them right out of line ups with possible decent suitors that were normal, caring, and even giving! I passed on the good guys and went right for the trouble and pain because that is what I was subconsciously looking for.

Years of feeling rejection from my mother laid a hefty pattern for me to first realize and then unravel. Before I did that, I purposefully sought out suitors who rejected me because it was so familiar to me and my parental conditioning. I was taking these rejection patterns and wounds, then projecting that out into the world. Like magic I kept drawing avoidant and difficult partners in. I did this because my core belief was that I was unlovable, it was like a self-fulfilling prophecy. A person stands as a mirror in front of you to reveal/reflect something important to you, about you. If you feel the person you are looking at doesn't love you, you don't love yourself. If you feel the person you are looking at is not good enough, you don't feel good enough. If you think the person you are looking at is a soggy chip (sometimes good, sometimes not enough), then you might be the soggy chip! If you see the person you are looking at as adorable, you are adorable.

For me, the same guy with a different face kept showing up and I fell for it hook, line, and sinker. I wondered what on Earth was wrong with these particular suitors that they couldn't see my value (hint: I was not seeing my value-even though it sort of looked like I was- because I was thinking I deserved more)! It wasn't their fault. I gave more and more to get the love I was longing for (which was the opposite of what I should do). It never came back, no matter how good I was. These were not reciprocal relationships I selected, or continued to participate in. I had this gap in me and my partners were just reflecting my issues. Holding up a mirror for me as a gift.

My other problem was also leaving each relationship before I learned my "lesson." Dr. Margaret Paul noted on her website (www.flourishtogether.com), "leaving your relationship-other than an abusive relationship-before discovering the inner fears and beliefs that led to you the relationship in the first place, is essentially a waste of time. You will continue to choose the same kind of person over and over; even if that is not apparent at first-until you heal the underlying issues that led you to choose this person in the first place." Indeed!

I learned I wasn't making bad picking decisions! There were reasons I picked these guys. I had a narcissist mom who was very resentful of even having me. We will learn later that the mom-child relationship leaves important imprints, but as a preview, I went out of my way to select mates to relate to me as my mother did. Prior to learning about self-love, the importance of my past, and how my feelings of rejection (and my projection of them to the world) were at the core - the rejecters were showing up like I vibed out. Once I became aware of why I picked these guys, I discovered I should've received an A+ in mate picking! I followed my subconscious mind's (ego) plan perfectly. These guys weren't bad guys, they did just what I chose them for and continued to reflect to me what I was projecting about myself.

A lack of self-love may also leave you feeling confused about your partner, wondering do they love me, do I love them? That is where the mirror comes in. What you see is what you are drawing based on your beliefs and then they are reflecting back so you can see them. I sat with that for a long time. It explained quite a bit.

Until this self-awareness and self-love about my life, I never got the love I was striving for because I didn't have it on the inside and it couldn't come from outside. Like I said, at first I questioned my suitor selection choices (really all choices I would make in my life) and thought each choice was worse than the previous; a function of low self-love. I could've analyzed this all day/night, but what was really at the core of my confusion was a little sign for me, I needed to love me more/better!! It was going to have to come from *me*, not another person or animal, period. And it was not going to be the phoned in self-love, it was going to be me practicing conscious self-love.

How do you know if you are high in self-love, or practicing conscious self-love? Well, think about this mirror concept and who is in your life right now. Are they all a bunch of soggy chips? Worse yet, are some toxic and abusive? Look at the people you chose. How are you treated in the community? I am not putting everything on you to make you feel bad. I am asking these questions to help you get some insight about how the people you are surrounding yourself with are treating you. This should be a good clue about how much you love yourself. Are you respected at work? Loved by your mate? Have friends who support you?

Look at the people you chose and the themes they are reflecting back to you.

When you practice conscious self-love, love will be reflected back to you. You will be satisfied in your love relationships and friendships, and these people will be kind to you. When you don't love yourself, harsh and sometimes unkind things will be reflected back to you. I often see posts on Instagram about how we are to ditch our friends who are mean, not evolved yet, and/or any platitude about being careful who your main six people are-because you become like them. In theory that sounds good, but those platitudes are only part of the story and not really helpful (unless you like repeating the same relationship mistakes over and over with different people).

The relationships we choose are what we are drawing in (based on what we are putting out subconsciously), and based on how we feel about ourselves. These relationships serve as a mirror for us to see how we feel about ourselves. So really, we need all sorts of people (even some undesirables ha) to show us something important about ourselves. We will eventually be able to walk away, but only when we become aware of them and we change, not them. This is not even about them. Everything you are doing is a projection from inside you and everything they are doing to you is a projection of their own subconscious and not even about you. It is complicated, in that, we are often not aware of our own energy.

Self-improvement and self-love. Even years into my soul growth work, I was still not getting it. I read numerous books on things to make my life better, to fix things outside myself: how to forgive others, how not to judge people, how to be kind, find my life's purpose, how to be a lightworker, the perfect parent, 30 days to meet your soul mate, how to deal with a toxic mother, and so many resources about how to fix my problem of the day. My outsides were shining up quite nicely, but there was still something seriously wrong on the inside.

I see quite clearly now, I could shine up and beautify my outside things (I now call my lotus leaves) all day long, but if my inside lotus heart, my seat of self-love, wasn't feeling good it would cut off my leaf supply. Inside the lotus - its heart - started to represent my self-love and I kept running into evidence that I was lacking! I was feeling unworthy of love, undeserving of love, and surprise... unloved. I was the queen of compassion for others, but showed no compassion for myself. I was unable to receive, unable to set a boundary, and just constantly put myself and my needs last on my list. I was the giver, doer, helper, listener, understander, and provider. All of that would be okay if I loved myself and wanted to be doing those kind activities out of love/joy (if you give for a good reason because you want to - hooray), but I don't think I was. I was doing it for some purpose - to earn someone's love and to prove to me (and maybe to God, to my mom, my kids, the neighbors) that I was indeed a good girl and that I was worthy of love. Ugh.

The world today and self-love. It is hard to get through a day without a reminder of how challenging the world can be with all the trauma and unkindness visible at our fingertips. I am a psychologist so I may see more, but social media and the news are a wellspring of hard stories to digest. I am so sorry about that. How do we love ourselves given the current state of affairs? How do we love ourselves if we didn't have a good model who loved herself, or worse, if there was active abuse or neglect? Well, you having this book suggests you have some call to answer these questions, even if it is outside of your awareness, that something in your life might need a little tweaking. This is indeed the first step to self-love (and the first step for most things according to Deepak Chopra), becoming self-aware. If you start with you, you will make such a positive impact for your whole family (and even their genome!) through daily interactions. The small or large positive changes you make will even impact the world and add to the collective, which would be quite a gift! Thank you!

My "self-sacrifice" (which was really unconscious parenting, too much and too conditional parenting) to demonstrate my love to my sons and others was for me - because of my unloved parts. I mean, I love them so much and still think about them all day long, but my actions were to get their love coins and not just because I was happy and fulfilled on my own. When I did become painfully aware of my over caretaking (to get the coins) it hit me hard. I allowed myself to grieve for some moments. Soon after I realized it was essential for me and for my children (and the world) to love myself as is and strive to practice conscious self-love.

When I began this process I saw time and time again how this self-awareness and effort to love myself (and my beautiful soul) allowed me to be an excellent example of self-love for others. A really neat side effect was my very own self-acceptance and self-forgiveness translated into being more loving, accepting, and forgiving toward others. I believe this self-awareness and commitment to love myself was my greatest gift to myself, my children, and other loved ones.

My detours were not easy. Before I go into them I want to say they have been processed and now I realize the important lessons each hardship afforded me. Most importantly, I am grateful for them as they helped me rewrite my story with more self-love. I didn't see that right away. There were times I didn't even want to process the pain or forgive it. I wasn't grateful for the lesson. I think that is okay. I am now, and that is what is important. There has been so much less pain and suffering for me now. Of course it is not perfect, and sure there will be challenges and things I am not comfortable with, but my default now is to be loving towards myself and it is a qualitatively different place. Still, I remain aware of what is really happening, check in with my emotions, and make adjustments when it is time.

First Relationships and a Lack of Self-Love

Terry Real (relationship expert and best-selling author on the topic) said, "We hold ourselves how we were held, but we can do it differently." I love that. I wasn't in self-love because of how I was held by my family of origin. I was subconsciously picking partners to do what I thought I deserved (which was familiar to me!). Then, my behavior towards the mate was reflecting the ups and downs of how I was feeling about myself (which was also amenable by their actions to me). When I saw that for what it was, it wasn't confusing at all. I believe the tipping point for the reality of ALL of our relationships is recognizing (through self-awareness) where we are with our very own self-love.

I retraced my steps and got to the place where I fell out of love with myself. I realized my mother who had narcissist personality disorder likely contributed, but I want to tell you even the most careful, devoted, giving, and generous in availability parent can turn a child off the road to self-love by how the parent loves themselves (hence what they are modeling to their children) and unconscious parenting. So it is important we ALL know this. Good moms, bad moms, all the moms and dads and siblings in between.

There might be something more challenging than a narcissist for a mom, or less challenging, where the mom seems normal, but is relying on the child to fulfill their love needs (this is VERY common). This stems from the mother's own lack of self-love. All are influential! All of those things have influenced you. Children (you) in each situation will repeat this demonstrated maternal relating into adulthood by treating themselves just as their mom treated them. If she abused you, you will abuse you (pick your poison here - you can berate yourself with your inner critic, use drugs/alcohol to numb the words you are now saying to yourself, etc). We will pick partners that remind us of how our mom/dad treated us, model how we were treated as a kid in this new adult relationship, and then subconsciously continue this cycle with our own children- whether it is in or out of your awareness. Even if you deny it, it is how it is. I am using mom here, but some people didn't have a mom, or some were raised by a different family member. I don't mean to be insensitive- please substitute your most influential caretaker.

Adding to the mysterious information transmission about a caretakers' level of self-love, is the fact that children are egocentric and biased in their thinking. They think their parents are perfect (whether the mom boasts this or not). It would not be normal for a child to know or even think there was something wrong with their parent without some context. Such context is rarely provided by others in our society because we don't comment on other's family relationships and often venerate motherhood. I (and likely you did this too) internalized all of our parents oddness as something wrong with US. Moreover, children, especially exquisitely sensitive ones, intuit how moms and dads love themselves and then replicate their intuition (about how the parent feels about themselves) in all future relationships. The disconnect between what parents say ("love yourself") and what we do (the kid sees how mommy is so mean to herself) can be stressful and confusing for children. The covert love we feel for ourselves (or don't feel) is the great teacher.

Let's say you were the son/daughter of a mom with depression and things revolved around the illness. Almost all of your time as a youth was spent managing your behaviors to not further disturb, upset, get in trouble, get in the way, you name it. This serves us at home, at school, and in all circumstances fueled by conditional love and where you are rewarded for being the good girl/boy. We strive for validation by being the good girl, the good boy, the nice one, helper, you don't rock the apple cart-it is like an addiction. But, the cost of this is you don't come to know your true and authentic self. You don't know your likes/dislikes, needs, desires (as a kid or adult), because your childhood was spent responding to another's mood. It serves us as youths because parents and teachers want obedient/good children and we want their approval. But this does not serve us in adulthood, whereby a different skill set is required to function in society and properly raise the next generation.

Moreover, the hyper focus on pleasing others will be detrimental. If you have not yet had the awareness that you are in hyper-drive, managing your behaviors to please others - and then done something to change it, you are likely now seeking out co-dependent relationships where you can please people, fix people, and help people as you did as a child. Your subconscious/unconscious is stuck in this pattern. We are often not conscious, not happy, and moving through life for other's love coins.

You have heard about the Law of Attraction or The Secret? It isn't magic, or a secret. This attraction process is you projecting out to the world what is in your unconscious (also referred to as subconscious) mind. Then, whatever is in there, determines your thoughts. Then thoughts determine your behaviors, and your behaviors attract to you exactly what you are subconsciously thinking about. The subconscious is sort of mysterious in that we don't always know what is in our unconscious mind, but it determines so very much. This understanding alone is super helpful! In this amazing book, The Biology of Belief, Bruce Lipton wrote," neuroscience has now established that the conscious mind runs the show, at best, only about 5% of the time. It turns out that the programs acquired by the subconscious mind shape 95% or more of our life experiences." Wow. And remember, what is in your subconscious mind is not even of your design and is most likely outside of your awareness….until you make it conscious!

We spend a lot of time keeping our subconscious problems, like growing up with conditional love, out of our consciousness (self-awareness) because it seems painful when we get a small look at it (when you feel triggered). This trigger, or message is more of a gift though. If you lean in to it and feel it and work through it, you have the chance to bring something unconscious to the conscious level. Only there can you look at it and make it leave your subconscious. We want to do this because it will be a much better life for you, if you run it consciously. Then you will have healthier thoughts in your subconscious mind attracting healthier things to you (via your behaviors and energy you give out).

What if you are starting to see the imbalance, the discomfort in some of your relationships, where you are fixing and pleasing people.

You may deny or hibernate more, thinking there is something wrong with the people, or maybe even you. You don't feel appreciated and are getting more resentful by the day. You might be getting triggered by other's behaviors or comments. These are the good signs! We want to lean in here and catch the message. It is time to make some changes. The discomfort is a sign that better things are available for you. You can lean into it instead of denying it, which would work to keep it repressed in your subconscious.

Being a child of someone with a personality disorder can also be very difficult for the child themselves. Indeed, it is really the loved ones of someone with a personality disorder who suffer the most. People with personality disorders don't think there is anything wrong with them. If they do have a relationship problem, they are more likely to blame the problem on the other person. Parents with personality disorders blame children for their relationship difficulties and don't make efforts to do better just for the child.

Parents and others with personality disorders wield a double whammy. First, there are outward manifestations toward you that are cruel (the obvious first layer of the abuse cycle), maybe some messages of conditional love, or maybe no love messages at all. Some people are starting to realize they can move away from such messages and poor parenting behaviors! There is the option of going "no contact" with an abusive parent. There is always the option of boundary setting (more on that later). The wonderful Dr. Shefali says we can even "divorce" our parents who are not practicing conscious parenting! I personally would have loved to know about these options about 20 years ago! The second problem (and maybe even more important problem) is when children come up with an explanation for the abuse, poor treatment, and little love and internalize it, which causes lack and unworthiness patterns to form in the unconscious/subconscious mind. This second and very important layer must be addressed to sufficiently stop the abuse cycle for your family. Unfortunately this is the missing link that is most often not addressed.

It is true my mom harmed me because of her overt neglect, lack of guidance and nurture in almost all domains of human experience (layer one). But I in turn, harmed my children because I didn't model a healthy self-love example because I kept up the negative internalization and subconscious beliefs about myself. I didn't take the second and equally important step in breaking the abuse cycle. I didn't recognize how I made sense of things as a child and didn't correct the way I was relating to myself. Neither mom is to blame (we might be tempted to blame one more, but there is really no need to do that as blame interferes with lesson learning). It was what it was, we can have compassion and understanding, and we can all grow from these experiences.

I was doing everything to tell my children to love themselves, and that I loved them, yet I saw my children in relationships where they were being treated poorly, taking on too much, and hurting their bodies with certain choices. I worried, prayed, and really just tried to get to the bottom of it. I did so well at parenting I thought, how could this be? My actions and behaviors toward them were so loving, so caretaking, so different than my mother's to me. I earned my mom of the year mug (for layer one, indeed)! Yet why were there these problems? *"They don't they love themselves, they don't think they are worthy of love. I wonder why that is?"* Then it hit me, oh no, it is because I didn't love myself and they could see it (I stopped the first layer of the direct and overt abuse cycle, but not the subtle layer two with its damaging consequences). Even if I took my bubble bath once a month and/or tried to demonstrate some semblance of self-care, they knew it was lip service. Because of my self-dislike I was up their butts with my caretaking and making them need me, trying to get my love needs met from them! So, the cycle continued from me to them. I was over-mothering!

Two layers to break in an abuse cycle. The realization of a two-layer abuse cycle is crucial. I was so invested in breaking the overt abuse cycle of my mother to me (as my gift to my family) and I did that! BUT and this is a big BUT, to stop the cycle of abuse you need to: (1) have the insight and make a conscious effort to not behave that same way toward your loved ones, AND (2) you need to remove the effects of the abuse from yourself. For if you don't, even if you don't outright abuse your loved ones, messages will seep out from your subconscious mind (via your behavior) that you are not worthy of love. These behaviors will model and confuse your children about how they should feel about you and themselves. And the cycle will continue!

So I will mention this again, breaking the cycle of abuse for you and your loved ones requires more than you not abusing your kids. It requires you undoing your parental conditioning and finding your self-love so you can model something healthy, and your kids can internalize something healthy. In that instance, and then for all time in your family line, you will have broken the cycle. It sure is something to behold and strive for, I guarantee you that!

Triggers. One clue about how you are feeling about your self-love and things in general is to become acquainted with your triggers. Triggers are helpful environmental cues that trip something in our experience to bring an unconscious pattern to conscious awareness.

When you get triggered your thoughts move out of the present and go to the past (most likely a subconscious fear from your past) and it is difficult to think clearly or problem solve. This process of what is happening is even outside of our awareness. We usually get upset while not understanding the real reason. We may also mislabel the cause because we are just not that familiar with our subconscious mind. I used to be triggered by the word "trigger" and to be so fearful of them and try to structure my day to avoid potential triggers or things that might upset me. Do you do this? It is really no way to live your life.

I see triggers differently now. I now choose to look at triggers how Anita Moorjani advised. She wrote, "Everything that seemingly happens externally is occurring in order to trigger something within us, to expand us and to take us back to who we truly are." Yes! Triggers help you realize something is not quite right and you need some adjustment.

When you view triggers like that, it is easier to see their value instead of flying off the handle or reacting to others/yourself inappropriately. The only requirement to catch something as a lesson and not suffer (i.e., react inappropriately, fly off the handle, be out of control) is your awareness of it, your interest in seeing it as a lesson, and you quieting your mind to hear about this lesson in absolute terms (more with curiosity as opposed to our traditional drama).

I really feel like a good solution to triggers is awareness and to LOVE YOURSELF. Whether you are triggered by an internal thought of your own, or an external event or comment, any scenario where you could be triggered, feel abandoned, unworthy, etc. can be dealt with by your positive unconditional regard for yourself - mind, body, and heart.

Marianne Williamson (1992) said there are only two emotions, love and fear. Love is divine, and fear is your ego. When in fear you can't be in love, and vice versa. What fear is your trigger eliciting? If you are not sure, it might be a subconscious pattern/fear. Is it bringing up something uncomfortable about your past, a concern about your future? It is not likely a problem right this very moment because most often the present moment is the sweet spot (if we took the time to be in the moment, we would know this), but we are often lost in fear! Some say there is no cold just an absence of heat, no darkness just an absence of light. If cold and darkness are not real maybe fear is not either, maybe fear is just the absence of love. Showering fear with your conscious self-love is likely the remedy.

To help us figure out where we are, I like to recommend we first get to a position of quiet, or else we won't even be able to hear what our soul is trying to tell us with this trigger. Once you get calm and quiet in your mind and body, then you can think about the trigger and try to bring some awareness about the reason for it and what this trigger is about. For me, my triggers were so important because they, eventually (after I became aware of their purpose to help me, and got much better at managing them and stopping my suffering), led me to realize my self-love problem and other problems (fear of abandonment, rejection, trust, and a few more even).

Strategy for triggers activity. Here is an early strategy for triggers (even before we get to the Daily Be and Daily Do chapters). Triggers are viscerally upsetting and can elicit the stress arousal response and pain can be stored in your body! It can cause you to worry about the future or ruminate about the past (so we have a mind component), and can cause you to behave unlovingly to yourself and others (heart). Because of this, we need a three-part plan of action to get back to a more loving and less fear-based state that involves the body, mind, and heart.

Body. In the middle of a fear moment I always start with my body - I get to a place of calm as soon as possible. This can be walking out of a situation (you can always ask for a moment), getting to your car, your bedroom, office, empty room, bathroom, a chair, and just physically disengaging from a situation with your body. I like to lay down. We will talk about more body work ideas in later chapters, but disengaging and slowing down is almost always effective for me. As soon as I disengage, I start counting my breaths. Becoming focused on your breathing is a sure way to calm you physically and it leads us to our next part, calming the mind - getting quiet in your mind.

Mind. When you are in fear your mind is running amok! There are things to do, say, be frightened of, and it all seems to be happening at once. After you tend to your body (by laying down or sitting or just noticing your posture in a safer place) and are now breathing in a slow, controlled way, you might've engaged the relaxation response, and that is one sure way to calm your mind. If your mind is still running with thoughts after you tried to just breathe slowly and calmly, then count your breaths. Count 1-2-3 as you inhale deeply making sure your stomach moves out, then count 1-2-3 as you exhale. You can do this for 10 times. You could even say in your head, "*inhale 1-2-3, exhale 1-2-3, inhale 2-2-3, exhale 2-2-3, inhale 3-2-3, exhale 3-2-3, inhale 4-2-3, exhale 4-2-3, inhale 5-2-3, exhale 5-2-3,..........inhale 10-2-3, exhale 10-2-3.* " This slow and steady breathing up to ten will for sure engage your relaxation response and your mind will be busy with counting quieting your thoughts leading to fear. Once you are in a more balanced body and mind state we can add in our heart.

Heart. One of the most effective things to do to get rid of fear/unhappy thoughts is to think of things we are grateful for. This usually warms your heart and brings you back into a state of love. You can think of something related to the trigger (maybe the opposite of it-say you were triggered because your friend said something that upset you or reminded you of past choices, but you are grateful for other friends who might not say that right now). You could also think of something to be grateful for related to the situation in general (wow, that brought up the past; I am grateful I am not there now, and I am recognizing it as the past and right now, I am grateful for this clarity). You could even think of something completely unrelated to be grateful for, your kitten/dog, the sunshine - just something to call to your mind, something that makes you feel wonderful and grateful. Really focus on and feel the happy, wonderful feeling of being grateful inside your heart, let your heart pump that great feeling all through your body, and be focused on the good for as long as you can. More on gratitude later!

You can also ask yourself: How can I be peaceful right now? Something peaceful and simple (most likely about being kind to yourself) should come to you. When it does, listen. It is a direct message to you from your soul! Honor it. Sometimes I put on some quiet/gentle music with no lyrics, pick up my cat, talk to my cat, call my friend, write in a journal prompt book, or listen to a meditation video from YouTube. After the gratitude and heart self-nurturing you can follow up with a related affirmation about yourself or the situation (i.e., I am worthy of love, I deserve love, I forgive others, I choose to live in peace) to help your heart feel good and you happy. Write that affirmation or a nice note to yourself and carry it with you for the day. If you pray, you can ask God, or whoever you pray to, to help you remove the pattern of that instituted the trigger (e.g., jealousy, feelings of not being liked or favored),*"Please remove my pattern of feeling jealousy and help me look for examples of love instead of not being loved."*

We can argue with our thoughts and/or try not to think them, but asking yourself to not think about the purple elephant usually makes you think about it more! We can try and argue with the person or the trigger while in our fear/agitated state, but I really haven't seen that be effective either. Try the three part - body, mind, heart plan and see if you like it as much as I do.

Exploring the trigger when you are ready. After you are calm and feeling ready you can look at your trigger objectively. Your discussion with yourself might look like this: "*Well that was interesting, I sure was triggered by my boyfriend ignoring me at the part. Of course this would be upsetting because it is upsetting to feel unloved and unworthy. I am feeling that. But wait, where is this feeling stemming from, what is this feeling trying to tell me? Oh man, this is how I felt when my mom ignored me.*" You can explore these things (again kindly and peacefully) then put them down whenever you are ready. You can either walk away from the trigger, or return to the person who triggered you in a kinder, growth-promoting way for possibly both of you.

Trying to find the simplicity in something complex can be so beneficial for help in processing all sorts of triggers, questions, or confusion. The right answer is always: *What is the simplest way to peace and love?* Calming your body and cultivating love in your heart really works with changing your thinking. It opens your spirit to hear what you desire in the current moment and then being able to trust it.

Another trigger assessment to make is to recognize most people are not conscious. Most people you interact with are ruled from their subconscious patterns (remember the 95%) and are projecting their unconscious problems on to you, so what they are saying is NOT even about you. Yes that is true, the other person who may have triggered you by reacting harshly toward you (or ignoring you) was doing so because of their subconscious. It is important to recognize what someone says to you is a reflection of their internal world in that moment. It is not even about you! I am guessing nearly 95% of all people's behaviors and words toward you are just projections of their own lack of self-love, or another problem they are experiencing. Don Miguel Ruiz wrote, "Don't take anything personally. Even when a situation seems so personal, even if others insult you directly, it has nothing to do with you. Their point of view and opinion come from all the programming they received growing up." Ah-ha!!!

What if your trigger activated a feeling of being unloved or not worthy of love, or some kind of condition of worth/love from your past - a parent, friend, partner, teacher? I want to go out on a limb and suggest all these triggers are reminders (subconscious or conscious), or blasts from the past that threaten our feelings of self-love (and our feelings of us deserving love and receiving love from another). Relating to yourself in a different way now (with your unconditional and conscious love) can help you change the way you perceive the trigger. You might've believed you didn't deserve to be loving toward yourself before our talk, but now you do, so it could be the case the next time this trigger presents itself, it won't even trigger anything.

What if some person, experience, or your job is constantly triggering you or upsetting you? Take notice! There is a message here for you and it is up to you to find it out! My triggers kept bringing to my awareness the need to fix my lack of self-love, feelings of unworthiness, and rejection (the triggers were the clues I had some unconscious patterns from childhood to fix). This discomfort and these triggers actually helped me figure out what I did need/want in my relationships, career, and life.

After I found my peace and did a little exploration of the reason for my discomfort, I was able to stand up for myself, set boundaries, make better choices about how I spent my time and I started practicing conscious self-love more and more. My triggers were all messages from my soul to live the happy, pleasant, and peaceful life we agreed to. I am so grateful I stopped avoiding my internal discomfort and triggers and chose to explore them and work with them peacefully. This is always your choice to make. The rewards are more than you could imagine, and it was only uncomfortable for a little while.

We choose our relationships and experiences in adulthood. We should choose things we like, make us feel good/healthy, and are good for us, but we often don't. One reason you would choose to not honor yourself and your likes would be if you didn't know what you liked. Another would be if you didn't feel you deserved to have what you liked (because of the subconscious negative patterns). In theory, it should be easy to walk away from a toxic job, toxic friend, toxic situation we previously chose to be in, but it can be difficult can't it?

The reason it is difficult is due to your lack of self-love and thinking you are not deserving of love, care, respect, or kind treatment. This lack of self-love caused you to manage your external behaviors for the love coins, so you are not instituting boundaries, putting your needs first, or even sending out resumes for a different job or partner. In my most challenging jobs and relationships, I can look back and see the little experiences as clues for me now, and how I could have responded if I had my self-love intact; with boundaries and speaking up. But I missed the message and kept my head down. I was managing my outside behaviors just like in childhood. I stayed at some jobs and in some relationships and the clues kept getting louder and louder. I endured and accepted lots of bad treatment. A few times I changed jobs or relationships and things looked a little better, but there was always a tipping point where the judgment/resentment/feelings of rejection came in. I just wasn't practicing conscious self-love.

Now that I am, when I feel taken advantage of, I say something, or disengage as I deserve to be respected at my workplace and acknowledged for the significant contributing I do. You can do this too. When you practice conscious self-love your behaviors change in such a positive way and you are less willing to be in a job or relationship you don't like. You don't necessarily even have to leave the job or the relationship if you can get to a better place in there. And remember lots of experts think we need to stay in the relationship and fix our subconscious pattern or we will keep drawing in the same kind of experience. What if you try engaging from a place of conscious self-love and see what happens in the situation.

For the other relationships with obligations, like family membership, you can still do these things (i.e., boundaries, speaking up, walking away if needed) too. It might be harder because the patterns of interacting the old way are deeply engrained, but it really comes down to you. You can institute a change at literally any moment. It all starts with you and also ends with you. At any time you can make the choice, even with your main and forever relationships, to take care of yourself and share or obtain your wants, needs, and desires. I have seen many books on how to do this (strategies, homework, pep talks, etc), but for me they all left out the most important fixer. Practice conscious self-love. We can have 5 pages of homework for you to stand up for yourself and set a boundary. You can read 200 pages about how to do it. But if you don't feel you deserve to be loved or have good things (because you don't love yourself) I don't think the books, master classes, or instructions are going to get you where you want to be.

I Love My Parts Activity. Right now, put your shoulders back, look at your hands and arms, marvel at how strong they are and all the things they did with you for all these years, how capable they are, thank them, love them, "arms and hands I love you." Look down at your chest, see your heart, with you all this time, you love your heart, "heart I love you." You just must love these inside and outside parts, all of them. Look at all your body parts and tell them you love them. Have a weird thought? Chuckle and love it because it came from the brain you love. The old story did not begin with you, but the new story does. Today when you next look in the mirror you smile at yourself, "You, I love you!" Put your arms around yourself and hug yourself. Sit in that posture for a full minute. Give yourself a squeeze at the end. It is time for you to see you, honor you, feel you, and love you. You are holding this book, that's how I know.

There is Hope for Self-Love no Matter Where you Are!

Once the ah-ha moment came for me, *oh I am most of the time NOT practicing conscious self-love*, it couldn't be unseen. For me, it seemed like that self-awareness of my condition of self-dislike was the turning point for me-the realization of my truth within. Everyone has different truths within. If what you are reading resonates with you, you might benefit from practicing conscious self-love. Can you think about it for a moment? Once I had this self-awareness, I could proceed from a more problem-solving space, a place of action instead of reaction, a place of reflection instead of projection, and most of all, a place of love for me and others. It was the one thing I was missing and greatest gift to reveal. It was the 25th on my Advent calendar!! With this book, maybe it can show up on day 1 or at least day 10 for you.

If you need to grow in self-love but don't feel you deserve it for yourself right now, do it for your children, cat, dog, rabbit. Get it started wherever the motivation comes from. In this book we will be viewing the parent-child relationship from both sides: when you were the child to undo some of the damaging messages/behaviors in the unconscious parenting you received, then some redoing in the form of healing your inner child. Then we can address your interactions with others. If you are at a place where you want to focus on only one of those places-then do that!

Even if you don't have/want children, your conscious self-love is essential in relationships with all humans. Before I had my important revelation I was forever sending love to people. You may have encountered this, or even done it. How nice! I would regularly surround loved ones, friends, acquaintances, or people I saw on the street/online in need of assistance with my projected love. I've come to think that even better than sending my love to someone else is helping that person access their very own self-love. Each person is their own healer and we can pray for others and try to help them, but it is really not ours to achieve for them. Send love all you want, but finish such an activity with a warm embrace for yourself too! You will see in this book I am pretty adamant about others not being able to supply your love, but I think we can send love to help another feel their own love - I am okay with that!

One problem with all my love sending was I was getting depleted (I wasn't finishing with my warm hug). I was so focused on helping others, being happy for others, and sending others love, and so sure that was the answer for life, yet I was always surprised when I felt resistance or an internal stir of discontent. How could this be? I was helping, I was doing what I was supposed to be doing for others. Right? Well sort of.

Interestingly, once I realized the importance of love for myself and started practicing conscious self-love I got to a better place where I was able to give more; but without the sweat and hard feelings this time. My giving came from a place of desire to give, not because I wanted or needed something in return, (I was already whole) but because it was fun and it brought me joy. It is a qualitatively different place than giving and doing to receive love coins. Once you get to this place you cannot go back. If you supply your own love coins (again and indeed, this is really the only way to get them), you will be full. When you help others from this place, you will like it more and they will feel your authentic joy in helping.

The beautiful irony (lesson) was, once I was practicing conscious self-love (and took care of me) nothing was about me anymore and I could be more helpful. I took nothing personally because I saw the truth in things. I was working for my soul and bliss and joy to be present in this moment of an interesting experience. I wasn't working for other's attention and love (who needed it - I already loved and approved of myself). With this new-found love and approval I decided how, what, and when I would express my love and generosity. Choices became much easier to make and my internal radar seemed more aligned, making *going within* to connect with my true-self easier, and even staying in the present moment became much easier.

Something else that became easier was my receiving other's love. If you are not receiving your own love and working for other's love coins you are over functioning and interfering with others who are trying to give you love. You cannot give away what you don't have, so when there is a serious lack of self-love you just can't give any love out. You need to receive some love (from yourself!). I have heard people talk about their relationships like, *oh I am the giver and he is the receiver.* It can't really work like that though (outside of the parent-child relationship). Both people need to give and receive. Reciprocity in adult-adult relationships (giving love and receiving love) should stay in balance. I believe a lot of the stress of the lovely people in the world is because they are not supplying their own love coins, certainly not expressing their need love to receive, and then getting a little confused and resentful. It would be challenging not to feel resentful. Things are out of balance indeed. We think changing the world would be too hard and we retreat. We are missing the easy fix that each one of us should just start practicing-conscious self-love.

Once you start practicing conscious self-love (and taking care of yourself, so your behaviors are loving toward you, to match those love feelings) you end up quite naturally and authentically giving out even more love to yourself and others (normal, healthy love, not guilty love, and recognize you deserve to receive love, too). Another lovely byproduct of feeling love for yourself and behaving lovingly toward yourself is you encourage your loved ones (even the ones who were slacking) to come up to you. Remember we lead by example. If you start loving yourself, they will love themselves and be able to give you a bit more in the transaction. You will see clearly what is happening and nothing will seem scary anymore. No loss, only more love. It is really the only way to change a relationship in my opinion. We will talk a lot more about you and your partner's role in relationships in the remainder of the book, and how relationships change for the better as a function of YOU practicing conscious self-love.

We really can change the world, but we need to start with ourselves, by practicing conscious self-love. When we do this, we will be kind to ourselves. If we are kind to ourselves, we are kind to others. The whole world benefits! Embarking on this journey will change the character of your relationship not only with yourself, but also with your family, significant other, friends, acquaintances, and society at large.

The goal is to free yourself from the lack-of-love mentality that interferes with us showing up for ourselves and others in a loving and fearless way; to free yourself of thinking love is something to obtain or seek outside yourself and working for those love pennies. When you release the idea you (or others!) have to earn love, you will become truly free.

Most often we have to *earn* money, respect, trust, and other things outside of ourselves. The one thing we all have an unlimited supply of, inside right now to give ourselves and others, is LOVE. There is nothing you need to do to increase your supply; you have it, all of it. It is totally free and way better than money, chocolate, or sex. Loving yourself allows you to worry less and open your focus to the joy of the journey. When you love yourself your choices are more about what is the authentic thing for you to do in the moment. The best way to honor yourself and the other person, and to experience joy in the moment. "Oh yes that's it, I am going to do that then." No weird things like passive aggressive behaviors, tests to see if someone loves you and how much, punishing, worrying about if you are being too nice, too mean, or pushing them away, expectations then resentment, questioning decisions, egoist behaviors or harming behaviors - it's just, "I love myself, I love you, what is the most loving thing to do here?"

Moral compasses rise because when I love myself I am capable of actually loving you. When I love you I have your best interests at heart and I could never hurt you, because that would hurt me too. Addiction and self-harm behaviors are ameliorated as we love our souls and bodies. There is nothing to run or hide from. I love my parts and here they are. Your love for yourself can become more important than the pain of the world. It is in this place that you can actually help the world. When you love yourself your choices honor you, others, and the world. In other words, it is hard to be an asshole when you love yourself for real.

Abraham Hicks noted on Instagram (@Abraham-Hicks), "Appreciation and self-love are the most important tools that you could ever nurture. Appreciation of others, and the appreciation of yourself is the closet vibrational match to your Source Energy of anything that we've ever witnessed anywhere in the Universe." How beautiful! Remember, in order to truly appreciate others, you need to be in appreciation of yourself first. You can't give away what you don't have! This quick shift in perceptions on a daily basis can make a tremendous difference in your life.

The chapters that follow provide more information and even suggestions about practicing conscious self-love, but if you got this important message in these first two chapters, and are able to incorporate it at your soul level, you could really stop reading here. This may be challenging due to years of mixed messages about self-love and the conditioning you received as a child and every day since then. That likely needs to be dusted off. I am hopeful the rest of this book will be of assistance. In the first section of the remaining chapters we clear the past by growing in self-awareness, undoing of the parental and societal conditioning you've lived through, and cultivating a willingness to move to a changed place. The next section is about strategies to start practicing now that the conditioning is understood in the form of Daily BEs (mindset) and Daily DOs (behaviors). Finally, we address how to help others develop conscious self-love in order for all of us to live in a more beautiful world. The very end of the book contains my conscious self-love library resources for you.

Chapter Three: Self-Awareness Clearing the Past

"No Mud...No Lotus"

Nhat Hanh

Your past is important in shaping where you are today, but only as important to the extent that its imprints are/were outside of your awareness in your subconscious mind (gently or loudly prompting you to either treat yourself kindly or unkindly, with self-love or self-hate). Your past and its negative effects can cease to be an issue just as soon as you see it for what it was. Take the reins back from those who hurt you, release the subconscious patterns guiding your current auto-pilot functions, and start living with yourself in a kind, accepting, forgiving manner, and with conscious self-love.

The first step in the change process is to become self-aware and to make sense of some things in your past. This chapter is important for all people, even those who have not experienced trauma, challenges in childhood, or conditional love. I don't know how many of those people there are though!

I don't want to dwell on unhappy things, nor on the past, but it is important we discuss your past in order to bring you to a space of self-awareness, especially about your self-love. How your parents behaved toward you, each other, and the rest of your family members, and how they modeled their own self-love (and all your internalizations of the above) were your first self-love teachers. Then your school, friends, other humans, and even the media impacted your self-love. We are exploring not to place blame, but to get insight, so we can make peace and move the heck on from the past.

The past is only a problem when we are not seeing how it is impacting us currently; and/or realizing it, but not letting it go. Your goal in life is to live well. Be happy. Be kind to yourself and others. Enjoy experiences. Presumably then, the way to deal with your past, abusers and all, is to refuse to treat yourself as they did and live well.

Will you please put yourself back in child mode. Think about when you were 10 years old. Visualize it if you can, and let's read the next few pages from your inner child perspective and reflect on *your* parents and their direct loving/unloving behaviors to you and those they modeled to you. It is most likely the case your parents did not practice conscious parenting. Let's see.

*Note to current parents. Where I am going in the next few pages might be offensive for you as a parent (in case you are doing some of these things). When I came to be aware of my parenting mistakes I was very offended by myself. But soon after those feelings I became very grateful to have the insight, as the changes that followed were the greatest gifts to my life. Keeping this in mind, I would like for you not to worry about your own parenting right now. The fact you are reading this book assures us there will be much time to correct anything you want to correct.

The Family Unit

Drs. Harville Hendrix and Helen LaKelly Hunt (1998), experts on relationships, authors of so many essential books on love, and creators of IMAGO therapy, wrote all your relationships are based on the foundational parenting blueprints offered by your parents. Indeed, they noted in their brilliant book, Giving the Love that Heals, "Whether a child learns self-acceptance or self-rejection has implication for every aspect of her relationship with those close to her, especially the intimate partners she will have as she gets older." Wow, right? Another important gem from the book, "we are unconsciously drawn to people who share characteristics with one or both of our parents, probably the one who was most problematic." Oh my gosh! The parenting role is crucial for literally all future relationships. The main idea being whether your parents taught you to love or hate yourself. It explains why you search out others to treat you the same exact way as your problem parent-in order to work though that early relationship glitch (lesson). I assume conscious and unconditional parenting leads to the love side, but the practice of conscious parenting (until recently and really is still) rare indeed.

One of my first resources to lean in to this idea that my childhood was rough and likely was still impacting me was a 7-day healing course focused completely on the undoing of the UNconditional parental love I received. In this 7-day healing course, each day is spent unraveling the consequences of the unavoidable and common mistakes your parents made in raising you. In the course we are encouraged to understand that all parents made mistakes. The parents do this because their parents did the same to them. This helps us understand their behaviors were not really about us, see they were "mistakes," and we can muster some forgiveness (if we can). Then course participants are instructed to go deep into the psyche - on a rescue mission to find your thwarted inner child. The inner child who was shamed and banished during childhood by being, "too loud," "annoying," "always interrupting," "a lot of work," "not good enough at basketball," "a terrible sleeper/eater," "only a B student," "not as motivated as your brother," "stupid." What was your inner child shamed and banished for?

This context afforded by the program and the others started me on my path to forgiveness, but there were still some blocks despite this improved understanding. As I mentioned, forgiveness and situational acceptance (and even gratitude for it) for my abusive childhood only came when I did my core self-love work. My self-love work came about through my self-awareness and insight, the release of subconscious themes and patterns from my childhood, and then finding the resources to assist me in processing all of it. Then all the lovely lotus petals, such as acceptance, forgiveness, gratitude, more conscious parenting, and understanding, became even stronger. Before my self-awareness about my lack of self-love, I was working on shining up my lotus petals and making some progress. Take it from someone who tried for years to focus only on the petals, they just keep falling off until we start to practice conscious self-love and tend to our lotus heart.

It may be important for you to consider how you grew up and the context of your parents' relationships with you and each other. As I mentioned, it is more than likely you have some baggage from your childhood as few people were practicing (and still are not) conscious parenting. Actually, I would say having no baggage would be atypical, and it might just be in that case the baggage is directing your current behaviors from your subconscious mind and outside of your current awareness.

The amount of baggage is something that can vary, but I don't think the variance is based the amount of abuse, but more a function of the seemingly less harmful unconscious parenting. You would think more abuse would result in more trauma and more current problems, but the relationship is not always so straightforward. We know about super-copers and resiliency (those from significant trauma who somehow grow exponentially in the face of it) and people who seem to have had a happy childhood, void of the appearance trauma, to report being weighed down with baggage and maladaptive behaviors. The truth of the matter is, we are not to judge someone's trauma, abuse, or what they may be experiencing. Everyone's perception and experience is their own. That means yours, too! You don't control anyone's anything (especially their understanding of their past) and you don't let anyone control your anything (especially your understanding of your past). Feel that relief.

With colossal baggage or unconscious parenting comes a real need to move on from the past. If we don't, we let the past continue to hurt us in our current days. Terrence Real (2008) calls this moving on from childhood baggage an "unblending" or reparenting our inner child. We do this by releasing ourselves from poor or even just adequate parenting, and we do this so all of our adult relationships, and the constant thoughts we have about ourselves, won't be affected by things outside of our awareness and control.

What happened?? Coming from a place of self-love, let me present the kindest viewpoint. Our parent(s) were doing their best (and as Artie Wu will tell you – people are just acting out how their own parent's didn't love them). So it was really their unprocessed subconscious pain blob who was parenting. Dr. Shefali calls this unconscious parenting. Moreover, even on the best, most perfect day, so many parenting triggers can be triggered, subconscious behavior patterns activated, generations of bad behavior modeled, distractions with their own life, and projecting their issues, or lashing out based on their frustrations, I could go on, but you know what I mean. Sometimes I look back at my mom's more memorable explosions and now see, wow, that had nothing to do with me at all! I didn't see that as a child though, and that is the big problem we as adults are facing, and someday our kids when they are adults, will need help to process.

Being a conscious parent (see Shefali Tsabary in resources section and via Google) is what we should strive for. Conscious parenting is different than mainstream parenting. In conscious parenting you are aware of your own issues and past and want to provide loving guidance instead of rehashing your unenlightened experiences of sitting at the table until you finished your dinner. In conscious parenting we allow the kid to love themselves as a separate soul and not an extension of us. We see them for exactly who they are, which is not really about us at all. We realize we are here to train and guide, to help a child love, trust, respect, and value themselves. Conscious parenting is not about us (let me show the world MY amazing child), or what they can do for us (fill our voids, fix our issues, fan our ego flame). Conscious parenting is not ego based at all. It is NOT, *"Hey look at my great kid" "See how much my kid loves me?"* and sometimes even, *"Do you love me, kid? I need you to love me because no one else does."* Those examples are not conscious parenting FOR the kid; these are examples of unconscious parenting for an adult low in their own self-love. Very few parents parent *for* the kid. It was likely uncommon for your parents to celebrate your unique gifts. Dr. Shefali wrote on Instagram, "Most of us grew up with unconscious parents where we were not seen for who we truly are."

A parent for the kid realizes, Well wow this people-making is challenging. I want to do a good job, but I am so irritated, triggered, not myself, tired. I am sure I am giving some mixed messages, or even blatantly harming my child's psyche. I need to stop it, but it is so hard. I want to be better, but how? I need some help here. Parenting like this (conscious parenting) for the kid is the exception, not the rule. I am sure you were not parented in this way. I think it would come about by really understanding and investing in learning about conscious parenting, but I also have to tell you, I think only parents who practice conscious self-love may be able to pull this off conscious parenting consistently.

In my opinion, conscious parenting is rare because so few parents love themselves. As a new parent I completed much research on childhood/parenting (I mean I have my PhD in developmental psychology) and really tried to get it right, but my mistakes were seemingly out of my control (likely subconscious). I've read many books on the topic; boy I sure thought I knew what I was doing. I wanted to pretend I did. During this time, it was me shining up my lotus leaf on how to be a good parent (without my lotus center of self-love intact though). The disconnect really interfered with my behaviors. I needed self-love to address my subconscious voice in a kind way in order for me to become a better parent.

Moms

I am bringing up moms now because we need to talk about the negative hits to your self-love in childhood for awareness. You just can't separate the effects of parenting on self-love until you have it (oh the irony). It might've been the case you didn't have a mom. You might've had a step mom, adoptive mom, two moms, two dads instead, or any variety of mom or non-mom possibilities. I do not want to be insensitive and I don't mean to be. If you can conjure an image of someone who you consider your primary care-taker then let's focus on her/him/them.

All the great (and not so great) women and men I know have something interesting to say about their mothers. The mother influence is gigantic and can lean toward one valence quite frankly. It is not likely we have an "eh" feeling about our moms - it usually is a totally "pro" or totally "ew" experience and recollection. I don't want to lose you here, but it is accepted in the spiritual community (and indeed made public in the amazing documentary HEAL), that we, as souls selected one person before we were born - and that one person was the lady to birth you. We knew this person was going to be important. How her importance played out for us is now our topic.

Being a developmental psychologist, I know the salience of the role of the mother in absolute terms (in human and animal relationships). The mother wields an insidious influence (covert or overt) over time that can really impact the self-love a child feels or doesn't feel. When mothers are out of self-love, and model self-dislike behaviors in front of their child AND make repeated negative behaviors toward the child, it likely results in what we refer to as the **Mother Wound**. Discussion of mother wounds can relate to cross-cultural and generational issues accounting for women's role in society, and/or it can relate more to parenting. For our purposes, we discuss the *mother wound* as it relates to parenting (although I would agree that the type of parenting you received is likely the parenting you will provide unless the wound has been processed, making this indeed a generational phenomenon). People with a *mother wound* did not have a secure attachment in childhood because of a lack of appropriate mothering (i.e., under-mothering, over-mothering, or confusing mothering) which causes problems in adulthood.

I don't think we all admit it, but it's likely we all have a big or little mother wound to think about. Even though I tried my very best and did a lot of research on parenting, based on my lack of self-love, I think my children would say I left a mother wound. But, good news, because of this insight, we are able to undo it now. Coming to recognize these problems is so very beneficial and that is the reason we are discussing this now.

Many moms are doing their best while some moms are not. It might look like they are really not doing their best, but with a little context we might see that this is the best have to offer at this particular time. The focus in that case should be less on judging and more about helping the children in the direct line of fire of this challenging situation.

Some moms are doing what they can to stay afloat from their place of not loving themselves and modeling discrepancies between their words and actions. Let's take a look at three mothering categories. These categories are really more about a constellation of similar behaviors than categories, but it may be easiest to understand as categories. In each category we will discuss physical behaviors (provision of food/shelter/clothing) and emotional behaviors (provision of love/nurturing/approval/guidance). We can follow the same example of a mom and a child's sporting event through each category. An example of under-mothering behaviors would be not attending the sporting event (absent provision of emotional support), may not have washed the child's uniform, or arranged transportation for the child to the game (absent provision of physical support). An example of over-mothering would be to not miss a game, yell at other children from the stands, email the coach about putting their child in (or other comments); more or less an interference with the normal process.

It also may be the case your mom was one category, but you packed it away as a different one. That is okay. You and your siblings may even disagree about your mom's categorization because even the same children from one house have different experiences with their mother. What is most important is your beliefs about your parent from your child's eye (your childhood story). If you had a horrible parent, but somehow packed it away as okay, then it is!

Going over these behaviors is not meant to upset you or judge you as a god or bad parent. The intent is to get insight on the relationship between some parenting behaviors and self-love, especially how you are relating to yourself now (which might currently be out of your awareness). Bring this information to your consciousness, so you can use it to practice conscious self-love will be very worth this effort. Requisite in this newer self-awareness, is seeing all things (you, your parents) through a non-judgmental lens. And recognizing their behaviors toward you were unconscious, and more about them and not really even about you.

Mom type 1: Appropriate mothering - mom doing her best and crushing it. We are thinking back to your mom here, no thoughts about your mothering allowed just yet. This appropriate mom doing her best and crushing it is practicing conscious self-love and conscious parenting! She is able to be consistently kind and good because she loves all parts of herself, so she can show up for others and model this amazing behavior and way of being. The behaviors she models for her child are consistent and self-love based. She is authentic in her relationships and has relationships, not to complete herself or fix something she believes is broken, but because she enjoys the other person and the time spent together. This is easy to see. There is a peace and joy to her. She doesn't over commit. When asked to do something she checks in with herself to see if she wants to do it. If she does, she makes plans to do it and easily, guiltlessly takes care of the details. She doesn't lie or make excuses; she doesn't have to, because saying no when she doesn't want to do something is a self-love bonus that is allowed. She would never let another treat her poorly without standing up for herself. She is on your side and helps you see how wonderful you are, but she is also honest and you can trust her. This woman loves herself, takes care of herself, makes good eating and exercise choices, accepts compliments, and believes she deserves to be happy. She doesn't check out with a bottle of wine after dinner to cope with her difficult day (okay she may have a glass), she is not on the prowl for attention outside of her marriage, and she is not poaching any of her friend's husbands. She is practicing conscious self-love and teaching her children to do the same!

In her outward behaviors toward her children and others, this mom is also crushing it. She encourages her child to make healthy choices and behave in the same self-loving way toward themselves. She sees the children in their unique and special way and refuses to project her disappointments and unfulfilled wishes onto them. She honors their very existence and is able to communicate her unconditional love on a regular basis. Indeed, there are no conditions for her love. She allows others to be themselves without too much input and generally provides great counsel when called upon; helping others see things clearly. She believes in natural and logical consequences for most things, but steps in to provide appropriate guidance or assistance when needed. She doesn't solve her kids' problems, she gives them confidence and nudges when needed. She is a master at communicating her hopeful beliefs so that others can feel encouraged and succeed while being happy, smart, and healthy. When a play date opportunity comes up, this mom checks in with the kid to see if they want to do it before accepting, not just accepting because she really likes the other mom asking. This mom steps in where there are sibling/friend disagreements and or roasting (and certainly don't join in on the roast, and doesn't say mean things to the child to get a laugh from others). They are great at listening instead of always bossing, lecturing, criticizing, fixing, or teaching. This mom motivates and encourages by believing in the child and figuring out what would be the best confidence booster at the moment. What do you think is at the core of these behaviors? If you answered she is practicing conscious self-love and unconditional love for herself and others you would be right. When you practice conscious self-love it is almost impossible not to love others. When you practice conscious self-love take care of yourself and it is almost impossible for you to not take care of others in a loving way. Did your mom do it this way?

    Stop for a minute and count the moms you knew like this when growing up. If you are an adult now it is unlikely either of your parents were like this. There was not a lot of information about conscious parenting, loving guidance, parental nurturing, and normal child development in the 1930s-80s. To the contrary, many parents thought children could be spoiled with attention and praise, and the authoritarian (tough love) parenting style was most popular. Children were raised from an authoritarian standpoint to follow orders, get a job, and be as successful as possible, which usually meant making money in business as opposed to the arts. The parenting was not warm and fuzzy. It seemed like this was sort of okay for my generation (outside of child abuse of course) as there was just one parenting style and it was very normal to not have a cool/nice parent. The normative and coming of age movies such as *16 Candles* suggested we (the children) were all in this together against our parents.

In the late 80s, the democratic parenting style (also called authoritarian by Diana Baumrind) surfaced and focused more on the child. It seemed like there would be a positive shift, and there were improvements (for parents and children), but this generation of parents is now raising the very first generation of children who are slated to not outlive their parents. I am sure we can all agree we have a problem on our hands.

There are increases in all categories of negative outcomes for our current lovely children, teens, and young adults (i.e., mental illness, addiction, death by drugs, murder, suicide, harming others, rape, bullying, tinder dating) than in any generation. Suicide is now the 2nd leading cause of death in people 18-34. This of course makes parenting challenging, but are there insights we can glean about parenting behaviors that can be helpful. I don't exactly know the mechanism by which these childhood outcomes so collectively took a turn, but I really believe it has to do with the lack of conscious parenting, a lack of parental conscious self-love, and something about the current children having some need to help us grow. I also believe conscious parenting (with conscious self-love at the core) is the answer. When we practice conscious self-love, and encourage our children to do the same, I believe we will have different outcomes.

Mom type 2:* Under-mothering - *Mom not doing her best. A mom looking like she is not doing her best can be as obvious as her physically, mentally, or emotionally abusing her child. Abuse can also come in the form of neglect and unavailable parenting. Moms with personality disorders like narcissism or borderline personality disorder (or any personality disorder) can harm their children on a daily/hourly basis. There is actually a new category of PTSD called C-PTSD (C stands for complex) to account for the insidious abuse/trauma a child may suffer over and over for years at the hands of an abusing parent.

Under-mothering causes constant feelings of rejection and fears of abandonment played out through the entire life. In the direct contact relationship, odd mothering behaviors look like they are on purpose to the child (that is why they intuit the lack of love, and possibly how they get so "sensitive" in the first place). Children don't understand the context of a personality disorder. There may be no physical scars to see (in superficial relationships no one would really know about a person's personality disorder - the behavioral manifestations are typically saved for the loved ones), but it is very real and hugely damaging to a child's self-love, self-worth, all the self-hyphen words - really all aspects of a child's life. Moreover, this type of parent-centered parenting can seem very inconsistent and unpredictable to the child; requiring vigilance, and an unhealthy focus on the parent, which robs the kid of a normal childhood. I recall my own mom would unleash a horror of verbal abuse one minute and then gently ask if I wanted some eggs within 5 minutes. She would yell at me at the top of her lungs in the car and then roll down her window and smile and say hi to the neighbor. I just never knew what was going to happen next and it was terrifying. I wasn't thinking about what my Barbie should wear, my homework, or what flavor of ice cream I liked best. I was thinking about how to manage my behavior so my mother would not be mad in general, or mad at me. Micro managing and personalizing (as children do) that my mother didn't like me interfered with all sorts of normal milestones I didn't reach; stunting my emotional and mental growth significantly.

When such a child gets older they will likely take over their mother's role in abusing themselves (via their adopted subconscious beliefs from these experiences) in which they don't believe they are loved, are not worthy of love. When someone feels they are not worthy of love they may grow to hate themselves. They may harm themselves (with inner talk and even harmful behaviors). They may do this for years to come. The circle continues as easy as that. Just so we are all clear here.

I want to be very sensitive about this next important part, and I hope it comes across as such. We usually honor the role of motherhood, believe all moms desire the role of motherhood, and are at least somewhat good at it. No one really knew I was being abused by my mom, but if I let it slip out when I was little that I was sure she didn't love me, the feedback from friends and even strangers alike was shocking. They would say in all sorts of different ways, "Oh no, your mother loves you." Um, no she didn't. Narcissistic people don't love others. People with other personality disorders might not be capable of loving their child or another human. Mothers with substance abuse disorders or other mental disorders are not really able to express normal, recognizable love to their children. That is the truth. Saying out loud, "my mother doesn't love me," as a child, and not being validated caused much angst. Saying it out loud and receiving validation (later) helped me to recognize it was not essential for my mother to love me. It was not essential for my happiness, joy, or life. But for children this would be a nearly impossible insight. If I would have taken the unhelpful rote responses from others to heart and not explored things further (as many do), I would've never had this important realization.

To respond to a child who confesses they believe their parent doesn't love them with, "No, that can't be true, of course your mother loves you," invalidates such a core human need. I can actually recall the two very important times it happened. It takes a lot for a child to confide in another adult like that. For the adults who invalidated the experience I believe they thought they were doing their best, but it was another unconscious parenting move. In truth it was also irresponsible, untrue, and shitty. A better response would have been simply, oh gosh I am sorry you feel that way, that must be hard. Do you want to talk about why you think that way?

And by the way, it is possible your mother didn't love you. Let's get clear about the reality of that idea pronto! If it didn't feel like love, I believe you. I am sorry. That must have been more than troubling for quite some time. How are you doing processing that? Do you know that it wasn't your fault and it was likely based on her lack of self-love, and not even about you? I am glad we are hopefully putting some context to that right now. I want you to know, how that important caretaker felt about you is 100% inconsequential to how you feel about yourself. We are becoming aware of the family conditioning that interferes with your self-love (and all the beautiful lotus petals that stem from it: joy, bliss, confidence, self-esteem, gratitude, forgiveness, happiness, contentment) and we are working to unravel it right now.

Moreover, there is such a *love your mother* pressure, to be good to YOUR mom, that people would tell me, "Oh well, try to get it straightened out before she dies" (?!), "She is your MOM you know," and the like. What? I promise you I heard such comments for years. Each time was a little insult I took to heart (not anymore now, but yikes how damaging, talk about triggers). Is there anything for you to write down here, like are you really angry about something? If so, please express_____
_____
_____
_____.

Moms with substance abuse or other mental disorders are also doing quite a large disservice to their children with a slightly different twist. The kid needs to muster up compassion for the mom in the midst of all of her neglect and poor treatment because she is ill. Can you imagine this child telling another about their experiences and feelings about their mom? Think of the mixed societal message for the child - what is she supposed to do with all of that? Moreover, there is a lot of confusion around love with an alcoholic or addicted parent. Rejection, shame, unworthiness, guilt, and trauma plague the child (for possibly the child's entire lifetime if there the child doesn't gain insight about it). This child thinks she is somehow responsible for the mom's very illness. Children are egocentric and internalize such things, especially without proper context by another adult. These children take on the belief they are responsible for this treatment, the mother's problem, and for fixing it. This results in the child leaving their own normal childhood growth behind to instead focus on how to make mom happy on a daily basis. Ugh. I would say for 9 out of 10 kids in this scenario, no adult is providing the proper context about their mom's problem, and the child is personalizing the situation to be about them. The number of mothers with a substance abuse problem or mental disorder is increasing daily. We are talking about a lot of children now in this group. It is no longer an anomaly we can turn the other cheek about. We must do better as a society, as women, as men, and as humans.

Now I know the truth that most moms are not using conscious parenting principles and lots of moms are doing worse, but it is not the child's fault and the children shouldn't have to suffer or feel guilt, shame, resentment, or fear because of it. We need to believe what we are hearing if a child shares important concerns. In front of others my mom pretended to be normal. It wasn't until I was a young adult and I challenged some of the emotional abuse and neglect that she was no longer able to control herself in public, and people caught a glimpse of the craziness. It was such a relief to have just a little understanding about what was going on, and knowing that I wasn't crazy, or to blame as she was insisting.

Have you ever shamed a friend or acquaintance for not dolling out the *love to their mother* without knowing anything about the context? Have you ever been shamed for such a thing yourself? Please stop doing it, and/or stop letting that be done to you! Either walk away knowing that person is crazy, or if you are up to it, tell them your truth within! They might learn something! In my 30s, when it still bothered me, I developed a little elevator pitch speech about what to say when someone asked me such and such about my mom. It served me well for years. Now that I don't need everyone to love me and approve of me for my love and acceptance coins (because of my self-love!), I can be honest and authentic in the moment. Sometimes I respond if I think I can teach the person something useful, and if not, I just smile and nod.

For me, my mom's under-mothering really stunted my psychological and emotional growth. There was just so little guidance and so little nurturing, so little love (for me or for herself - she was constantly berating both of us). I really had no clue about appropriate behavior with peers and was just winging it out on the playground. This was only effective for me about 50% of the time and the other 50% I dealt with the negative consequences of being just too weird for my friends. Remember I said I was an expert at behavior management, but only around adults, and when it came to kids my own age I let it all hang out and assumed it would be cool. It wasn't. I could see there were differences between my peers and I, and yet I didn't really know what to do differently. I didn't have the mom instructions guidance. I watched a lot of television and gleaned information from *Mr. Rogers, The Brady Bunch, The Love Boat,* and later *Friends*. Thank goodness for those programs. A lot of the things I learned during my youth served me now, and I am grateful for it, but there were some tough years. I am sure you can all relate. The problem is those shows aren't on now.

When it came to mothering my kids I said I would do the opposite of the mothering I received. I did that, but I didn't practice conscious parenting, and I had not fixed my self-love problem. As a result, I over-mothered in terms of lessons and guidance to correct what I experienced, but I overcorrected, and it was still about me and unconscious. For my kids, I had a lesson about every possible encounter, every possible outcome of the encounter, to think of each other child's possible response, just too much of a focus on others and how to be appropriate with peers (because that is what I missed out on). I am sure my kids were exhausted. I would have been far better off teaching them about self-love, but alas, it was a concept I wasn't familiar with until they were much older. This leads us to the third type of mothering, the over-mother.

Mom type 3: But wait, my mom was a saint (over-mothering). There are different ways over-mothering can manifest. Over-mothering can manifest covertly were it is confusing and it looks like the mom is nice and doing a lot. She sure is complaining a lot and doing a lot of running around, feeling ragged, and full of resentment. Over-mothering can also manifest overtly, whereby moms make direct bids to be the center of attention and the kid's life (i.e., "no one will love you as much as mommy does," "my child and I are best friends!"). On the outside the over-mother may look fantastic and very devoted. Her children might have a lovely home and she may drive them to many after school classes and activities. However, anytime a mom is not communicating her **unconditional love and acceptance** to the child, and practicing conscious parenting (where it is about the child and not the parent) a mother wound can develop.

This is where a mother's practicing conscious self-love comes to be so important. Even though the over-mother appears to have it all and be doing her best, this mothering without her own conscious self-love will be similarly passed down outside of awareness. Over-mothering causes feelings of incompetence, not trusting yourself, anxiety, and shame, which can be continuously and unconsciously played out throughout the life of the child. If your mom did a combination of sometimes under-mothering and sometimes over-mothering, based on her own unconscious patterning and wounds, then we have both sides of the negative consequences, causing a lot of confusion for the child. Also, putting yourself (as a mom) absolutely last on your list day in and day out will inevitably result in resentment.

We will talk later about balanced relationships. Although your parent-child relationship isn't a balanced give and take one, if the mom who is doing all of the giving (which is mostly how it will go) isn't taking care of herself she will become exhausted, overwhelmed, and resentful.

In the parent-child relationship, the parent should not expect to receive from the child, but she should be providing similar care/love to herself (that she is for the child), or there will be an imbalance and resentment.

There is something to be said for the sainthood of mothering and I tried it. I think one of my son's friends even referred to me as a saint once lol. I got a heck of a lot of enjoyment from running here and there, seeing to everyone's needs, but never my own. It was ego filling and soul crushing. I would also guess the resentment and irritation building inside me was hard for my loved ones to ignore. My children saw me putting on a good show, but my bright kids knew something was up. How confusing! Also, the deep and denied maternal resentment can slip out at important moments and make a child bleed on the inside just like the lady razor (or negatively impact their self-love).

Let's consider a different child angle: did you ever feel guilt or shame for all the stuff your mom "sacrificed" for you? Some moms even tell their children they quit college to have them, or they would be further in their career if they didn't stop to raise the kids. Outside of sacrificing, some moms tell their children they were "an accident." I can't believe I wrote that, but within the time I have been alive I have heard this quite a bit actually. It may be the truth, but a child will not process this correctly. I can see that because how do you process being told your mere existence was an accident. Hm. If any of these off-handed comments were shared with you, how do you think this impacted you, your good feelings about yourself, feelings of worthiness, and your ability to love yourself? Sometimes I wonder, wow, if a mom can say that in public, how are they relating to their child in private? My guess is they have not processed their parent wounds and are suffering from obvious resentment? Think about it just for a minute.

Other problems caused by over-mothering are guilty feelings and anxiety in the children. This guilt and anxiety can get stuck in the body! Did you ever think there were conditions attached to all that your mom was doing for you? The conditions I am thinking about here and related to this discussion could be to prove her worth and deservingness of love from you, her spouse, or anyone by showing she was doing good things worthy of love. She may have really wanted to do these things because she adored you so and just wanted you to be happy (a good reason, but again unlikely). If she instead was doing those things because she was trying to be a good mom for some external reward or approval, guilt, shame, or to fulfill herself (an ego-based reason based on a lack of her very own self-love), the child will sense this and their self-love will be negatively impacted. Remember we are not blaming here, we are sharing this experience of insight and self-awareness to help us process our past.

There is a related concept in this over-mothering area I want to bring up, and we refer to it as *failure to launch*. Parents are often chastising their children about their child's launch failure, but I am certain this is more a failure of the parent than the child. The over-mother fails to let go either consciously or unconsciously, and her sweet kids pick up the slack however they need to, to get their love! Remember over-mothers are not fostering a child's self-love. Instead, over-mothers are so far up their kids' butts, they quite honestly interfere with the launch! I don't think parents do this consciously (it is unconscious parenting indeed). When you give too much direction and help, a child can internalize messages of incompetence, needing help, and they can't or don't want to do anything on their own and need us. This implicit message strips courage and one's belief in their ability to succeed without constant input.

I was a big-time over-mother. I did love my boys and wanted to do well as a parent. Since I hadn't processed my mother wound by the time they were growing up, I did the best with the under-mothering I received. I knew I wanted to do it differently, but I overcorrected and then over-mothered. Remember about the **2-step process to end the cycle of abuse from Chapter Two**? I saw the abuse and knew I didn't want to do it, but I didn't fix its impact on me, so I was still parenting from a place of self-love lack. Because of my over-mothering, my children received the messages that they needed me for most decisions and guidance and they needed me to supply their love (I wasn't fostering their own self-love).

It is important to remember our beautiful children are sovereign souls. We need to cultivate their relationships with themselves and get them to trust their instincts. I am not saying we let our four-year-olds guide themselves, but I am saying we scaffold and allow (as they grow) them to be themselves and be supportive, instead of being too directive.

I have a lovely friend who was so into controlling her children they didn't really get to be themselves in youth. Of course she was doing the best she could, but both kids (28 and 30) have yet to live their own lives. They are doing what she wanted them to do and directed the heck out of their precious formative years. One moved away, but the other is working at a job the mother wanted. I think both the kids are successful actually, but I don't feel their lives were really been about them yet. It's true, a career as a Star Craft gamer is less desired (from a parent's perspective) than an engineer, but I don't know where we draw the line and I don't know if when he is 50 he will have regrets.

It is tough to balance this loving guidance while still allowing each child's special gifts and soul to grow. In my friend's case, her intentions were good, but her hyper child-focused parenting (and no focus on herself-from her unhealed mother wound) made it look like everything she was doing was for them. She often spoke about all she had done to help, but it was really just busy, interfering work that didn't even need to be done. She spoke about her plans, that she always wanted to be an engineer, but her parents didn't support that, so now her child was becoming an engineer! She had no insight about any of this. She wanted coins for her parenting efforts, AND she led her children to believe her plans for their futures were more important than their own.

Remember the most loving way to be in a relationship is not to control others and not to allow yourself to be controlled. This applies to significant others and your children! As a college professor I heard repeatedly from students they didn't really know what they wanted to do and that they were in college because it was their parent's wish for them. I also heard some students tell me they wanted to be pursuing a creative art, but their parents insisted they go with a science career or one with more "potential" for their future. It always hurt me to hear that. We brag on our children's accomplishments as if they somehow reflect our accomplishments, or the job we did as parents. We praise our "old-soul" children, or adult-like children who take care of their family members and mind our wishes, but is this what we want for them and how does this impact them?

It is the best-case scenario that parents love their child! That is what we want to communicate! How can we do this and retain the beautiful attachment relationship, but allow them to navigate what is right for them and foster their very own self-love and approval? This way, they won't want to run away, be confused, or not love and trust themselves. It takes effort and conscious parenting to pull this off.

Right now in the news, parents are being implicated for paying colleges and others to admit their children. I know the peanut gallery from the Internet are taking a harsh stance against these parents, and of course I do see the problems with this situation, but the vehement judgers are likely being triggered (remember seeing/disliking something in another often represents a message for you about you). Whether we are irritated by another or admire another it is because we see that beauty or beast in ourselves reflected (or else we wouldn't even see it). At any rate, I don't think we should be judging. In all honesty if we had that money and our kids' futures could be locked because we "helped" them get into a wonderful college, can you honestly say you wouldn't do it too? From just my limited understanding of the situation, and my just guessing, I feel like those behaviors may not have been so ego driven (to make the parent look good), but more a case of maternal love (caretaking) gone wild. Say what you will, but certainly we've all "helped" with some homework to help our child out of a jam - some might've even done it so our kid or us look good. Or what if your biggest dream was to go to

Harvard, but you couldn't and now your kid can if you do this one thing. I mean there are a myriad of reasons (ego driven and just wanting to give them what they or you most covet for themselves or you, let's be honest). The intents might be different, and that is sort of important, but the message to the child is the problem here. "Mommy will fix this for you. I am here to meet your needs and you don't have to." I know this. I've done it. Mine was on a smaller scale based on what I had to offer, but if we are honest I think you can say the same. Wanting the best for your child is a gift of love. Helping them to love themselves and feel confident in their ability to achieve is the best and supreme gift of a lifetime.

I added this current day information about launching and college payments here to help you understand something important. Now think back to your parents. Were you encouraged to do something they wanted? Did that make you feel adored, trust yourself, grow in your own self-love, or were you many of your decisions about pleasing your parents? When you pushed back did you feel less than, not worthy, that you were making a mistake? I feel it might be hard to make decisions or trust yourself if that was the case. Can we agree that your parent's intention might've been good, but the effects might be a bit challenging to process without this very important self-awareness? Please do think about it.

The best question to ask may be, what can we do to support our kid's very own soul growth. We can realize they are an extension of us, yes, but they are here for their own journey, and they need to love themselves to make their journey better. It is not easy. I will address this later in my "helping others grow in self-love" section. If you can't wait for that, here is a fantastic quote from Dr. Shefali Tsabary, the expert on conscious parenting, "Love without consciousness becomes neediness, dependency, and control, all in the name of *love*. When we merge paths and take over for children, spouses, or friends in order to affirm our feelings of love and security, then we are using these sovereign souls to fill OUR gaps. Don't lie to yourself and think it is the other way around making yourself the saint. That is not the case." Wow, she really tells it like it is!

If you can reflect, where was your mom's self-love meter (not objectively, you don't have to ask her, but as you perceived it - perceptions are actually more important than reality as our perceptions are our truth within, and really that is the only truth to be had). Maybe she didn't loathe herself, but did she ace that test on practicing conscious self-love, or was she was somewhere in between? Were there any confusing messages? When you are somewhere in between, can you sometimes behave towards others in a loving way, sometimes take care of yourself, and sometimes take good care of others? The times when you are not doing these things seem to be stressful though because you see/feel the dichotomy and you want it to be positive all the time. The outward manifestation of the "sometimes self-love" are better than no self-love, but that still looks confusing to children and others. Plus, the inward manifestation of the "sometime confusion" starts to add up in the body and take a toll.

_____

Please put your mom's perceived self-love on the continuum

_____

1   2   3   4   5

never   rarely   sometimes   most of the time   95-100%

Please write down some messages you received (either directly or things you intuited) and how they made you feel.

_____

_____

Thinking about it now, is your mom's self-love and yours similar? How do you feel knowing this? Does this make you want to change things?

Other mom behaviors/issues. Less obvious (and outside of the context of a mental health problem) not-doing-their-best mom behaviors can be accidental or purposeful and portrayed through toxic or harmful messages, lack of support, promotion of competition between children, lack of supervision or too much supervision, absence of boundaries, lack of guidance, no protection of the child from another's sexual or physical abuse, a focus on improving the child constantly, suggestions they are not worthy of love, lack of attention or too much attention, and disbelief in the child. Let's add a few more of your own to this list right now. Just go ahead and spill it, what did your mother do to you?_____, _____, and don't forget _____!! The list can go on and on and is personal. It's likely no two people have the same constellation of how their moms might have contributed to their lack of current self-love. By getting honest and seeing this situation with compassion, we don't have to blame anyone; we can just extract the lessons and love and leave the stuff we don't need in the past where it belongs.

Narcissistic mothers. As I was trying to figure out where my self-love went astray I kept running into resources on narcissistic mothers. There are probably hundreds of books on this topic! Based on the sheer number of resources about this topic, I infer there must be a significant number of these mothers in our society. There are also a lot of empaths now. In my limited experience I surmise empaths are the children of the narcissists (remember from before- empaths are often working completely around the mom and her parent-centered parenting) who later seek out relationships with narcissists. This would account for the increase in empath-narcissist relationships.

What also makes sense to me is that narcy and empath behaviors are on different ends of one continuum. I apologize in advance to the empaths for that statement (I feel like many empaths are reading this -

that is a good joke because it is empathic). It is a continuum of somewhat problematic behavioral attributes and has something to do with a lack of self-love! In both cases the empath and the narc have extremely low self-love. The difference is the narc is completely and detrimentally *self-focused*, and the empath is completely and often times detrimentally *other-focused*.

It is like the empath has full compassion for others and no self-compassion at all, which could come to pass if you were raised by a narcissist and everything revolved around them, right? The narc has only self-obsessions, but again it is likely a response to how they were raised and have no self-love. Although it appears on the surface they are in love with themselves, the irony is, they hate themselves and seek an external love supply. The empath seeks an external love supply as well, because of a refusal to have self-focus. This is truly a symbiotic relationship.

Sometimes relationship roles can switch and it really may be the case that all people not in self-love will do things to get love from another. It may be the case we are all narcissistic to some degree. It will be healthy to be a bit self-focused (not obsessed, but not ignoring your needs either!). It will be healthy to have a bit of compassion for others (not to the point we have no self-compassion, but some compassion for others and ourselves). Who is to say this empath-narcissist relationship isn't light-dark/yin-yang where both sides are needed to deliver the understanding (via processing and integrating). Later I present more information about how to achieve a healthy balance of give and take in things related to self-love.

There are many, many things the narcissistic mother can do to mess with your growth and development. It seems like a very common problem these days. I read numerous books on the topic making the undoing for me was really beneficial. I was unable to forgive my mom, even though I tried so hard, until I took the keys to my self-love safe back from her.

Before I was at a good place with self-love I had to go *no-contact* (a technique for dealing with narcissist family members) with my mother just because I was not able to withstand her abuse. I recall Dr. G, my therapist (who also had a narcissist mother!), telling me I could consciously choose to go no-contact or not, as he was able to have contact with his mother because he didn't let her negative comments or behavior get to him. I was not at that place and marveled in how advanced I thought he was! I can see it now myself, the difference between no-contact and "upgraded conscious self-love contact" on my terms, but at the time it was not right for me to stay in contact.

If I would have been practicing conscious self-love, had awareness about the situation, and realized her behavior had indeed nothing to do with me (but were her projections of self-hate carried out on me), I would have been able to do as Dr. G did. But, I was not at that place. There were no options for me setting boundaries either because the minute I declared a boundary, like a 4-year-old having a tantrum, my mom pushed back and used that exact boundary information against me.

If I had the opportunity to repair my self-love before she passed I am confident I wouldn't have needed the no-contact separation to stay healthy even in her presence. Still, no-contact for me was a step in the direction to get to my place of self-love, so it was personally essential for me. It was a glorious two years to tell you the truth. Despite friends and strangers warnings that I would be mad at myself after she passed (yes all people seem to say that to children who are abused) I was not!

Another word about **boundaries** and conscious self-love. I just don't think you need boundaries in conscious self-love. When practicing conscious self-love what another person does or says to you is not a threat. You can take it or leave it. You can instill a boundary by telling someone to stop saying a particular thing to you (that's triggering), OR you can stop letting the trigger bother you. It is your call. If you are practicing conscious self-love and own your power, even if you do get triggered by another's projection, you soon realize this. You more easily see the sheer ridiculousness of such an ignorant comment or behavior. It is funny, not scary. You don't have to plan your response (I would work on those responses for a few days before this time and then never even say my peace). Once the veil was lifted, my mother's behaviors became so obviously ridiculous they were not even hurtful anymore. At first I would laugh almost. Then I felt a little bad for her. I didn't need a boundary. I needed more conscious self-love.

Remember, every relationship comes to you to teach you something. If you set a boundary you might miss what you are supposed to be learning. What if your lesson WAS to stand up for yourself and speak your truth, okay then the boundary was the lesson. If, however, you have no problem speaking up and sharing your needs I say you can skip the boundary and go for the juicy part of not letting what they are doing upset/control/impact you negatively. See the comment as interesting, recognize it is about them, and it is likely a reflection of something both parties are projecting (about themselves!).

My mom also had a problem with my mere existence. I think this was in addition to the narcissism and reflected a deep-seated resentment for having me. It was family knowledge that I was supposed to be an abortion. Her obvious irritation and resentment about my dad encouraging her to not have the abortion was palpable on almost every interaction. This led to a tremendous feeling of rejection with a whole array of negative consequences for me. Adding in issues to the parenting mix can create extra colossal baggage for you to process - and be grateful for later ha. Ameliorating rejection patterning from our childhoods is a sure step in the right direction to positive mental health and the road to self-love.

In the face of the rejection I tried my best to win her (and then others) over with gifts, great help, being good - you name it. I was always buying her thoughtful and generous gifts (as a child and adult). I never ever felt like the gifts (or anything I did for her or in general) were enough. For Christmas she might get me one or two gifts, strange sale-item things, and I had at least 10 thoughtful gifts for her (it was like this for most holidays!). One Christmas I went to her favorite store she always talked about. I was so happy to go in and ask for the shop owner's help in selecting the perfect gift for my mother. I identified myself and said I was Mary's daughter and she just looked at me blankly. I repeated and said, "Oh you know Mary, right?" She said, "Yes of course, she comes in all the time, but she only has a son." I said, "No, I am her daughter," and she really pushed back saying, "No I am sure she only has a son." She must have said that three times! I walked through the shop thinking, *oh my gosh she can't even tell her friend she has a daughter.* For a long time that feeling of being unwanted and so unimportant that she pretended I didn't exist really upset me. It would slip out of my subconscious at times I am sure and impacted how I related to others in my life until I was able to process it. Now I think it is so ridiculous! But you can see how in all my later relationships my problem was not feeling appreciated by my mate, but feeling claimed by them and acknowledged as important to them. You can also see how this would be an impossible ask given the fact I only seemed able to pick "avoidant" attached partners. When you are with someone with an insecure attachment style you cannot look to them to help you feel secure. You must do this yourself, outside of the context of that relationship.

Each Easter I made my mother a beautiful Easter Basket because she would mention every year how she never got one as a child. As she said that she wouldn't marvel at the good stuff she was getting now, it was just like the basket transported her to her past deficits. She was missing the joy of getting the basket now from me not realizing she was depriving me of the same thing she was so hurt from. It was important for me in this situation to make sense of it. It was challenging indeed, but I added to my suffering by noticing everything and taking it personally. Who remembers what their parents got them for holidays? I did, because I was constantly searching for feedback about how much I was loved. This is not ideal. In addition to trying (to no avail) to win the coins, I was becoming resentful myself.

Now I am hoping your relationship with your parents may not have been so bad, and I am so sorry if your stories are worse. Sharing stories can be therapeutic. Knowing we are not alone in suffering takes some of the shame away. Changing our understanding of the story, that it was never our story anyway, helps us to let it go. I kept circling back to thinking, *wow, she did enough harm, I am ready to let go of her power over me* (by me carrying the emotionally charged stories). After sitting in that place with the stories they became less and less emotionally charged and are now just facts about bad parenting we can use to learn from. We are covering a lot of ground here and possibly brining things to your awareness. This is really the place it needs to be for you to break free from the inappropriate conditioning and anything worse that might have happened. Just sit with it and know you are okay right now. I did quite a bit of processing of the trauma through various techniques I will share just a bit later, but I always knew I was going to be okay and I believe you are too.

Because of my mom's lack of love to me I spent a lot of time trying to make even other people (mates and friends) who didn't like me, like me. I did this because I didn't love myself, grew up in a house where no love and acceptance were modeled, and I was emotionally abused and neglected. Before these facts got sprung from my subconscious, I picked partners who were emotionally unavailable and not interested in me, and worked very hard to make them like me because that is what I knew. I stayed with mean spouses who really didn't care about me because that is what I thought I deserved.

All the books I read about narcissistic mothers were helpful about her role, but I didn't really get everything solved by the new information. It wasn't until my frame of reference changed (self-awareness about how my self-love was impacted) and next my refusal to adopt her modeled hateful inner critic - did everything else change. Let's just say it was a challenge to climb out of my personal self-hate state and stop accepting my mother's projection of herself to me, her subsequent and over-judgment of me, and my internalized judgment of me and her, and start repairing my relationship with myself (and ultimately all others). But I did it. So can you!!

One thing that helped me make the transition from allowing myself to be abused by my mom (and going no-contact with her) was considering karma. I don't know how you feel about karma, but I came to realize I was actually helping my mom's karma by not allowing her wrath to impact me (no more bad karma for her if I didn't let her mess with me, my beautiful soul, or negatively impact my self-love any longer), and even less bad karma for her if I stopped the family pattern of abuse. If you are not a fan of the idea of karma then I have a science analogy for you. Your family genome gets imprinted and passed through generations. Your psychology (thoughts and behaviors included) via epigenetics gets transferred to you from past generations and passed from you to future generations. One reason to clean up your genome is fixing thing for all future generations (karma or not).

Karma was a tool for me to use, but the truth of the matter is, if you stop agreeing to this role of hurting yourself because your mother did (and likely her mother before her) behind us, we can help our children and their children. We can stop the chain by loving yourself in front of your children, undoing past conditioning, and living happily and peacefully. If you do, you clear a whole family line of self-hate genome or karma (whatever you want to call it). It was a real gift for my family and their future families. If you don't have children and don't plan on it, this work will also help all other relationships in your life (not just the parent-child relationship).

Processing the Mother Wound. Most of the really wonderful people I know experienced a mother (or father or other main caretaker wound). My doctoral dissertation was on the effects of moms modeling positive and negative expressiveness patterns. I was a walking around with this wound outside of my awareness even in psychology graduate school. No one even picked up on it! Well, one of my professors did and even told me my mother was a narcissist! I didn't circle back to that term for 20 years, but thanks to Dr. Michel ☺. Now I see clearly there was the wound and also a purpose to the wound! It made me feel a lot better about the wound that it had a purpose ha. Still, I don't think "the purpose" requires we suffer! The lesson/purpose is here to learn from, so we can move on in a kinder and more loving place when relating to ourselves. The last thing we want to do is end up berating ourselves up for years on end. What if we progressed from lesson to resolution in one tenth of the time! That is my goal!

In thinking about your mother's behavior, what do you think was at the core of these behaviors, lack of self-love or maybe even self-hate? When you loathe yourself you don't take care of yourself, so it is almost impossible to take care of and to love others. This does not excuse the abusive behaviors, or require you forget about her behavior, but if offers you some context to recognize it had NOTHING to do with you AND it is time for you to move on. Take the good parts of this lesson, so you can be led to self-love and joy and let the pain and negativity go. That is what the lesson really wants you to learn. The very last thing we want to do is choose the other route; to accept, take on the role of new inner critic, and then perpetuate what was modeled or taught to you (subconsciously or consciously) about how unworthy you are, or how much you don't deserve your very own love. Agreed?

Do you see what I mean, how it is so very challenging to get mothering right on a daily basis for 20 years? I am not saying it was easy for our parents. What I am saying is-now you know it was not about you- and completely about them and even unconscious. What are we going to do about it!? We need to leave it behind.

There is no reason the rest of your life must be spent riddled with guilt, shame, feelings of unworthiness, or lack of self-love (and the physical and mental pain occurring in the body as a function of these stuck feelings) because of someone else's unconscious parenting mistakes. In almost all instances there is at least some family conditioning around to interfere with your self-love and all the beautiful lotus petals that stem from it. Try to bring it to your awareness, so you can see it and get rid of it.

For you, or people you know who experienced significant trauma. I don't mean to minimize something horrible that happened (abuse) and we do need to acknowledge that no one deserves to be abused, especially from your parent! We know that the problem was completely outside of you in this case. I could tell you about how your parent may have been abused and that might help. I could tell you to forgive the person/situation and move on, but really? Do you really need to forgive that reprehensible behavior from your caretaker? Contrary to the forgiveness texts I read, I will just say, no, I don't believe you need to forgive your parents right now in order for you to practice conscious self-love. I do believe though that only when you practice conscious self-love may real forgiveness for them may be possible.

Let's try on, "I am no longer willing to hold any negative feelings in response to what happened." Period. How about instead of forgiving another for that harm and trying to see the good about it (vomit), you forgive yourself in the context of the relationship (I forgive myself for hating him, I forgive myself for being angry), maybe forgive the relationship (I forgive myself for hating this relationship), forgive the lesson (I forgive myself for being angry at God for letting this happen). I always think forgiveness and gratitude go hand in hand and I absolutely know the power of gratitude. Still, it is hard for me to muster up feelings of forgiveness for a child abuser or gratitude for such a lesson. Someone should say this out loud, right? There I just said it. I just can't do it. I know I can't go around full of lack of forgiveness and gratitude though, because then I will suffer.

What if we change it up a little... look I am grateful I survived that! I forgive myself for hating her, or being angry at her! We can change the target of our forgiveness (to us!!) or gratitude (to us!!). If our current society suggests we need to forgive or be grateful for lessons, let's realize we are in charge of the targets of both -you can do it how you want!

What can you forgive and be grateful for about this situation related to whatever it is you want to forgive or be grateful for? Is there anything? You decide. You don't owe anyone anything (certainly not your forgiveness or gratitude). Plus, there is nothing for you to feel bad about. How can you get to a better place? I forgave myself for being angry at my mom (in addition to a huge inner critic of myself I also carried around a lot of guilt for being angry!).

That forgiveness gift TO ME, of me was a big turning point. I gave lip service to being grateful for my experiences because they would ultimately help me help others, but in the early days before I practiced conscious self-love I was mad I had to have this lesson and quite frankly and thinking why me (I am just being honest here). How is that supposed to be helpful to another person-it wasn't. Thanks to a helper I had changed the question from *What am I grateful for about my mom sucking so bad and harming me?* to *How did I benefit from her not loving me how I needed?* This small shift changed the dynamic and I found several things to be grateful for (related to MY resourcefulness and strength).

Even though a trauma like that occurred, does it help if I say you can still release it as part of your past and not part of your present or future? I am more than certain this is the case, but you may need some help to get there. If you are reading this book and that is all you need, amazing! If you are reading this book and you need additional assistance, please check out the resources section at the end and see what resonates with you. Trauma in all forms needs to be processed, and if you need the help of a therapist, please get the help you need. It will be worth it and you deserve to take care of yourself even if other's didn't.

Dads

Ah yes, your dad. With the majority of health and psychological research on men, I am surprised there is not more data on dads and fathering! That is sort of a joke ha. From being a developmental psychologist I know the importance of modeling an appropriate dad-type guide/teacher. I was the chairperson for a dissertation about dad's roles in daughter eating disorders and can tell you they matter. I also know the devastating effects of a no dad-type guide/teacher on children in terms of later substance abuse and other challenges.

I want to talk about my dad for a second. He was the best! I think I had my awakening to the idea I needed to love myself in midlife because of some early messages he instilled. I also want to express my belief in the observation - you just need one good parent (or adult figure) to get to most of the good stuff. Let's pray you and everyone has at least one! I weathered some pretty tough storms in my youth looking back and I just kept getting up and dusting off each time. I think my resiliency might have been the self-love imprint left by my dad in my early years (he died on my 15th birthday).

I marveled at my dad's loving skills. I think he should've had high self-love, and I think he did at a time, but my mom and her cruelty hit him hard as well, and I think she tried to steal some of his self-love for herself too (a narcissist supply need). I could see pain in his eyes and he had a drinking and smoking problem (self-harm behaviors/habits). But the things I recall most now were those beautiful loving gestures (from his heart and not for stuff) and the fun we had when my mom went out. From his behaviors I could tell he really valued and respected me as a person. He taught me to value and respect myself. I knew he truly enjoyed spending time with me and he honestly tried hard to shield me from the overt cruelty of my mom. He once snuck in a McDonald's hamburger to my bedroom where I was locked in for not eating my mom's homemade dinner I hated. My mom found out and kicked my door in (ripped my cat poster) and took my burger! That was harsh, but the main thing I remember is my dad sneaking it in with his finger on his lips…shhh. The behaviors to convey this love for me were obvious to me even as a child. I could tell he valued me as a human and if he did, I should too! I don't know why I didn't embrace HIM relating to me and instead adopted my mother's words for my subconscious experience of myself. Isn't that interesting! I forgave myself for adopting my mom's voice for my inner critic instead of my dad! Is there any chance we can help people focus on the good parent experiences? Why not :)

Dads have been taught even less how to nurture than moms. It is really more than likely your father was present (if indeed he was present), but not too involved. How a child comes to understand this relationship is pivotal for self-love and their later parenting. I believe what's important is a dad's demonstrated availability to his child, communication of unconditional acceptance, validation/approval, and communication of unconditional love in the context of loving guidance. It would be important for a father to be in a child's life. If not, there may be consequences whereby a child feels rejected, unimportant, and possibly not worthy of his or another's love. It is obvious the father should voice his acceptance of the child in most areas. Discipline should be doled fairly and with the child's psyche in mind (remember the internalizing). Even passing comments about weight like, "Are you really going to eat that," or career choice, "A teacher, why do you want to be a teacher?" will be heard by the child and thought about for years to come. My own boys thought their dad, with all his obvious foibles and parenting missteps (some cringe worthy, like all of us!), was a superhero in their formative years. How challenging to overcome damaging words from such a revered man.

Father Wound. A bit more significant than fathering foibles is a Father Wound. Each person will likely have a mother or father wound to process. By process I mean will experience negative ramifications from the wound unless and until a person becomes aware of the wound and corrects their subconscious story. The mother/father wound will manifest differently in males and females. I have seen some males with an unprocessed father wound have a real hard time being in an intimate relationship for fears of compromised freedom. A father wound may interfere with their good parenting because the new father is stuck in an adolescent-like mode (likely where the wound started) and gets envious attention is not on the child. Daughters with father wounds may look to males to provide for them or take care of them (prince charming) if they missed out on that, or maybe they will not trust men. One thing is sure, a lack of child-focus, validation, and/or presence from a father to son/daughter contributes to the father wound and the wound can cause relationship problems, commitment problems, and attention seeking behaviors, and unnecessary competitions (poaching). If you have an **inner child wound** (a father or mother wound) then I highly recommend you keep reading AND you consider doing some **Inner Bonding** self-healing process developed by Dr. Margaret Paul (please see resources/bibliography section).

My best friend since I was 16 had a narcissist father. She didn't figure this out until her mid-life either! That is a long time to go under the guise of us being "horrible" offspring with all the associated guilt, shame, and resentment. That's a lot of years and a lot of people with no or low self-love walking around (children of narcissists and other problem parents) doing for others and not themselves, or expressing their self-hate outwardly. I wonder if that has anything to do with the state of our society today?

Moreover, Louise Hay and so many others claimed these damaging and possibly repressed negative emotions get trapped in the body - outside of our awareness - and can cause physical manifestations (pain and disease!). We need to get better at recognizing damaging parental influences sooner, and engage the debriefing of negative parental programming sooner. We need to help all the children who are suffering and learning to hate themselves at the hands of those who are supposed to lift them up. One thing we can do is help people feel love for themselves, so they can treat others (loved ones, children, strangers) with the love they feel for themselves.

To sum up, the dads of both sons and daughters play a significant role in a child's self-love and self-esteem. For a long-time, conditions of worth were sort of doled out by the man/father (maybe he saw that as his role). Think of the power of those words. What if he was an absent dad? Would that make you feel unworthy of attention and love? Whereas the mom's lack of love or interaction with you may manifest as you thinking you don't deserve to be taken care of (traditionally her job), a dad's lack of love or interaction feeds into your feelings of esteem and how you regard yourself in the world. What does it mean if the "head of the household" is at odds with himself or you? It means a lot! Even behaviors and words that were coming from his "good" intentions (based on what he thought would be "motivating") can have significant negative effects. A lack of approval, modeling of their own self-destructive/self-hate behaviors (drinking, smoking, infidelity), flippant comments, and overall disinterest in parenting will impact both men and women. This challenging impact may manifest as lack of trust of men (or people in general), dislike of men (or people in general), confusion around men/man things, feelings of unworthiness, confusion, and you guessed it, low self-love.

What messages (overt or covert did he send about your worth and how you can feel about yourself, self-love)?

_____

_____

_____

Thinking about it now, were these two things related? How do you feel knowing it was not even about you? What do you want to do now when it comes to how you relate to other people?

    Changing the game. Let's wrap up this section with some advice even before we get to our Daily BEs and Daily DOs chapter. Because it's unlikely our parents demonstrated unconditional love to us, or conscious parenting, we need to create a situation of unconditional love and acceptance for ourselves.

We must do this to be happy in our lives, to stop the cycle of conditional love in our families, and to positively impact the lives we have been charged with raising. It is not a platitude to ask you to take back the life baton from these other people controlling how you feel about yourself, how much love you should have (deserve), or how you should let other people relate to you. It is not an outside game by any stretch of the imagination. Your self-love, self-acceptance, and self-forgiveness are controlled by YOU. If you don't take back the baton, you will be ruled by the outside, watching from the sidelines in your very own life, where it is very chaotic. It is an uncomfortable feeling to be detached from your true self. You must get the baton back, today.

Self-Awareness Activity. You start by becoming self-aware of the influence of your past on your present. You were likely not taught how to relate to yourself in a healthy way. You might not have been taught how to relate to others in a healthy way either, but let's put a pin in that for right now. Right now the one most important discovery is *how* you are relating to yourself? This can be both an exciting and uncomfortable realization. Uncomfortable, realizing you have not been relating great to yourself, but exciting to realize it is all YOU now. There is really no need to even consider how much time it wasn't you (I figured you went there). It took this amount of time to get here today, so this is the perfect timing.

You say: I am now willing to develop a conscious and loving relationship with myself. Take yourself out for coffee. When a situation pops up, you say, "*hm, how would a person high in conscious self-love react to this. Let's pretend I have high conscious self-love right now, what should I do?*" You can also give yourself the same kindness and understanding you would give a friend out to coffee. You and your friend only show the light to each other, but for you, you know your dark as well as light (and maybe that is why you are mean to yourself, and practice the conditional love). This may even be why you don't think you deserve love. It is not true.

We all have both dark and light inside our heads. Just because you know yours and not the other person's doesn't mean they don't have any. You can make a conscious choice today, right now, no matter what, to surrender this darkness in you (these negative thoughts about others, your expectations, your disappointments in others and yourself, all the "shoulds" for yourself and your loved ones) for you own conscious self-acceptance. Why the heck not? All that stuff is here to teach you about yourself and others and relationships anyway. It is okay. Treat yourself as if you were talking to your friend, without judgment, with kindness, compassion, understanding, support, acceptance, and love. You are a master at helping others to see they are wonderful and deserve forgiveness for each and every foible. It is your turn now.

Let's reread this sentence....**I see my problem, but I treat myself to my very own kindness, compassion, understanding, support, acceptance, and LOVE without judgment.** Just a little more every day, more love, more kindness, more patience for you and your thoughts, feelings, behaviors, all of it, all of you. You are that little person who longed for the unconditional love and acceptance of your loved ones. Well, here it is, just for you. You are the adult to you (yin-yang!). She focuses on her flaws BUT you remind her no one is perfect. She berates herself for a bad choice, BUT you remind her you would've done the same thing, and point out what a great learning experience it was. She says she doesn't like herself, BUT you tell her there is nothing she could do to make you love her any less. She is at full love capacity with you! Reach for your love. Allow your inner child, your insides to feel and receive this love. Love yourself. Honor yourself. Forgive yourself. This is what you are here to learn. This is your soul's and the Divine's wish for you. I am certain it is truly this.

The Parental Unit Relationship Model

Information about relationships is also conveyed via how your parents related to each other. This relationship serves as a model for you for your whole life (until you do this introspection and attain some self-awareness of its impact on you). Think about how much their relationship (problems/successes) are blurring into your current ideas about partners and likely causing damaging expectations until you do the "unblending."

Did you ever have a weird reaction in your relationship about something you didn't really see coming? This reminds me of the Catch 22 gift giving scenario when you tell someone you "don't" want a gift and then they don't get you a gift. Who does that? I did! Maybe your mom always said that, but your dad always showed up with a gift, it was their thing. If you want a gift you can go ahead and say so. I spent many holidays with no gifts (that I absolutely wanted!) because my mom had always said that weird thing, and I adopted it as my own as I thought I should. My problem was my mates did not receive the memo that I was lying!, so I was gift less (at my request) far too often thinking people didn't love me. I was 100% interfering with my receiving love because I felt like I didn't deserve a present!

What if there was constant bickering in your parent's house? Do you seek out a partner for drama and bickering? That is what you know to be "love," you long for that. Is that the healthy way for you though? If one of your parents was absent and rejecting are you avoidant in relationships and dislike commitment or intimacy? We can explore and un-blend from our original family unit. If we don't, we just accept and assimilate that model we watched as the model for our own adult relationships, which will inevitably cause some chaotic expectations your partner has no clue about.

Was there an affair in your parent's relationship? Do you believe your partner will cheat on you? Are you constantly worried about that? Maybe it feels normal to be deceitful, lie cheaty, or always on the lookout for someone better. It could be anything. It is important that you smooth this out because it is not really even about your or your essence or preferences, it is simply a pattern you saw when you grew up. You put together what relationships should look like from that. If you have problems in your relationships now you might want to move away from your parent's story and evaluate what YOU want. Also, practice some self-compassion and make choices that would be in your AND others' best interests. What would feel good for you right now? Getting to this place of what would feel good doesn't always mean you need to find a new partner either. You can redefine your relationship goals, desires, behaviors at literally any moment! It is important to step out of the conditioning and imprints and clarify what WE want. That is when you honor your soul and the people who chose to be near you on your journey. The parents weren't even our choice!

For me, there was cheating in my family and no one was high in self-love, so there was a lot of external searching for love. In retrospect I selected my first husband for this very reason! He cheated on me while we were dating, while we were engaged, and then surprise - when we were married, twice! I think Harville Hendrix would say I picked someone untrustworthy and unavailable because I lived that way. I could add I picked someone untrustworthy because I didn't believe I deserved a good guy because I was unworthy of true love (because I was lacking in my very own self-love). It wasn't that I was a bad picker (which I thought for several years - and was afraid to make any decision) and it wasn't that he was a horrible person (which I also thought for a little while ☺). I picked him for this reason - that he was unavailable and really not that into me - so I could relive what I thought to be right and true. Moreover, he was likely playing out his own abandonment/feelings of rejection issues with me (so his cheating was about how his parents related to him, ugh, the circle continues, doesn't it?). Moreover, his behavior was a projection of my insides (remember all these people serve as mirrors for us) and I was full of self-hate, so why should he like me. His mirror message/lesson to me was, *"Hey girl start loving yourself."* I can thank him now!

I struggled with understanding the thought process of the men and women who "poach" married people and this helped me displace my anger for a little while, but I realized poachers of course had their own parental issues they were dealing with. Perhaps they felt their target parent liked a sibling better and were trying to get their desired attention from their unattainable parent? People who poach are most likely acting out their very own unworthiness beliefs translated into self-sabotage choices and behaviors. Wouldn't it be great to solve all these things with healthy self-love before entering into a relationship, so there wouldn't be the extra burden of the infidelity and poaching stress?!

I can tell you my anger over the situation (toward me, him, and these other women) was uncomfortable for me. It was a tough time, and I just kept blaming myself for getting it wrong and then moved about my life not trusting men, women, or myself. I spent a lot of time shining lotus petals and other more superficial stuff to make myself prettier, skinnier, etc. I got on that track because one of the only people I told about my husband's affair was my mom, which was of course a big mistake. This is starting to get like a horror movie where I keep going into the garage alone. Anyway, my mom said of course, that the affair was my fault for putting on sweat pants when I got home from work and not making fancy meals where we sit at the table. She told me all men cheat and I should be happy he isn't gambling.

Even after coping, correcting my mother wound, and dating again, I would keep picking partners this way (unavailable and uninterested) until my lesson was learned. The learning of that lesson came via the very self-awareness of the situation and my activities to practice conscious self-love. Then it was over.

We know some families discourage discussions about emotions and even the expression of negative emotions can be prohibited. I remember right after my father died I would cry myself to sleep, and my mother told me to "stop crying because all the crying in the world would not bring him back." It is difficult to learn to work through difficult situations and feelings when there is a prohibition on displaying emotions.

Are you longing to discuss emotions with your partner, but fear doing so because it is not what you think is okay based on your imprinted relationship model? My mom also told me my dad's death was MY fault because I caused him stress. That's some pretty significant emotional abuse and possible guilt and shame for a new 15-year-old to process alone. I was so ashamed/guilt ridden to talk to anyone about how I missed my dad and for sure way too disturbed in my thinking to ask someone if it really was my fault (it obviously wasn't, but I held on to that for years). It also made me feel very responsible for other's sheer existences (a big precursor for my future controlling behaviors with the kids. I believed if I wasn't careful or if I caused anyone stress-they would die because of me). Who could I tell that to when I was 15, or even 40? No one. Just the other day I was on the phone with my young son and he was saying he was feeling depressed. I heard his dad in the background saying, *"oh great, here we go again,"* chastising him for him expressing pain instead of showing up with compassion or a place to discuss a negative emotion. I am not chastising my ex-husband, but I am pointing out our society's challenge to let others express emotions-especially negative ones. Did my son trigger my ex? Did he take it personally? What he said was not a conscious parenting response (so it was more about him than my son). My point with that story is it is still happening today.

Just think about some unique aspects of your imprinted parental relationship. Note the first three things that come to mind (he was constantly on her about money, she would go out with her friends and he would get jealous and yell at her, he was rude about her cooking). Now, think about your expectations in or desires for a mate. Do you see any similarities? Again, just this awareness is a gigantic step toward your growth and happiness. If you get triggered because you don't get your flowers on your birthday, you might say, "Oh, I don't even want flowers." That was my mom's definition of love. If you decide you do want the flowers you can tell your mate - my dad always brought my mom flowers on her birthday. I don't know if I even want that, but it is this parenting pattern that must be triggering me. Just get real about your insights and share them with your mate! Can you imagine such a thing! Now that would be an interesting parental model for your own children to watch, wouldn't it!?

What was my parent's relationship like?

_____

_____

_____

_____

_____

What Do You Want Activity. This activity can be used for absolutely everything. For this moment right now let's think about what you want your relationship to look like, regardless of the parenting imprints from their relationship and regardless of your conditioning about what you deserve. Let's believe you deserve great love!! Close your eyes. Take some deep breaths. Think of your cat, dog, a bunny. Smile. Hug yourself. See yourself as happy and fulfilled in your relationship (whether you have one or not). Feel that feeling. How are you receiving love? What are you receiving. How are you giving love? What are you giving. See the possibility. Realize how much easier this will be if you are practicing conscious self-love and know you deserve to be happy and have your OWN relationships regardless of anything in your past. Love is who you are. Love is what you give. Love is what you receive. How does that look. When you are done, breath and be content. It is not a matter of going out and finding the perfect partner. It is a matter of you connecting to and practicing your conscious love. You will feel your love for yourself. You can't help to relate to others this way. They respond in kind. The best way to get what you want is to start giving it. Even when it is hard! Try this in a few of your relationships starting today!

People Who Don't Love Themselves are MEAN

What if your parents scored high on self-love, but you still feel low. Our self-love feelings can be impacted by parents, siblings, mates, friends, the media, and other things. Let's explore that now.

Media. If there is one thing I can get behind consistently is respecting (and loving, of course) people's creative works. I find it so confusing when people criticize other's creative endeavors and think, *wow, why judge that* (unless of course it is destructive, sending a bad modeling example, or harming another in some way). How can we criticize a person's expression of themselves - what is inside their soul and mind? Then I remember, *oh yeah, not everyone loves themselves yet*. Indeed I believe the trolls (as we call them) on the Internet and in public have so little love for themselves they lash out in unloving ways because that is really all they know to do. How unfortunate for all of us. Still, it is essential we practice our conscious self-love, so we don't let this new and unchartered territory of the media and social media cause further havoc.

Does it help you to know the reason the trolls are being mean is because they don't love themselves? It helps me a little bit. Even the covert cruel behaviors offered by trolls that make you question yourself are coming from a place of lacking love from the source. We get so irritated, but that is only because WE are not loving ourselves either! If we loved ourselves, then the trolls (passive-aggressive people included now) and their behavior would NOT even matter. Their inappropriate behavior is not about us (we can see this when we are practicing conscious self-love); it is just directed toward us because we are in a certain place at certain time.

If we don't take these behaviors personally and/or allow them to impact our own love for ourselves, we grow even stronger. We stand firm with our beautiful flowered mirror to the troll (while not even being triggered) and help them see their lack of love for themselves is really at their core; and that it is okay because they are still worthy of their own self-love. We help people see their own path to love through our modeling, advising, and extending more love. The correct answer is always......... more love.

I am on Facebook, Instagram, and Twitter myself. I've seen posts of people advising others to kill themselves, bragging videos of humans beating other humans or harming animals - we could go on for a while here, right? There is cyber bullying, likes for posts of abuse, you name it, all in this anonymous and unaccountable venue. I would say it would be a challenge to be high in self-love growing up with social media unless you (or your good, conscious parent) limited your media exposure and/or really went out of their way to help you cultivate self-love.

Self-love may even be impacted by consumed media (non-interactive mediums like movies and television programs and interactive mediums like video games), especially for children. I wish Mr. Rodgers was still on, don't you? Our generation was lucky to have more positive children's programming than negative. Unfortunately, that is not the same today. Even if we did sneak an adult program when our parents weren't supervising they were so qualitatively different than the adult programs available for consumption now. Children and adults of all ages are consuming media that rarely, if ever, demonstrates self-love or care for the human psyche. What do you think about this? I don't like it!

Relationships with friends or others low in self-love. During my lack of self-love decade I berated myself, could barely make decisions, and then always hated my choices. I certainly provided a bad self-love example to my children. Behaviorally I LOVED my boys, but as I mentioned I engaged in quite a bit of co-dependent mothering and "caretaking" (both are bad - in fact, co-dependent activity is thought to stem from feeling unworthy!) in order to prove I really was worthy of love. I was out of control with judging my (and the world's) conditions of worth. It was less harmful than what I went through, but still, no picnic for my kids I am sure. I was really trying to get it right. What about the parents not trying to get it right? Yikes.

Did you have any challenging relationship experiences that you now think might've impacted your self-love? Sometimes we refer to these people as toxic. If someone doesn't value you in general, or what you bring to the relationship (either by telling you directly or by more covert techniques), everyone who sees it will suffer. Even relationships where there is an unequal balance of give and take can cause a disruption in self-love.

We continue to search for external sources of love and go to great lengths to prove to others we are loveable, when who we really need to prove is ourselves. Relying on others for your love is even less effective than shining up your lotus petals by doing your healing work and loving yourself. Plus, you can shine the petals all you want, but the major repairs are not going to happen until you address the lotus center, heart of the matter who supplies the life to the petals. It is not an option and you just must practice conscious self-love if you want your petals to shine.

People assume they need to find a new partner who loves them more. This idea that your repairs in self-love can be delivered by another is creating an expectation (expectations are not great), will likely lead to resentment (which is even worse), and cannot, and will not, pan out. We could save a lot of money on couples counseling and divorce if everyone came into relationships with their own self-love in-tact.

Relationship influences to self-love can start young! When children start "dating" now, no one really has high self-esteem yet, especially about dating. You go in low and are attracted to others who treat you as you treat you. If you are low, do you want to be with someone who treats you well, or gives you the love that heals? That answer is no. You want to be with someone who sees you like you see you.

Do you recall your first few relationships? Think about what it is like today for young people. It's likely worse because the consumed media in our society has dramatically shifted from *Happy Days* to *Cheaters* and *Dateline* (seriously how can every episode be about a spouse killing the other, for a while my only dating criterion was: *not gonna kill me*. Also people, let's learn from *Dateline* to please agree to the prenup if you are asked because you'd rather get out with your life than killed... I am just saying).

I recall my son's first girlfriend. He was in 8th grade. He was nervous and really doing his best, I thought. I, of course, was bringing him all sorts of lessons and advice on how he should do things (and give), but I completely missed the boat on telling him what he could expect to receive. Until one day. He brought home his 8th grade yearbook and we were looking through it as you do, and I couldn't wait to see his picture - he took a great picture that year (you know how hard that is). I turned to his page and saw that his girlfriend signed his yearbook across his picture page (over his picture) with a black sharpie and drew a mustache, glasses, and squiggles all over his face (what we used to do to enemies in the old days). He was - I am not even sure how to describe this emotion/reaction - but it was upsetting for me to witness as he tried unsuccessfully to show no facial expression and make light of it. He confessed she did that (drew over his picture) in all of his friend's yearbooks she signed. It was 8th grade, when I still had some oversight and we talked about why this girl wouldn't be good girlfriend material, and I politely encouraged him to end the relationship. I think about what type of imprint that left. Does he still question his worth in relationships? What about that girl? Does she remember that? Does she still dislike herself? Have the media, public, your friends been cruel to you?! What messages have you taken away? How do you feel knowing it was not even about you? What do you want to do now when it comes to how you relate to other people?

What about our current school system? Well, I have a bit more bad news to report (or good news depending how you are taking all of this, in acknowledging we can do something about it). It starts young, like in preschool, where kids should mostly be running around, but instead are learning letters/numbers, being evaluated, and learning about all their mistakes (why do teachers always top the paper in their red pen with how many "wrong," like with a -4). Why not a +96 - isn't that so much better!?! I told my son's teacher this in first grade because the minus marks were really getting to him. She said she would consider it, but nothing ever changed. When he brought a paper home I would take a red pen and write, the flip side plus score for him and talk about that. That particular child was so fearful by the "helpful" college readiness sessions mandatory in high school he could barely apply. He was sure he wouldn't get in. With both boys I would pray our traditional school system just do them NO HARM (sort of like our traditional Western medical system, right? But alas, both of those systems s are really messing up their constituents - how unfortunate!). Do you see how our current school system sets us up for a lack of self-love?

    The lack of understanding about ADHD and autism by school personnel is creating another huge problem for our youth (in terms of self-love, them thinking they are failures, and their actual futures!). Schools, teachers, and administrators are calling meetings, scaring parents, making children feel like failures/flops, and inappropriately diagnosing ADHD (and inappropriately suggesting medications!) at an alarming rate. I always thought this was because schools are busy and must teach to the middle to stay afloat. If you take your child to the pediatrician and say he has a problem with attention you will be able to leave with a stimulant medication for your child. It is really inappropriate for medical doctors to be diagnosing and treating mental disorders. I am not mad at teachers (or even pediatricians), but our country doesn't revere teachers or schools (but can you think of a more important profession? I can't). We revere the medical profession, but the gross lack of self-care caused by medical school/residency programs and then the crazy amount of required work hours by doctors - I mean there is likely a significant lack of self-love in both groups. Our whole country has this systemic problem of lacking self-love!

Do you know in Finland school teachers are venerated? In Finland they know that kids have challenges focusing (ALL kids - and ALL kids would prefer to be running around than sitting there taking in some dribble ☺). In Finland, school classes are an hour to 45 minutes of information and 15 minutes of play and exercise. Finland's school system is consistently ranked best in the world. What is the problem whereby our country refuses to emulate successful educational and medical systems? Is there a lack of self-love in our very institutions?

How the External Imprints Affect Us

We've spent a lot of time talking about how others can affect us. This is insidious and even possibly outside of our awareness. The worst part is, if we don't recognize it, we are likely to take the baton in treating ourselves poorly from our parent's/friends/media for the rest of our lives. This is a very common and normal occurrence, but what kind of life is that? Why do we even do this? Well, we do this because the subconscious mind gets conditioned and these damaging beliefs about ourselves sit there and run 95% of our show on a daily basis until someone steps in to process the subconscious and conditioned imprints from your past.

The Subconscious

The subconscious mind is where we hold all of our self-hate OR self-love programs. The programs run on autopilot and influence literally all of our thoughts, interactions, decisions, and the like on a daily and even 24-hour basis (the subconscious is even active during sleep). Our subconscious mind was developed when were children (between birth and age 10). We didn't choose the messages and lessons (you recall Chapters 1 and 2), we absorbed it from our surroundings and via our parental and family beliefs, modeling, and interactions.

Subconscious mind's contents. The thing about the parental conditioning is just the same as Pavlov's stimulus-response idea. Take a cat and can of tuna as the example. If you keep pairing a can opener sound (neutral stimulus) with a can of tuna (conditioned stimulus), cats begin to salivate when they hear the can opener (conditioned response). This is a simple example of how stimulus and response (S-R) associations come about, by the over and over pairing, which results in learning WE created. That cats learned based on their conditioning that can openers were good. It wouldn't matter what Pavlov picked as the stimulus. Just as it didn't really matter what my mom did, it was the meaning I gave it at the time that was important. It was all those conditioned responses I made (i.e., fear, self-hate, not feeling worthy or good enough). True, they were based on her odd stimuli (mean words and nonverbal cues, and neglect and abuse), but I could've not taken them personally, then such associations may never have been created. But this is what children do and why we need to break the cycle.

Knowing I was the one creating the associations and conditioned response is good news and gives me my power back, because if I learned it one way I can recondition myself! Some people refer to this as reconditioning, reparenting, repatterning, really there are lots of names for it.

You can break the association between the stimuli and conditioned responses! You should, because those S-R connections you made as a kid is now your automatic pilot and determining your thoughts and behaviors! This automatic pilot is housed inside your subconscious mind. The automatic pilot/subconscious mind runs 95% of your daily on goings (according to neuroscientists) and is most of the time completely unconscious to you.

To stop being unconscious of what is happening behind the scenes in your subconscious is easy. It just requires you become aware (conscious) of the association, you can see it in real time as it is happening, and then consciously replace the negative conditioned thoughts/feelings/behaviors with self-love and acceptance. Have you even driven somewhere, gotten back home and thought, wow, I have no idea how that happened, I wasn't present, the car and my automatic pilot did a great job taking over? When skills become practiced over and over (experts say it takes 10,000 hours of something to become an expert) the skill is internalized and becomes automatic. How many hours did you witness, hear, see you being treated like you are worthy of love? How many hours have you witnessed the opposite? What thoughts about you have been internalized and become your automatic pilot?

Spending time in taking care of yourself helps you develop fond feelings for you, unravels the unworthiness, and helps you commit to the process of reconditioning. It is up to you now to make positive and adaptive S-R connections, so they can become internalized and be your automatic pilot! Then, over time even activities that might've irritated us, such as making your bed - when viewed through your conscious self-love lens can be seen as a self-care kindness to ourselves. Through relating with yourself with care, love, and soul nurturing your lens changes and it gets even easier to be with ourselves in a kind way. Over more time, this way of being with yourself and others in a kind, loving, and compassionate way becomes your new automatic pilot and your subconscious patterns of critique and abuse are replaced with acceptance and kindness for yourself and others. To facilitate the process you must internalize the love, acceptance, and kindness for yourself first (practice conscious self-love) as you just can't give away what you don't have.

The Subconscious Story

I was talking (commiserating) with a friend about the shitty childhoods we had. Comparing war stories like whose was worse. The "I bet I experienced more trauma than you" game. He was telling me about how his brother is so bitter and not seeing any value in his life experiences (the story). Still, my friend would go on and on about his father almost every time I talked with him. I don't know if it is because I ask good questions (maybe that was the case), but maybe he really does have an unresolved father wound on his mind every day. Where does the trauma sit? It sits in the subconscious.

Freud and many others maintained that the subconscious mind was the ruler of most all our thoughts/emotions/fears/behaviors, but this ruling was going on undetected and outside of our awareness. Remember the Wizard from OZ, like that! The subconscious is the Wizard. It would be better if your Wizard was operating with a good story. I don't think that's common though. As I look up I see in my bookshelf these books, The Emotionally Absent Mother, Difficult Mothers, Mean Mothers, When you and your Mothers Can't Be Friends, You are Not Crazy-It's Your Mother, Mother's Who Can't Love, Toxic Parents, Children of the Self-Absorbed, Difficult Mothers, Toxic Mom Toolkit. These are just some I picked up throughout the years and I tell you there are so so many more. There are other issues outside of parenting to cause trauma. I can go on and on. The point I am trying to make is.... a shitty story filled with being unloved, unwanted, abused, neglected, and otherwise traumatized is much more likely the norm unless your parents and the adults you encountered were all great, conscious people, who practiced conscious parenting. What are the chances?

I don't think the nature of the trauma, or other story and the details of it are what I want to deal with today. What I want to share is - this story, just like a molted alligator skin can be shed. Zipped off. See ya! Bye Felicia. It can be an easy or hard to shed. You know my motto, don't make anything harder, so if I were you I would go with the easy route.

An unexplored subconscious with your trauma story is like a silent business partner. The unconscious memories parlay into unconscious robo motions (current-day conditioned responses to unexplored parental and other conditioning and other trauma stimulus). Each day, each minute, we try to protect ourselves by engaging in more projection, negative thoughts, bad feelings, and environment tinkering to avoid more pain. We get triggered, reactive, we try to cope and set a boundary and avoid the trigger. We are constantly on edge. This is the vibe we put out and the things we attract to us are simply the things sitting in our unexplored subconscious mind. That is indeed the Law of

Attraction. We actively search out experiences and thoughts that are familiar with how we are feeling in the subconscious - the self-fulfilling prophecy.

We already talked about this, but if you are feeling bad about yourself do you want to date someone who adores you? No, because that is too weird and confusing. You seek out others who treat you like you do, crap. How would one fix that, keep finding different partners (saying you want someone to be nice, but really only setting on the crappy ones). No, you address this by becoming aware of what is in your subconscious, see the story, the patterns, how they are running your current show, and put a stop to that by becoming conscious, practicing conscious self-love, and watching yourself make different choices because of it!

Story creation. It is our story from youth. To be clear, we all experienced parental conditioning. We all put 2 and 2 together and paired responses to our environmental stimulus. Our subconscious just contains a volume of S-R connections we put together. The main S-Rs in the subconscious were put there from birth to 10 and were from our parents. That story lives in our unconscious mind guiding daily, hourly, thoughts, behaviors, words to ourselves, words to others, our parenting, our relating to our partners. It is really just a truth we must realize.

Some people have good conditioning/stories/subconscious contents and some have bad. I don't mean to demean anything, but it doesn't really matter the story. All people must step out from the stories from the environmental conditioning. Like an unzipping of a conditioned skin step out of it and let that snake skin fall on the ground. See your new and improved skin.

Some "childhood" conditioning lasts for 10 years after childhood, some for 20 years. For some the childhood established S-R connections last a whole lifetime! The point of the story is to step out of it. I personally think people with bad stories may be better off ,because it seems to me those people are so uncomfortable with their boiling subconscious stories they get the itch to become conscious (become aware of the subconscious program) sooner and make adjustments.

The adjustments are simply to step out and away from that story. The story could be from your childhood, it could have continued on and been the main theme of your first/second/third marriage. It doesn't matter when you realize your story is just that - a story, a bunch of S-R conditions you put there when you were like a baby. Your story is a little gift for you to help you realize you are here to live your beautiful life where you get to love yourself despite a story.

Once you recognize the story is just that (and not the truth of you) YOU can choose to become aware of its effects on you. This can happen at age 13, 33, 83, or not in this life. If you do have that insight of self-awareness - Glory Be! - then it will be up to YOU to choose to leave it behind, or keep it with you.

I decided not to keep mine because it was icky, made me not like myself and others. My story was a present to help me realize I needed to dump it. I didn't really need Cognitive Therapy to change my thoughts, I didn't really need to keep talking about my mom and processing my feelings. What I really need it was to just decide that story was nothing but a story, and it was time for a new and improved one.

My new and improved story shows me as strong and vibrant. I mean, think about it. I was supposed to be an abortion, right? Well, wow, that was some fancy footwork of mine to instead be sitting here writing this. What a strong gal! What a gift I found out that part of my story so I can see and appreciate my strengths. Just because my mom didn't want me, look, I came out anyway. Someone wanted me. Maybe it was me :)

The trick is to reprogram the subconscious by undoing is to become self-aware of how you think about yourself (what do you say about you, your triggers, your reactions). Awareness bring the subconscious to the surface and that's where we can change! We will discuss more strategies to do this in Chapter 5 of your Daily DOs!

So now what! My future got a lot brighter because of my awareness and conscious practice of self-love. My growth in this area was a process. I had many experiences and resources I will share later. You will resonate with some and maybe not others. The most important thing is your awareness and deciding to practice conscious self-love. The next is understanding, when you release all the pain and trauma and hurts, you make a place for true love to enter!

Your self-love can fluctuate and I experienced this when I started out knowing I wanted more. I looked for more love outside to fill my tank, but then soon realized, self-love is not a tank to fill, but more a conscious practice (hence - conscious self-love). It wasn't an overnight change, but the awareness of my desire for it was the tipping point for sure. Having the knowledge to understand that the past is past and letting that go is key. You and your true self/soul/heart center can rid the negative patterns from your thoughts and emotions. I think that awareness, and then my intention of wanting it, was really about 70%. If you see it and you want it, you are at a really great place right now. We are moving on from others and our pasts, to US!

After reading this chapter you have successfully completed the contemplation for change part (this was when you picked up the book, well done!), then the motivation for change (you graduated from Chapters 1 and 2), and now in this chapter you have self-awareness (you must recognize there is a problem for you to make some changes). Well done! If you turn the pages to the next chapter you are considering preparations for change. This is a very big deal! Next will come action and changing behaviors. We are stepping out of the mud now and waving at the nice lotus leaves as we step into the juicy center of the lotus heart, where all the good stuff sits. We are doing this for us, for our loved ones, and for the world.

Here's an important quote from John Mayer from Instagram: "Someday everything will make perfect sense. So for now, laugh at the confusion, smile through the tears. Be strong and keep reminding yourself that everything happens for a reason." I will add that the sooner we embrace the reasons and lessons, the sooner we reduce our suffering. It is not difficult to face these facts, but we avoid it because we think it is. We are correcting things from our pasts and generations of others' pasts imprinted in our genomes. When we make the most of and best out of our reasons we minimize our suffering, so we can be happier on a daily basis. It is good to live happy and peaceful lives full of love and joy and to help others do the same. I think that is the best part of us being here!

"Awareness is like the sun.

When it shines on things they are transformed."

Nhat Hanh

Chapter Four: Practicing Conscious Self-Love

Daily BEs

"Everything we hear is an opinion, not a fact.

Everything we see is a perspective, not the truth.

Very little is needed to make a happy life;

it is all within yourself, in your way of thinking.

You have power over your mind - not outside events.

Realize this, and you will find strength."

Marcus Aurelius

What I am going to say now was hard for me to understand, until it wasn't. It relates to my understanding of how the petals won't fully shine up until you focus on the heart of the lotus and your self-love. A conundrum exists whereby when we think about how to become more peaceful and in love we are using the ego mind. Just the mere action of using that ego mind (and our intellect) prohibits us from leaving the ego mind and letting go to where we need to be. How will we get to the place of sitting still and quieting our thoughts and mind (or at least not attaching to thoughts) to hear the truth from our True Selves.

This reminds me that the very the act of consciously loving yourself and growing in self-love requires both instruction and then letting go. We need the ego to help us learn how to do things, and then we need to trust when it is time to move through life through more of a soul level. This chapter is all about things that may help you practice self-love (words and instructions), but really this choice to actively and consciously love yourself is already in you and simply needs to be accessed. It can be accessed by choosing in the moment to love yourself and over time you most likely won't need more instructions and will just be always moving from your soul level and your true authentic self.

There are no techniques I will offer (like the petal shining) that will work as much as you just deciding today, that today is the day you will begin to consciously and actively practice love for yourself, warts, boils, bad choices, cringe worthy past behavior, cellulite, all of it/you/and your beautiful soul, whatever it takes. Of course conscious self-love is more than that, but it really all does start with you. Of all the people who did and didn't love you in your past - can we please just count on YOU for some love, kindness, and compassion, for yourself. Yes we can. Let's just go ahead and commit to fall in love with yourself. Could it be that easy?

It is our decision, based on our new-found self-awareness of the benefits, placing context to our story, and putting some parts of the story down, and then walking away (thanking the story for it's important lessons as the door hits the old story's ass on its way out!), and then deciding things are changing today for ourselves and our loved ones, for future generations, and forevermore. There could easily be a victim consciousness here, and no one is going to blame you for a pity-party, but that is really ego-based and not going to get us to the happy place. We must and we will actively choose differently - not for grace for the others or to get love from them, but to get love from our very own selves!!

Instead of beating yourself up all the time with your inner critic you will instead change harsh thoughts to curiosity to ask your soul what you are supposed to do with such thoughts. But your default will not be the critical mother or friend you grew up with. Your default mode of "reacting" - will no longer even be reacting. It will be acting toward yourself and others with awareness, acceptance, mercy, and unconditional love. Unconditional love is - love under every and all conditions, events, thoughts, feedback. Let's try it, repeat after me - *"I love me and I treat myself warmly and with love no matter what is happening around me (feedback from others OR my inner critic). From now on!"*

We are talking about changing yourself and the way you relate to yourself. You can get a new job where they respect you (and you should!) and that is a positive change that may be nice for a while, but it is also an external thing. The bigger and even more important thing to change is an internal one - you becoming understanding that you deserve more respect and now make all choices (jobs, partners) from that viewpoint! Can you imagine!

Now I know I just said the self-awareness and the desire for this should be enough, and it might be or it might not be. It sort of reminds me of the paradoxical ease and challenge of meditation. We know the goal of meditation is not exactly to think "no thoughts," it is the even *easier* version of looking at the thought and letting it go. Just like here for conscious self-love, we know the goal is to just love ourselves, but in reality because of all our previous internals and externals we might need some assistance. If we didn't have the troubled conditioning, just telling you today that you should love yourself could be very easy. If it is, great! Yes, the goal is to just love ourselves, but the unconscious conditioning often requires we undo a bit more and have some tricks up our sleeve for the non-loving thoughts.

When practicing conscious self-love you regularly check in with yourself at your job or with your partner to make sure you are feeling respected, and if not, you communicate your needs. You recognize so much earlier now when you experience a little discomfort - it is a sign about you feeling disrespected and you can do something about it. Although changing your circumstances can be good, it is not exactly about that - that is ephemeral and not permanent. The permanent change is your self-change. This is profound! Such a gift to yourself, and the world! Oh and once you do make a change for yourself in this positive direction of conscious self-love, it is hard to go back! You protect yourself and recognize saboteurs, and you are immune as long as you keep practicing your self-love.

As I mentioned before about boundaries, you can choose to institute them or not. Boundaries are about other telling other people to stop affecting you negatively. Conscious self-love is you taking their power away without them even being involved. Once you get into the practice of conscious self-love behaviors and kind treatment of yourself it will likely generalize to all sorts of other behaviors reaping benefit over benefit for your lovely self, with boundaries instituted or not!

Remember self-awareness is key and the decision to relate to yourself in a conscious and unconditionally loving way is the answer. How many tools you need to help with both of these things may depend on the day, where exactly you are with your self-love growth process, a particular situation, your past, or anything. What I pray is that your lotus heart center is warming and that we can start from there! Even you being willing to consider this idea of loving yourself more and the expanded possibilities that entails for you, your loved ones, and the world is making a big difference in you. I hope you can see and feel it!

What are Daily BEs. Your Daily BEs are ways of *existing and being* and are very important. Like a personal motto. When people describe you, these are the adjectives they use. How do you want to be described, how do you want to BE? It is completely up to you regardless of story, old patterns, thoughts/feelings, and relationships you currently have.

People who practice conscious self-love will also practice good Daily BEs. Daily BEs are not things to do, or behaviors, they are rather a mindset. Still, someone can tell what kind of Daily BEs you practice. I can see this (and I presume others can, too) just by looking at your face and body. People who are aware of their Daily BEs (and make an effort to have some control over them) smile more, are kinder, and take better care of themselves and others. People practicing conscious self-love are masters of their Daily BEs!

When managing your Daily BEs you are protecting and guarding your core in an easy-breezy, loving and kind manner that benefits you and all the lucky people you come into contact with on a daily basis. It is HUGE to have a good Daily BE as your internal set-point. If you think that this is how we change the world (one person at a time getting their shit together) then you would be correct! Even if you aren't at a job where you make hundreds of peoples' lives better, you walking into Walgreens with a good Daily BE is just as important.

I want my Daily BE to be in a state of conscious self-love for me and others. For me, this is accomplished by a way of **be**ing grateful, accepting, peaceful, unconditionally loving, conscious, understanding mercy, and having compassion. You protect your peace and other BEs and are aware of your subconscious programs and work with them continuously. The Daily BEs determine your lens and are your characteristic ways of being. If you wrote down three to five things you wanted to be today or every day, what would they be? Do you like mine (unconditionally accepting, compassionate, peaceful, and grateful)? I will spend a little time now trying to convince you of the importance of these BEs.

When our Daily BEs are grounded in self-love, we are making a conscious effort to understand how our ego fits in our love puzzle. By practicing a self-love mindset, your viewing and hearing lenses see and hear love. Engaging in this love lens for one experience, 10 minutes, one hour, one day, ends up determining the quality of your years and even life. The fact that you alone filter (and determine) the character of all external events and internal thoughts should make you need to go get a glass of water right now.

Although you like spending time alone now because you are the only one you can count on you not to upset yourself (most of the time lol), you now can easily spend time with others when practicing your Daily BEs. Even if they accidently or purposely "try" to upset you, you don't have to perceive it as such. Your day to day interactions with others (even though they include a second person) are still completely and totally guided by you and your lens. What happens inside of you has nothing to do with them. We also know from the previous chapter - even words meant to upset you shouldn't be interpreted by you that way (all is projection), and all is mostly showing up for you to give you an important lesson for right this very moment! We don't need to get angry or irritated at the person, ourselves, or lesson, yet we can instead be grateful, in charge, and growing in our consciousness.

I am not saying I never had pity parties for myself or my lessons. Of course I have. That is okay, but that is certainly no longer my default. No one comes to our pity parties (for long) and there's no cake after! If there is cake, you end up feeling guilty for it. I am a fan of peace parties now and the cake tastes great!

If I continue to wallow in my lessons' effects without seeing it as a growth opportunity (and asking it what it wants me to know), or if I ignore the lesson; no matter what I do, the lesson keeps showing up. The universe is not out to get me, and it is not the case that I have a greater share of lessons to learn. The fact of the matter is we draw the lessons to us by what we are putting out. And what we are putting out is determined by our subconscious patterns (determined by our unpacked and unprocessed childhood experiences).

Importance of Daily BEs. If you Daily BEs are putting out good vibes/energy (because your subconscious suitcase is unpacked), you will see and draw in good. Some people call this the self-fulfilling prophecy, the Law of Attraction, your karma, The Secret. I like to use Dr. David Burns idea from his book, *Feeling Good-The New Mood Therapy*. You are in a good mood, so you move about the world pretty happy. People like that and they react happy back to you. The opposite would be true if you were acting sad. Over time, these daily experiences of you giving out and then receiving back good or bad start to become your regular state. Either way you think about it (law of attraction or Dr. Burns' idea) there is no magical secret or universal secret at play here. It is really the case of you looking for things in the external environment (and possibly internal environment -your thoughts) to reify what is in your subconscious mind. This is actually pretty scientific.

If our subconscious mind is not explored and you are working off old family patterns, it is possible you are putting out victim energy, judgments, lack of acceptance for yourself or others, of unworthy and unloved feelings? When we do this, it is very likely we pay attention to, look for, and/or draw those things in to us. When my main subconscious patterns were mistrust I drew in cheaters; when my patterns were rejection I drew in the avoidant partners. Once I started dispelling my unhealthy subconscious patterns and allowing myself to adopt the exact opposite limiting beliefs I was more gracious and loving to myself. I felt more worthy, abundant, full of self-love, and I started to draw to myself experiences, friends, and partners who felt the exact same about me!

Speaking of drawing things into us, we can talk in terms of big things like the subconscious' role in our partner selections, but we can also talk in smaller terms of drawing things in on a daily/hourly basis. These smaller things can be *attracted to the magnetic force of your subconscious mind*, or your current mood, or mindset. If that idea of a magnetic force bothers you, think instead about you just plain looking for evidence to support what is in your subconscious mind. That is why it is so important to protect your peace, because when you are peaceful and happy you draw more of that to you (or, you look for that and find it)!

On a pity party day you are likely to draw in and actually perceive all stimuli coming in as a bummer (this is Dr. Burns' idea). We have all done this, right? I was really looking forward to a long Memorial Day weekend to work on this book and indulge in self-care. Then I went to the grocery store and saw party napkins and mini decorated cupcakes (yes, napkins were my trigger!). Then my whole day changed as I was reminded I had no plans for the weekend (my own choosing really) and everything coming in (even my previous joy) was a bummer. I sat with my feeling of perpetual aloneness and decided it was a remnant of my mom's lonely life. I talked to my best friend, got some context, canceled the pity party, got right with my Daily BEs (only ate two mini-cupcakes) and had a tremendous weekend with myself! Who better to spend it with really? :) It was not magic, a secret, or the universe being cruel (or nice). If you keep asking "why me?" you will draw in things to be upset about! They will be all you see. It is YOUR lens and you have complete control over it! Maybe we should refer to it as the Law of Lens :)

My self-love status is now inside of my awareness and consciousness and I am pretty good about checking in with my Daily BEs and keeping tabs of where I am. But more importantly, my default now is to deal with others and myself with self-love (consciously), so that it is so much more likely I am doing it. In the past, things could bother me for a long time- people could really get to me and I would say mean things to myself. Those things might still happen, but from the time it starts to the time it's finish is so diminished, because I catch it and take care of myself. Still, I am not perfect and no one is. I still regularly practice both Daily BEs and Daily DOs, whereby I check in with my thinking lens and engage in the self-acceptance, self-care, and soul nurturing behaviors (some days more than others). I do this because I love myself and I know that I am worthy. I know that YOU are too!

Some of my Daily BEs can look a little like Daily DOs, and we will veer into that territory in some ways in this discussion of how to BE, but I believe the things in this chapter are more about mindset than activities.

The Lens of Protecting Your Peace

A beautiful goal for yourself is to be peaceful. Gosh, when I am walking around my day with my Lens of Peace on (peaceful on the inside and peaceful on the outside) I love my day and I even know the people I came into contact with might've benefited. When was the last time you were around a peaceful person? It's a real gift, isn't it. You can be the peaceful person!

To protect my peace on a daily basis, I wake up and think of my Daily BEs. Taking 5 minutes in the morning to pray, or think about love, will set up the rest of your day for love and joy. You could pray, meditate, just think, journal about your emotions/day, or look out the window and set your lens to positive and helpful things. Try this tomorrow and then the next day and the next and you will see it is so much better than popping up and fretting about your to-do list, watching the news, looking at your phone, or popping up and taking care of someone else. Attend to your soul first thing in the morning and just be with her. That is more than enough to give your loved one (you) the positive attention she deserves to start her day.

So I've got that morning thing going for me. Once I notice I feel a sort of discomfort during the day, an inkling of ick (lesson, trigger, inner turmoil, someone being rude, my inner critic having something to say, me feeling scared or threatened), I just stop what I am doing and assess what is happening with me? Is it an external or situational issue? Is the ick coming from inside me, a thought or feeling (likely representing a subconscious pattern [internal]), or is someone/something bothering me [external])? **I take a moment**. I check in with my thoughts and feelings. I get present.

Get present with thoughts and feelings. The first step is about getting present. Present in this moment now. You can ask yourself, what am I thinking about? What am I feeling? What is the difference between these two things!?

Thoughts and feelings are different things and many people describe the relationship between them. Some people only think thoughts are valid and we should ignore feelings. Others believe the opposite, or suggest the two are related (either thoughts determine feelings, or how you are feeling determines how you think about things). Here is my take. Thought are mind words, ephemeral, can be easily dismissed if you don't attach to them, and can be changed and turned to positive with just that intention. Feelings are more visceral, in my stomach area more so than mind, likely coming from my soul to tell me something (gut feeling). Feelings are more of a state and harder to push away and just a little harder to change than thoughts (for me). If I am thinking a lot of critical/negative thoughts I can start feeling bad. Similarly, if I am feeling bad I think of more negative things. We can just easily use two feeling words of good or bad and that is fine. If you want to get specific try and name the feeling you are experiencing (e.g., joy, bliss, anger, jealousy, irritation, frustration, boredom, peace). It is helpful to distinguish between thoughts and feelings when we are talking Lenses.

Present moment *thoughts*. I had some problems learning how to get present because my mind was full of thoughts about fixing things. I was forever in list mode. I was kicking myself out of the present moment/essence with my head's thoughts about some future thing. I wanted to get everything right and I needed lists. The Power of Now was an excellent book for me. In the Power of Now we learn most psychological unease has to do with us ruminating about the past and being anxious about the future. If we all lived in the NOW moment where things are juicy and our senses are alive, then we would likely be happy, or at least peaceful. The moment of now (as compared to the past or the future) is the only thing that is real in our lives. This is such an interesting and incredibly helpful idea. I pray most days that I will be in the present moment for myself and the people I am with. I do actually say a prayer about it!

Something that helped shake me out of list mode (fixing thoughts) was surrendering. Surrendering is not throwing your hands up and saying *okay universe do what you want*. It is more of a belief in the perfection of each moment YOU are creating - via your soul and True Self in the context of the Divine world. It is you who is making the moment via your choices and actions and it is perfect. You don't actually need to plan, write out a script, or have a list when you just start being and existing from your soul and True Self level (your essence). You are free to surrender to a moment's perfection. When we surrender to the moment we are creating and believe that what is happening right now is the perfect thing to happen we can find peace. When I go to the grocery store and forget my grocery list, those are always the best trips. I get what I need exactly and also seem to forget the Diet Coke ☺. At first I feel frustrated, but then I remind myself, oh if I do forget something that was likely okay and even good! When you can see a purpose or reason behind my possible forgetting, or just trust in the moment (the art of surrendering) I move out of frustration to gratitude. Maybe I forgot to buy Diet Coke at the store because it was bad for me. You could try this activity next time you go to the grocery store. Just get what you remember to get at that visit and see how it works for you. There may be something to this! My son slept through a doctor's appointment and had to reschedule it. Instead of me chastising him or freaking out I immediately saw the benefit (he was not going to get a refill on a prescription I was questioning just then). I didn't note that to him, or mention surrendering, I just gently excused him from the shame and blame he was chastising himself by providing compassion and asked him to do the same for himself.

The other thing that helped me get out of list mode was to practice conscious self-love. Once I become more self-confident (because I was practicing conscious self-love) I realized there was nothing more to "fix," so I felt reprieved from planning future fixes, or putting off happiness until I had everything on my list. I was good now. My Amazon purchases even became less frequent!

When a non-peace thought comes in I may ask myself, in this present moment, What is this that is disturbing my peace? Is there something I can be grateful for? Is there something I can learn about me, my subconscious, or life in general? Am I being judgmental (which means I am not accepting me or another or a situation)? Am I lacking compassion in this very moment? Am I even in this moment? These are good questions because lots of time we aren't even present in the moment. I may see your eyes looking at me, but are you thinking of what to say next, what to eat, how what I said reminded you of something your mother said years ago, or what will happen when rent is due next month?

In those thought spaces there are questions, confusions, and troubles. Most often, in this very moment now, we are good and we can have positive thoughts. When we veer to thinking of the past or fretting the future our thoughts turn from peace to either regret or worry. It is nice to spend time in the moment. If I am not in the mood to process a negative thought by analyzing it and questioning it I will just say, *oh hey, NO,* and change that thought to a positive one. It is easy to do this. I know I can return to processing it later IF I want, but I also know if it was just a cray cray thought that popped in I can tell it to leave my mind and it will listen if I can think about something else, or get back to my present activity.

Present moment *feelings*. What if a *feeling* presents itself and you feel fear, grief, worry, overwhelmed, or hopelessness? This can be more visceral and more attention getting that a few rogue thoughts you can change to the positive in a moment. Feelings can be changed, but should they? Lots of times feelings are carrying important information from your body to your mind - heart to soul, so you can know something important about something in your internal or external situation.

In the past I would run away from bad feelings and try to resist them, avoid it, or deny it. They were sometimes overwhelming and I didn't like that feeling (so like a double bad feeling). I learned to take the overwhelmed feeling away and look at instigating feeling more objectively. Even though feelings are more visceral and palpable than thoughts, I learned they can be made less so, and also that I am in control of these feelings (just like the thoughts), which is crucial to know. We can't be overwhelmed or overcome by feelings because we are in charge of them. We can easily just say no, or I would like to feel differently at literally any moment.

When you don't attend to or change your bad feelings they don't likely go away and they may actually get scarier because we don't learn how to deal with them. Different than thoughts (where you can have a lot of thoughts in your head at one time positive and negative), feelings seem to be one or the other.

I think feelings are more like the stress arousal response - either a good feeling or bad feeling in your present moment. Did you know that, either your sympathetic nervous system is engaged and you are stressed, or your parasympathetic nervous system is engaged and you are relaxed - it can't be both. If you start a relaxing breath (or anything else to start up your parasympathetic nervous system you will stop your stress arousal response in its tracks! So, if you have a bad feeling, you can replace it with a good feeling (by intending to or changing something). But sometimes you can get some useful info before you do that.

Before I arrived at the idea that I was in control of my feelings too, I thought feelings would have control over me and I would need to be a victim to their coming and going, their power, and their unpredictability. I worked my hardest to set up a "safe" emotion and feeling-free environment for myself; that was how I protected my peace. So, so many boundaries. As you can guess, this didn't work. My relationships were disconnected, I was lonely, a little weird, and constantly on edge to protect my space from anything out of control. I decided to just process the bad feelings to get them the heck out of my head. By process I mean, look at them, see if there is helpful info for me here, then let the bad feeling go and replace it with a good feeling.

Some people believe your emotions (feelings) are just as important as your other five senses. Other experts maintained we spend too much time both thinking (getting so lost in thoughts) and feeling (getting overwhelmed by emotions) and both are ego activities taking us off our true soul path. I have come to think of it this way. If you are willing to explore your thoughts/feelings with self-awareness for important information about you and your journey and then *let them go* when you are ready (so they don't overwhelm and control you) then they are helpful. If you are not in the place for such exploration and you are stuck ruminating all day/every day, rather than releasing, then if I were you, I would take a feeling break.

One more note about your feelings/emotions. You may feel them spontaneously, or they get triggered. Let's hope they are the cute and good ones like peace and joy. Even if they are heavy and challenging, like stress, or shame, they are likely here to help you move to a much more exquisite place via their special message for you. If you have time and look at even these difficult emotions as important for your life (they are here to help you with something!) and process them accordingly, you will regain your peace.

Greeting the feelings activity. I have a few techniques about a positive *greeting the feelings mindset* (feelings processing) to share. When I get a feeling I don't like I think, "Oh interesting. Here is a feeling I don't like." I greet the negative feeling with curiosity. I try to figure out what the feeling is and where it is coming from. Am I feeling discomfort, loneliness, boredom, fear, joy, insecurity? Let's say the feeling is coming from outside, maybe someone is asking me to do something I don't want to do. I know I don't want to do it because I can feel my body screaming at me to SAY NO!!!. Still, I might want this person to like me and/or I feel obligated, so I have conflict (my needs or theirs). Step one even before I speak is to greet my feeling in my body and hear her out. You may not know the feeling exactly, but you can guess if you want. I don't want to do that activity because I am super busy and just don't have time. I decide to share the feeling because this will be helpful in this situation. I will say something like, "I am feeling a bit overwhelmed right now and I would like to help you, but I just can't." Often when we are worried someone won't like us - we will do things we don't want. To avoid such a scenario I always pretend they already like me and I have no obligation. You can share your feelings and do what YOU want with people you have known for years, or people you just met. Just share your feeling about their request and then follow through!

Maybe the negative feeling to greet is coming from inside (and no other person is even involved). Maybe I am thinking I should be doing something, *like I am not doing enough*. This can be a good lesson too. Most people have a pattern they are not doing enough, or even they as a human *are not enough*. We are always in Do mode and can feel uncomfortable just being. Knowing this can get you to have a discussion with yourself about how you are doing a lot and can prioritize and/or say no, or set a boundary, and/or get comfortable just being and resting. Am I feeling overwhelmed? If so, I can rethink what I have taken on and make adjustments. I can ask for help, more time, to get out of the task. I can change my mind at any time and that is okay! Maybe I can ask to receive instead of giving in this moment. Having this information can sure be helpful.

Maybe I am feeling afraid of something. Is the fear real, like I shouldn't go out in a thunderstorm, or is there a snake? Is the fear coming from an irrational source, my ego, or based on a subconscious pattern I have? I am worried my partner is cheating and I feel jealous. Is this based on something that is currently happening, or my past baggage about being cheated on? Am I just searching for clues he is attracted to other people? What if I search for clues he loves me. I can think about this.

Feelings don't likely pop in out of thin air. Problems are not solved by sheer luck. We need to look at them and figure out the solution. We can't do this if we don't understand the problem though. If we run away from the problems, they will follow us. It's best to stop, turn around, look this emotion objectively and just ask it, *"What do you need me to know?"* What am I afraid of? The answer usually comes quickly. Then I know what I am working with, something rational or irrational. So, Step #1 of greeting my feelings is looking it straight in the eye and not avoid it.

Processing the feeling activity. After you recognize what you are feeling, you can process it. You can do this now or decide to do it later. I start processing by talking to my feeling/myself as my best friend would. *"Oh, you are bored. I am sorry. Is there something you can do now to get you out and about, or up and doing something you enjoy?"* What if you are stuck in an insecurity loop and your mind starts running to, "Oh no, I am sure he is cheating, he likes the other person better, I will always be alone." **What would your friend say to you? What would someone who loved themselves do/say?** These two questions are SO helpful. I bet the answers would look something like...."Calm down, stop looking at his Facebook likes, this is likely your old baggage showing up to tell you something important (you are placing too much energy on this person and not yourself, or something like that)." You can process the feeling for now just so you start feeling peace again. We don't have to spend a lot of time in feeling mode, especially if they are troubling. Just greet them and process. By processing you can decide if you need to learn something, take action, or just let the feeling move on.

You can ask a feeling to move on softly or loudly. You can think, *"Oh, of course he is not cheating on me, this is just a common feeling I have based on my past. I am choosing to let this feeling go and get back to my work/exercise/cleaning."* You can visualize your feeling floating away downstream on a little floatie. You can thank it on its way out. Sometimes I actually turn and walk away from where I am standing when I am thinking something negative. Break it up physically, then I get back to my task at hand. It is for me to decide what to do with the feeling. I am always in charge of my feelings (the greeting and processing) and can drop it at any time. I am in control of my feelings.

Sometimes after you attach to the feeling for a long time it may be harder to see it floating out. In that case you can ask your feeling to leave loudly. My favorite Instagram account (@mariia_healing_light) has a great technique for this! She advises we yell at the feeling/energy to STOP, or ENOUGH and follow with, "I Refuse to feel _____ right now. I Refuse to believe _____." Refuse it and mean it. If you are fed up with a certain feeling, or just tired of it, ask it to go. I personally like to feel happy/joy most of the day.

I will process my negative feelings because I am a curious person and interested in learning (even things about me!) and try to absorb my lesson. When the processing of the uncomfortable feeling gets uncomfortable itself, I stop it and get back to what I am doing. I am in charge.

Protecting my peace means something much different to me now, thank goodness! It does NOT mean I set up my environment to be trigger or bad-feeling free. It DOES mean I go about my day in a relaxed way knowing what comes to me will be okay. I am likely to have good things come to me because my daily mindset (lens) is peace and even if an apple falls from the cart, or even if the whole cart tips over, I trust myself to process the feeling about it and let it go when I am ready. This understanding affords calm. There is nothing special about me that would suggest I can do this and you cannot. We can all do this! We will talk more about how to keep your Lens of Peace throughout the day in the next chapter!

The Lens of Self-Compassion

Self-compassion is very important in conscious self-love and it gets its own section. Compassion is a concern for another (especially their suffering) and a willingness to help. The definition of compassion differs by who you ask. Most dictionaries have the two components above (concern and willingness to help). There is a **third component of compassion** where we extend kindness and understanding instead of harsh judgments for failures or mistakes. Implicit in this component is the an acknowledgement that **no one can be perfect and there will be many many mistakes over your life**. Is this new information for you? It is always new and surprising information for the empaths, children of narcissists, perfectionists, and children of perfectionists I work with.

Okay, so self-compassion is when you (1) apply concern, and (2) are willing to help, AND (3) you or another person are exonerated from harsh judgments for your foibles for yourself (body, heart, mind, and soul). Let that sink in for minute! How are we going to have conscious self-love (which requires conscious self-acceptance) if we are constantly judging ourselves and criticizing us, and constantly judging/criticizing others! We are not. We need to start implementing this third and very important step of compassion for ourselves and others right away!

If your parent's didn't practice compassion toward themselves and were constantly beating themselves up I can almost guarantee you are doing this too (from their over modeling this behavior AND their overt projection of perfectionism on you with criticism, advice, and raised eyebrows) unless you found the awareness and are choosing to do it differently.

I know you want to have compassion. I especially know you want to have compassion for others. I know that because you have made it to Chapter 4 of this book (nice work by the way! and thank you ☺). As I mentioned earlier, you cannot give away what you don't have. You just can't authentically project compassion to your friends' mirror and it can't be faked. If you are going to harshly judge yourself, you are going to harshly judge others. If you are going to be an uncompassionate jerk to yourself, you will have the capacity to be a real jerk to others. I am sorry.

All the good things we want to be and do will not be ours to BE/DO until we get them inside us authentically. It makes sense! I wonder where the breakdown comes in. I see a lot of people showing concern for others and a willingness to help, but it seems like the third step of understanding about the normalcy of mistakes and the inability to dismiss harsh judgments is the problem. I wonder where that comes in? That is rhetorical; it obviously comes in because the flip side of judgment is acceptance.

If you are self-accepting, you are other accepting, and you are not judging. If you have mercy for yourself you have mercy for others. People who are not practicing conscious self-love are not self-accepting. How can we grow to understand such a thing and pass this on? The world seems to be even more judgmental than when I was a child. Is it social media? Is it because information and things to judge are just so readily available at our fingertips? Is it because we have access to so many people now? I don't know that answer, but I believe if we want to stop judging others we need to spread the good word about self-acceptance and self-love (the conscious varieties).

So what I am saying is, if you want to practice compassion for others you will need to start practicing self-compassion. Especially that third step. This third step when it comes to self-compassion is even harder to muster. I inner critics and harsh words to ourselves are really habitual and the default mode. We need to start working on this right away. It is essential to have both compassion for others and self-compassion. It is best to have both in a measured/balanced way.

Measured compassion. Important in this idea of self-compassion is the notion of measured compassion. If you have too much compassion for others and none for yourself you will end up doing things you don't want to do. Getting resentful. And really as I mentioned before you will be judging the heck out of these people and situations because you can't give away what you don't have. This compassion you are giving away is likely not authentic and it feels, okay, but not like it is supposed to I bet. Something is a little off you are feeling. The feeling is because you are not practicing self-compassion. Especially the third step!

What to do when your compassion for another (other-compassion) is in direct completion for your compassion for yourself? As with all things, we need a balance. An example of imbalanced and unmeasured compassion is when I was growing up and trying to earn my mother's approval/validation. I was putting my mom's needs (or another's) before mine and honoring hers and not mine. I was doing this because I was not practicing conscious self-love, uncomfortable with saying no, trying to be a good girl, working hard for my self-love coins, and people pleasing. I know you have never done that ☺

It is easy to see how one can get resentful doing this for a long time. Maybe you have been doing this for your children (compassion for them and not for you). I did. Remember I said the relationship wasn't reciprocal, but I did NOT say you should only have kindness, compassion, and love for them and none for yourself. That is certainly not the answer.

With my lack of self-compassion, some days I didn't know if I should discipline my kids at all, or just keep understanding and having compassion for their experiences. It is not a perfect science. I can tell you things got easier when I related to myself with conscious self-love. It helped quench my desire to label, judge, control, and fix others.

Getting other's to be more responsible for their actions and me less responsible (for their actions-rightly so) came to me via the process of understanding my true self and accepting her. I can rely on me to have appropriate/measured/balanced compassion for others, myself, and to take appropriate steps (speak up, be "not nice" if discipline is needed, say the truth) for me or them when necessary. Sometimes the appropriate step is to deliver something that is not so pleasant, or disappointing to others. That is okay. I am only okay with that because my self-love and guidance system is now intact. When there are questions about whether you should practice compassion for another or compassion for yourself, you can always ask for guidance by getting quiet and listening to your soul (love place) and not your ego (fear place).

Blame. In our society we are in constant states of blame towards others and it is happening so quickly now with social media. Often times regular, normal, shit happens (things we could respond to with the 3rd step of compassion-understanding we all make mistakes, it is normal to do that); but in the case of social media, people are ALL OVER IT. The Peanut Gallery is misunderstanding intentions, projecting, reading in, exploiting people in an even harsher manner than the original sin they are complaining about! You've seen this. I have also seen people taking the side of the perpetrator, as opposed to the victim, to appear politically correct. I have seen some really astonishing behavior from who the *bleeding hearts of the wrong cause*. It is surprising when such crusader's bad behavior is not self-recognized, especially in the context of their super-charged blame for others' mistakes. Everyone is so busy reacting and projecting (loudly) and without any concern for others. That is NOT conscious self-love. People are not thinking before they speak, not taking their moment to contemplate. So many people are still unconscious and the world is a bunch of egos running around attacking other egos, trying to decide if it is their turn to be the victim or attacker. There is no in between place being represented. The conscious self-love place where the actual power and peace reside.

I can't tell you what your truth is, but hopefully we can all become aware of actions, quit reacting, and practice some compassion (self and other). Plus if we are going to take a stand and go balls-out on some topic, please do so with measured compassion (where we try to understand and honor both sides). I am guessing the people reading this book are compassionate enough towards others, but not themselves. It is others who won't read this book who need help with the idea of other-compassion (for you nice readers :).

Spending too much time in blame is not great because it is a negative emotion, very low in vibration, and it is another thing that gives your power away. If you blame others for your problem of the day, then what power do you have to solve this problem? None, because we can't control anyone else. If the problem is appropriately ours (we take responsibility for only our problems) then we can find a solution.

It is empowering to take responsibility and stop blaming others for your problems. We don't want to go too overboard though with self-blame. Just as you take responsibility for your problems, you let others take responsibility for their problems. When parents fail to do that (and take responsibility for their kids problems) there is enmeshment, codependency, lack of child growth/responsibility, lack of child confidence, and lack of child self-love. We can help with other people's problems. But, in order to do so we must first see the problem as belonging to that person. Then we can help determine the actual problem from their perspective (not how we see it), ask what we can do, and provide support and love throughout the process. That is far more helpful than hijacking someone's problem for your fixing (for both of you!) and when you do this it usually isn't effective.

Managing expectations activity. Believing things will go your way is hopeful and good, but expecting them too and having a tantrum when they don't adds suffering. It is wise to step back from controlling situations, others, and expecting things to always go your way. It is important in keeping the balance. I can't tell you how many actual arguments I ran through in my head, speaking both sides, I will say this, he will say that. What a colossal waste of time! Where is the curiosity. Why all the advanced planning about these fights? What is the point of having a discussion if you go in having a preferred outcome in mind - you will miss the whole point of the discussion. Best to empower people by giving them the chance to speak and be heard.

Sometimes you will feel safe if things go a certain way and you try to control a situation. Instead of controlling the situation (through lies, or demands), try to express your wants and desires and then to let the situation unfold. It is more fun and interesting that way. You manage your behaviors and the others will manage theirs. Thinking about what you want to happen and trying to make sure it happens all the time is a lot of work and really impossible. If something involves at least one other person-we have a crap shoot on our hands. What if a situation involves more than two! Practice using your I messages and expressing your needs in a healthy way..... I think _____, This makes me feel _____, I would like _____. All day, every day!

I practiced the *I thinks, I feels, and I wants* a lot! I got a lot of good stuff I wanted :) My communication skills improved, I was experiencing more harmonious relationships! There was also a different shift! Relating to myself in this way where I considered my wants and desires got me to see I deserved stuff and was worthy of being heard. I internalized the I think, I feel, and I wants and held these discussions with myself. Sometimes I announced them, other times I would just go about providing for my own needs. There was a shift. I was starting to practice conscious self-love. When I felt more at ease expressing my thoughts and feelings and ACCEPTING them and practicing conscious self-love I became even more relaxed and had even more belief/faith/hope in good outcomes, instead of the need to control situations and outcomes. I started listening to others needs, being present, practicing compassion for others AND myself in a balanced way. This resulted in more harmonious communications and relationships! You can learn and know that whatever happens, you will love yourself anyway. This should help alleviate fears that lead to controlling behaviors.

The Lens of Forgiveness

Remember I told you already to forgive or not to forgive is up to you. I even said in some cases, you might think some people might not "deserve" forgiveness. I am okay with that and I want to encourage you to be too. I was reminded of a Bert Hellinger idea (Hellinger, 2002) that people actually shouldn't forgive egregious, or other harmful acts because it is not a person's place, and or it might upset the karmic balance (this would pertain to the parents/child relationship too). Hellinger preferred compassion over forgiveness.

Still, others recognize forgiveness is key. What I am willing to settle on right now is - please feel encouraged to forgive some aspect of a situation. Even if you decide to not forgive your abuser right now. Even if you decide not to forgive the person you are angry at right now - even if they apologized, even if they didn't know right from wrong. If it is not possible for you to forgive THEM, then that is okay. Still, we agree (according to the psychological literature) there seems to be something important about forgiveness for US.

Whether you choose forgive or not is up to you, regardless of the details. If you are not willing to forgive, it may be a clue you are not yet done processing your anger-and that is okay! During my first parent problem unraveling experience (that course I mentioned in Chapter 2) I heard my mom probably had a hard childhood and her intent wasn't to hurt me. This was actually the first time I had considered such a thing! At first thought, oh I should forgive her-it wasn't even her fault. This was helpful for a little while, but then actually caused ME some pretty significant grief/guilt and other negative emotions. I was still low in self-love at the time. I immediately had so much understanding and compassion for her (and not me). I pulled my trick of taking responsibility for absolutely everything in my immediate environment. Now, this little nugget of *her not intending to hurt me* - hit me hard. But, the fact remained she did hurt me. It was a truth of mine. Having compassion for her (and not me) and forgiving her (and not practicing self-forgiveness) held me up for too much time. I wish someone would have mentioned I would be okay if I didn't forgive her :) I was! I am! And spoiler alert, I did end up doing so. But this was only possible after I implemented self-forgiveness (remember you can't give away what you don't have!). Also, it was the freedom to choose forgiveness or not, and ability to forgive other parts of the situation and me helped me melt my self-hate and get to self-love.

Back to my mom and your target of possible forgiveness or not, making excuses for her/them, and having compassion for them only didn't actually help me get any closure, or to a better place. It also actually interfered with me processing the bottom of the barrel anger I still harbored for her. I knew I was "supposed" to be in forgiveness toward her and I tried, but the little anger sentiment left at the bottom of my mom barrel kept sneaking up and I additionally thought I was failing at my self-growth and this great opportunity of forgiveness. I believed forgiveness was supposed to be the answer. I just kept thinking, *oh my gosh how many times do I have to forgive her, look I forgive you, what the hell do you want from me?* I was still angry. I had some more processing to do. Now that is some good information to have that can ultimately lead you to a happy place.

There is another thing I want you to think about. Remember we already discussed how the people we are looking at are really mirrors for us and our self-love (and other self-things status). Perhaps why I couldn't forgive my mom really meant I couldn't forgive myself. That's when the real change happened! I didn't even need to forgive her, it was me!

Something I would really very much encourage about forgiveness though (especially to foster your conscious self-love development) is self-forgiveness. I started small and started to forgive myself for my new guilty feelings. I forgave myself for not being uber understanding to my mom and what she went through. Then I would argue with myself- *tough shit, I thought she should have figured it out and wanted better*. I forgave myself for still being angry at her. I forgave myself for all MY behaviors related to the mom situation. I forgave myself for how all her harm negatively impacted my parenting and partner picking. I forgave myself for picking this woman to be my mom, not realizing sooner she was abusive, and for letting her make me feel like a victim for 40+ years! I found this forgiveness for me, compassion for me, and kindness for me to be much more helpful than forgiving her. I kept remembering, and hopefully everyone else remember (unless they are a sociopath), most people are doing their best at any given time.

Let's talk about forgiveness in general and then you decide what you want forgive. That is certainly not my (or anyone else's) place to tell you! Still, some suggest not forgiving another person for something they did to you is allowing them to control you or your emotions (likely the feeling of guilt for you, anger at them or the situation, frustration). I hear that, and in that regard, forgiveness is a means to that end. Not forgiving a parent, partner, or anyone allows them to continue to control to your thoughts and emotions. But what if you are just not ready or willing to forgive their bullshit that ended up harming you? That's Okay! Don't! But, just for you, can you change the negative thoughts/feelings you hold in response to what happened. You holding onto those negative thoughts and feelings is like you drinking rat poison and expecting the other person to feel sick (I read that somewhere, but I am not sure where). It is not essential for you to forgive others, but it will be SO helpful to take back your power, reduce their continued control of the situation, and release the negative feelings with some forgiveness in the picture. How about we start with you!

Self-forgiveness. It is important you understand the vicious cycle of self-hate continues with a lack of self-forgiveness. How are you going to give someone else forgiveness if you don't forgive yourself? You can't give away what you don't have! If you are finding it hard to forgive someone (like I was with my mom in the beginning) I needed to explore what I was still punishing myself for, holding myself accountable for, unwilling to show me some mercy and forgiveness.

It is quite likely true - if your mom was a real meanie, she was treated poorly, and so was her mom, and her mom. She didn't forgive herself and she couldn't love herself. It was possible she extended this lack of forgiveness to you (for even existing) and even lack of love. You can sub in any person or even system for "mom." Remember I said you don't have to feel sorry for her, or even forgive HER. What would be important though to get back some semblance of control and power to change this- dynamic is: (1) understanding it wasn't about us!! and then (2) forgiving something about this situation (your feelings about the situation). Just think, it can be you who stands up and breaks this family cycle - for all of us! Learning is the best part of what we are here to do. We acknowledge things, forgive ourselves, maybe forgive others, and then take the experience as a growth opportunity that will ultimately help ourselves and others in the future. Just taking these steps can be liberating to help us grow in conscious self-love.

It is possible you have shame, guilt, and have been blaming yourself for stuff you did or didn't do for years. Do you think you can muster some forgiveness of that or whatever, for you?

Other times when I am feeling bad about something and don't really know what it is, I can ask myself, *"Who do I need to forgive?"* Often the answer is - ME! A favorite person for me to Google when I am down is Matt Kahn. He has such great information for us all. One of his

Golden Rules of life is "You've done nothing wrong." Take that in for a minute. Let it wash over you. There is nothing to fix. You've done nothing wrong. All the things you've done (even bad choices, misinformed behaviors) were all needed, to be carried out just as they were, to learn about us and our soul. That is why we are here on Earth, to learn.

The reward for forgiving yourself for whatever is hanging over your head (that you are beating yourself up for either consciously or unconsciously), is your new perspective that helps your soul grow (that you wouldn't be privy to if it didn't happen - so it really was a good thing!). Matt Kahn says the outgrowth of the rule, "You've done nothing wrong," is the soul attribute of self-compassion. You have done nothing wrong and you deserve your mercy and self-compassion! Matt Kahn defines self-compassion as "the ability to be at ease with yourself no matter how harsh the world, or ruthless your past."

A good rule of thumb is to treat yourself as if you were your best friend (and talk to yourself this way too!). Often we are not giving ourselves appropriate slack and beating ourselves up about a certain decision, action, or thoughts. We are judging ourselves so harshly and then really letting us have it! Next time you catch yourself doing this, just completely stop it. I think to myself, what would Gloria say to me right now. She might say, "Hm, that was an interesting choice, I can actually see why you made it, but now we know the results, so next time try a different strategy." Then she would tell me to let it go. And I can too.

There is something about taking to ourselves as our friend would. If this is hard, then think of it like your friend came to you with the exact same problem/issue you are currently beating yourself up about. What would you say to her or him? What if your child or a loved family member came to you with this very same issue? Start to relate to yourself with unconditional love and kindness. The world is harsh enough with its lessons and natural consequences. We don't need you to add to that by beating yourself up mentally or even physically (punishing yourself with substances, foods, unhealthy behaviors). We are practicing a new kind of kindness, compassion, and love for ourselves. I can feel it! Try this one....*I request forgiveness in my relationship to myself and my success!*

When you are ready and if you want, some words about forgiving others. We can extend this grace and mercy of forgiveness to our moms (bad and good), our dads, the media, our teachers, friends, and all people who had a hand in threatening our self-love. We are doing this for US, not them. They may not even need to know!

As I mentioned for so long I was very reluctant to forgive my mom. It was like I was hanging on to that last piece to really stick it to her. But she didn't even know. I was the one suffering from my lack of forgiveness. It wasn't helpful for me in any way. Not forgiving others was hard for my kind spirit and soul and I was conflicted a great deal. I don't even know how many years after Dr. G told me to forgive my mom that I finally did. When he first told me to do it I looked at him shocked, "But wait, you want me to forgive her? I spent weeks telling you all those things she did to me and how it negatively impacted my parenting and literally all of my relationships?" He said, "Yes," but I wasn't seeing why I should do that. It felt like I would be giving her a pass, or not standing up for myself, or what if I forgot then and let her keep doing it. I later learned that she didn't even need to know if I forgave her or not, and that my forgiveness of her, was only a gift for only me to hold. It was liberating!

I sometimes think we don't forgive others to serve as some sort of reminder to keep our guard up so we won't get hurt again, however, this lack of forgiveness is only hurting our own psyche and even our bodies. So I tried forgiveness. I read books on forgiveness and was really trying to understand how to be forgiving. I was motivated to be forgiving, tried so hard to do it, thought I did it, but it kept getting revealed I didn't succeed and there was more forgiving to do. At one point I was asking, how much freaking forgiveness does this women want from me?? Then it hit me, OH!!! I can't give away what I didn't have. I wasn't practicing self-forgiveness so the inauthentic and confusing "forgiveness" I was giving out to this other person was not even that. I had entered the forgiveness sticky wicket; whereby I forgave her, but not myself. This realization caused a different sticky wicket. I thought I arrived at forgiving others, but it wasn't until I started practicing conscious self-love and self-forgiveness that I could authentically and normally forgive others.

To this day if someone brings up the challenges about my mom I think about it and forgive her, myself, realize we BOTH did the best we could, and anything related to the situation immediately. The time for turmoil is so very brief and I do attribute it to my understanding of self-forgiveness and my commitment to myself to relate to me with love.

I can tell you to be forgiving, but you may not want to be. I can tell you about conscious self-love, and the important of self-forgiveness and you will likely just become forgiving of yourself and others. Then you will reap even more rewards (self-love and self-forgiveness, a real win-win). Before we get there, can I ask you: Is there someone you need to forgive? What would that take? Would it be as simple as you being willing to think, "Wow that was pretty shitty what you did. I didn't deserve that. I am going to forgive YOU as a gift to ME, and then wish you well." What about you? Is there something you need to forgive yourself for? Try it!

If you are mad at someone, think for a minute how and why their actions are impacting you. Is there anything useful for you to take in? Take what is helpful and then let the rest go. Forgive yourself for something related to the situation. After your pondering, say out loud, "xx I forgive you. I forgive myself for being angry about this situation and xx I wish you well." Then see how YOU feel.

An important word about resentment. Academically, resentment is defined as having been treated unfairly, and a combination of disappointment, anger, and fear. Wikipedia says, "When directed toward the person resentment can be experienced as remorse." You can be on the butt end of continual demeaning comments, unreasonable demands, or other real injustices against you, maybe from childhood, maybe not. Your current relationships can suffer and it is hard for you to be happy. Your anger grows deeper and lingers. You think you need a new partner because you are sure it is not you, but the same things and feelings return in each different relationship.

I believe resentment creeps in when there is a perceived imbalance in giving/receiving love. Resentment occurs when we use expectations, judgments, and entitlement. Resentment occurs when there is about a lack of forgiveness about some aspect of a situation. Resentment occurs in conditional love (love with perceived strings attached). Do you have a friend or child who you would do anything for? You do these things and don't keep score. That is a relationship with unconditional love, no scores. If we moved through all of our relationships with unconditional love, there would be no resentment. We don't though until we unconditionally love ourselves. Resentments live in your body. They are a *note to self* that you are not loving yourself or taking care of yourself. Something different needs to be done and it is YOU who needs to be doing it and/or making sure it is done.

After reading the first three chapters of this book, think about what is your diagnosis and who is mad at who here. You may be thinking: *"Now I am drowning in my boiling hot liquid of internal resentment and xx is reacting to me being a bitch, so I am getting pelted internally and externally based on my resentful thoughts and behaviors. I am bitter, my face is not smiling, I cannot muster my good Daily BEs. I hate the situation, others, and I am starting to get mad at me for letting this happen!"* Have you been to this volcanic island - Mount Resentment? It is the worst. You think, I won't be happy, I will not have a nice day, and each negative though takes a big hit on the body. I want to be floating around in joy and happiness each day. It is my choice after all. Why am I choosing the opposite? When I used to get like this I didn't realize I had the power to just stop it. Stop it and just start thinking a positive though. Getting off of Mount Resentment will allow you to see the purpose of this resentment and get you to a better place quickly.

This person you are resentful toward is standing there with a mirror to let you know something needs some tweaking in YOU. Most likely you are not speaking up about some authentic need you have. You let the imbalance in your relationship fester without YOU doing anything about it. You didn't speak up, you didn't set a boundary (in your head or out loud), you didn't try and remedy the imbalance, or tell anyone (even yourself) how you feel. You let your subconscious feelings of unworthiness run your show. You took what you could get (hating every minute of it) and now you and your resentment partner are miserable, because guess what, he did the exact same thing. Oh bother! Having mounds of resentment for another person is a ridiculous turn of events isn't it?

Resentment is the Ultra Max Life Poison we drink when we are uber mad at someone and want to hurt them, but what happens is we die a little bit inside each day in our resentment practice. The loser in the game of resentment is you. There is just no other way to behold this phenomenon. I can say I am so resentful of xx because he is such a jerk to me and just doesn't get it. Great. Based on this internal negative thought, I will likely be a huge bitch to xx, hold grudges, look at his actions as never enough, have kindness blinders on, and keep searching for clues about *HIS un*worthiness.

Have you known people to internalize this resentful attitude and take on a character quality of bitterness? When this happens the resentment is engrained and even minor infractions and/or "normal" interactions are seen as injustices. An engrained resentment lens leads to kindness blinders and us being on the lookout for opportunities to grow in resentment (for others and from others). It happens. It is hard to pull out of this vacuum, but it is possible! It is essential to dig out because over time resentment can lead to your personal unhappiness, anxiety, depression, and other negative things to impact your mind and body. The resentment takes away your power too and we are at the mercy of the person causing our resentment. It is always best to turn away from victim mode and get your control back.

Psychologists and marriage counselors know resentment is a formidable foe to happiness and relationships. Forgiveness (for yourself and others) is an antidote to resentment. Practicing conscious self-love is also an antidote to resentment. Let's go over both ways to dispel resentment.

When practicing conscious self-love you take care of yourself. You share your authentic likes and dislikes (I prefer that type of sharing to the *setting boundaries idea*) and speak up if you are being treated unfairly or don't like something. You don't *over-give* and you DO allow yourself to receive. The giving and receiving in relationships must be in balance, or it will be too easy for resentment to slip in. Lots of time people *over function* all on their own without even being asked! These are the first people to win the *I Resent You* race! They are doing this to get external love coins because they don't have enough on their own.

If you first mention your disappointment, or likes, or dislikes (as we should be doing in a kind way and taking ownership of our part), we can communicate with our I messages, learn more, and solve problems. When we don't do this, the disappointments and anger keep pouring in unabated (maybe because we don't feel we deserve better, don't like confrontation, you name it), but do see how these are all problems with us. Still, we develop resentment for the other person. Why do we do that? Soon we are walking around ruing the day and looking for clues/examples of other's shityness and developing our escape plans.

Please, for the sake of you and your loved ones, speak up. Do it in a kind way, using I statements: *"I feel unappreciated when I make a special meal and no one says thank you."* Sub in whatever you are getting resentful about. *"I feel xx when xx happens."* Open first by taking them off of the hook, so they will keep listening to you, *"This is not your fault, but when xx happens, I feel xx."* Let's see if the other person can respond and do things now to make you happy. Some people can and want to make you happy! Some people (maybe narcissists or other wounded people) cannot.

Be careful before you diagnose your relationship partner though (remember projection). Whatever you think he has.... may be exactly what your problem is! He is not appreciating you OR is it the case you not appreciating you. He is not loving you enough OR is it you are not loving you enough. He is a receiver and you are a giver, but you are getting mad about the imbalance (you want to receive some stuff too), but you are not saying what you want; and maybe even interfering with the love he is trying to be provided to you? This is good information for you to use to make wonderful changes! Practice your: I think.... I feel...... I want..... and see how it works out!

For a long time I thought one of my partners didn't want me to be happy. After looking at this with greater self-awareness, I realized it was me who didn't want myself to be happy (because I felt didn't deserve to be happy and didn't love myself). If someone is truly not into your happiness (after you mentioned things they could do to make you happy and you gave them an opportunity to do them), then you can think about their wounds (with balanced/measured compassion). Think about problem solving actions you can take for yourself. We won't ever be able to control how someone treats us, but we can speak our truth and then make decisions from a point of greater awareness and love for ourselves and others.

The other antidote to resentment is forgiveness. A heart break story of mine (but with a happy ending!) is one of my partner's perceived injustices of mine and the huge ball of resentment toward me he was carrying. I don't exactly know what it dated back to - as his parents are both loving and mental well. He just could not see the good things I was doing (he could do this with other people though). He could only focus on my mistakes and was not amused by my foibles and cute shadowy parts. He had kindness blinders on for my acts of love and literally needed to be reminded of huge favors I did for him that he was not paying attention to. He seemed to not be grateful and was not a giver. He was not a narcissist, but he was just so deep in resentment towards me (maybe women) and he couldn't get out. I was happy to stay with him because he represented a familiar figure to me (my mom) who felt the same exact way toward me. Fortunately, I figured this out while we were still together and was able to implement some remedies for both sides! What worked is when I realized those factors above (I wrote about him) were really mostly about me. I was withholding love from myself AND I was interfering with his ability and actual process to give to me.

Good news, I got to forgiveness first, and when I did could see things clearly. I went back in knowing it was my role to shine this light for both of us through unconditional love and acceptance. I did it with love and forgiveness and kindness throughout. To stop the resentment cycle I needed to clear out my resentment and stop projecting it out! My first job was to take all of the responsibility for all of the problems. I knew I was not responsible for 100% of everything, how could that ever be? Still, that was my initial peace offering and it seemed to melt a lot of animosity and opened a problem solving dialogue and much better communication from a much more informed place of mine. Next, it was my job to lean back and let him give to me how he was comfortable doing-outside of my control, overstepping, judging, and fixing (all lack of self-love spots), and without me taking everything personally.

It only takes one person to fix a resentment problem. To this day when I feel the resentment eye squint come over me, I stop it and refocus my attention on his goodness and my gratitude for what he did to "right" that day. I change my attitude and focus (lens!) and the whole landscape changes! Not only do I feel better, less angry/irritated/resentful, more joyful and appreciative, but he starts acting with more love too. Complete win-win.

Changing your lens to focus on the positive is a great answer to resentment. It takes your power completely back, empowers your partner to do nice things for you and themselves. This lens also frees your mind of recursive resentment thinking, so you can hear if you have a real problem to solve with your partner (he really should take out the garbage and how you can get your need met kindly), or if your resentment is a clue for you about you, that you need to practice a little more self-compassion or self-love.

The Lens of Gratitude

There are books and courses and meditations on gratitude! There are Daily DOs to promote gratitude (next chapter) and Daily BEs to cultivate an attitude of gratitude. Being in a state of gratitude is different than these activities though. A state of gratitude is an inside-of-your-heart-and-mind way to be thankful for you, me, your very life, all the lessons, snakes, flowers, and all things. Something I learned was, whenever I am feeling a lack of anything (I know this is a big no-no for the Law of Attraction) I recognize I am doing it (self-awareness) and I stop, drop, and start appreciating what I have and thanking the universe-I thank God (that is my spiritual preference, yours may be different).

Sometimes gratitude is easy to muster. I look at my cats and just marvel in their beauty and am just so grateful to see them and be near them. I think this is why kittens are so wildly popular on the Internet! They are adorable and immediately make you feel grateful. When people ask me if I believe in God, I of course say yes, and they ask how do I know, and I say.. kittens. ☺ I can call up feelings of gratitude when I think of my children too. Your kids might be younger and live with you, so maybe you cannot relate 100% (lol), or maybe you don't have kids, but think of something pure and beautiful.

There are the times when you are going through little or big things and it is harder to be grateful, of course. Still, try to get to that feeling of gratitude for something in you or outside of you and extend it to the challenging circumstance. You could also just try to be grateful for this circumstance - surely it is carrying valuable information for you to be processed now or later and for that we can be grateful.

There are many many positive consequences of gratitude!! Having grateful thoughts and even feelings of gratitude changes your brain. Such positive grateful thoughts send positive energy through your entire body. You end up with more optimism, a quiet body (this is healthy) and more resilience and better health. When I am feeling grateful or having a grateful thought I just look better. It is wonderful if you also believe you deserve the good things you are being grateful for! *I am so grateful! I deserve to have these nice things!* We can do things to maximize our ability to be grateful. You can be grateful for things in your past, but that exhilarating grateful feeling in the present moment is the sweet spot! Whenever you feel a lack thought, or a feeling of not being enough, quick just turn around and see something in your direct view that you are grateful for and hold it in your mind and heart. Gratitude changes feelings of lack to feelings of appreciation. These feelings give out energy at a much higher vibrational level, so you will attract more things. But even if that weren't true (I don't want it to be like we are "using" gratitude to get stuff), it is better to feel your positive energy whenever possible.

Gratitude for stuff. We know from Instagram platitudes about the universe, the fastest way to get more stuff is to be grateful for it. When you really feel that deep down you already have what you want, you shift from being in a state of lacking to being in a state of gratitude; your whole mood changes. I don't know if the universe senses this and provides more things, but I do know that when I am in this mood I am a lot more likely to draw that in from others. This good gratitude lens also makes me try harder because I believe deserve to have these nice things. If I visualize something it may or may not cause the universe to materialize it, but I know it makes me **believe** it is possible. Remember what we said about belief? If I believe it, I can make it happen! That is magic, whether the universe or I am making it happen!

Gratitude for all of life, not just the stuff. Cheryl Richardson coined the term "unconditional living." She explained "We can be HAPPY regardless of our circumstance or condition." This is taking gratitude to a whole new level, a deep, deep gratitude for living and life. Yes, we still make our gratitude list each day, and yes we can love things and people and be grateful for them, but we are also in love with life, even where there are challenges and things are not going our way. That is when we win life really. Maybe that should be called conscious gratitude ☺

Gratitude for life lessons. *But, Jill how can we muster gratitude for all these challenging life lessons?* Let's think about that. I spent a bit of time mad at my lessons. I was irritated and in a "why me," sort of victim mode, why do I get these lessons (even from a young age) and I see people skating by with no lessons! On a good day I kept my head up, but I can tell you about the resentment building up inside. Who was I mad at? The universe? The lesson? That is no way to live or get more stuff. I don't recall the day it changed, but as usual I can tell you there was a qualitative shift from not getting it to getting it and for sure it had to do with self-love.

There are lessons for our positive transformation inside every difficult and painful experience whether we like it or not. Recognizing this may help you not only transform and grow, but it may help you move from the **pain place** to the **peace place**. Let me give you an example. I told you my dad died my sophomore year of high school. No adult type person at my school approached me to be of assistance, not even my counselor or teachers. In fact one teacher (during a class about a week after my dad died) asked me (in front of all the other students) what my dad did for a living. I just stared at him unable to speak. Which caused him to make fun of me! Thankfully my best friend Anna was sitting next to me and she saw me start to cry and yelled out, "Her dad is DEAD." He apologized the next day, but that damage was done, processed, and fettered to my subconscious to hold on to for decades. Also soon after my dad's passing I kept falling asleep in French class after lunch. The teacher would stand over my desk and make fun of me too. He actually looked a little bit like Professor Snape now that I think about it. Do all children have these problems? At any rate, I felt bad. The next year, my junior year, I was walking down the hall and my counselor came running up to me to ask me a favor, "Oh, um, Jill, one of our freshman girls just lost her dad! Do you think you can talk to her or help her?" I can call up that moment in my life in an instant. I guess my counselor DID know about my dad? I guess this gal deserved assistance or acknowledgement and I didn't? Did my dad die because I am supposed to help people cope with death? I hated all of those ideas. I felt like I was too young to be having such questions and no one to talk with them about. Remember my mom was not a great sounding board to say the least and actually said it was my fault he died. There was no context for me at any turn. I just kept taking everything on as traumatic and sending it to my subconscious unconsciously.

    Anyway, I was kind of mad at this "lesson" of my dad's death, my mom blaming it on me, and people not recognizing my need for help, but expecting me to help them! This anger lasted for several years. During that time I was not anywhere near a self-love place. It was a very egocentric place that is true- but kids are like that! I took everything so personally and no one was around to hand me a copy of The Four Agreements, or provide context. I see it now as just something that happened, not even about me-it was my dad's life path. It impacted me because I was with him, near him when he was on his journey at the time- doing my thing. My "lesson" was something I chose to see, something not done to me, but something I could make good use out of if I chose. This view was much kinder and loving. Whenever in doubt, that is my litmus test question.....How can I be more kind and loving to myself or whoever? What a miracle to make good use out of a challenging situation. The lesson of missing my dad and no one caring about me (taking care of me) taught me I was responsible for those things. The lesson of my narcissist and emotionally abusing mother led me to understand about self-love, remind myself I deserved it, and help others return to theirs. I am not grateful for these things and that is such a much better feeling to have inside me. Still, it would be hard to ask how you benefitted from a loved one dying and I don't think we should ask or answer that question. I can say I did benefit from my mother not loving me and her abuse and neglect. It helped unfold my nicer and better story.

If I didn't ask those questions though, arrive at the answers, or explore my subconscious story, that story would be the same one she left me with and running my life 95% of my time (vomit). It is incumbent upon us to explore our stories and these questions..... How did I benefit from that _____ lesson? Ask yourself. We can be grateful for even the smallest amount of benefit afforded by a lesson.

What this looks like (the attitude of gratitude about our lessons) is a two-parter. First, say *"Wow I am so grateful my self-awareness is seeing these things (past and current) as lessons as they were/are."* I think about those past ones and say, *"Oh, I do get it now. Thank you."* Then, the second part, say *"I am grateful that happened, because look where I am because of that now. Thank you."* Something frustrating about the lessons of the past was the sheer repetition. ☺ I wonder what state I was in to just not be getting them. Now, because of self-love, I see my current lessons pretty clearly; much sooner, and often times almost in real time as they are unfolding. I am immediately grateful for my self-awareness, *"Oh, this is a neat lesson. Thank you!"* When I do that the lessons seem to abate.

These two steps I feel are essential to feel (1) the gratitude for the self-awareness of the lesson, and (2) then the gratitude for the actual lesson itself. This two-step process really takes me to a different level each time and allows me to move away from the lesson. My gratitude helps me see, "OH there is a message for me to sit with." I sit with it, do some soul searching, evolve, thank the two steps, then put the interesting lesson package down, and walk on.

The Lens of Receiving Love

Are you interfering with other people giving you love? Are you withholding love from yourself and then denying the receipt from others (and then complaining about them)? We need balance here too. You can't be the sole giver or sole receiver of love in a relationship-with anyone-and expect it to flourish, or stay harmonious.

I can't tell you how many times I have heard, *"well I am the giver and he is the receiver in our relationship - it works for us."* Like one person is going to get the good stuff all the time and one person is going to not get anything and just keep doing and doing. I have heard this a lot, even in a therapeutic setting! The first person I heard it from was me. Remember my mom required me to be the giver (and her the receiver) in our relationship, so it was just very natural for me to find a new receiver and to keep on my giving, but never getting, path. I thought I was just a generous and kind gal. I would receive a gift and immediately think about who I could give it to. I would never eat the delicious looking cookie or cupcake given out at work meetings; I would squirrel it away in my briefcase and save it for someone else even though I would have really enjoyed it. All prizes from meetings, work gifts, gifts with purchase; always handed out and never appreciated by me. Big things, small things, I passed them on. I don't know if I was generous, crazy, or feeling not worthy of receiving gifts.

I knew something was off for me though because I was starting to feel bitter a lot, feeling like running away, was pissed no one stepped in to give me something once in a while, and getting real irritated as everyone got stuff, but I didn't seem too. Now remember, in the parent-child relationship, the parent will be mostly the giver and the child the receiver (the child should never save their cupcake for the parent obviously); but I wasn't receiving thank yous either (which kids can give to parents), and the main problem was I wasn't giving things to myself or practicing conscious self-love (which we must do in the parent-child relationship to stay happy). I realized I was actively interfering with receiving from all sides by over functioning, care-taking, martyring, feeling guilty, and unworthy of love. You know how when you give someone something they say thank you and then you are supposed to say, you are welcome! I wouldn't even say that. I would drum up an, "oh, no problem," or "happy to do it." I wouldn't even receive their thanks with a "*you are welcome*!"

In adult, romantic and friendship, relationships the goal is not to find someone to receive your nice gifts of always giving. The goal is not to find someone to give you gifts all the time either. The goal is for you to relax a little and allow yourself to give AND receive, and grow together. There should be an equal balance of give and take in all relationships. It is not the case that there is a relationship "role" where one is giver and one is receiver! It is the case that in all healthy and growth-promoting relationships there is giving and receiving (give and take); but each person must practice both all the time, or the relationship will be unbalanced and unhealthy.

Talk about resentment, expectations, over-functioning, stress, judging, and a harsh inner/outer critic, a lack of gratitude, and a lack of joy and happiness! To have more love, and more daily happiness you must strive to avoid having one person be the full-time giver and full-time receiver. Let's say you are in this situation now. You can change it up by practicing conscious self-love and institute a new plan. Not everything must be recorded, tit for tat, or scored, but there should be a balance. You must receive, you must also give. If you are feeling resentful, judgmental, irritated with your partner there may be a give/take imbalance. I have found (interestingly) that it is not only the giver who gets resenty! The taker/receiver has a lot of irritation (often unspoken cuz who wants to mess up such a good thing); whereby their lack of giving love is being blocked! That doesn't feel good either.

Receiver your love! Accept your compliments, gifts, kindnesses afforded by others. It is okay! Plus doing that gives your loved ones an opportunity to give to you (which is joyful for them) and necessary for their self-love development! And good karma! It is okay to receive love and you see this when you practice conscious self-love. You are worthy of love, enough, and good at receiving. It is important to give, yes. The balance of giving and receiving (in all things and especially love) is vital to a harmonious connection within the context of all of our relationships.

You can do nice things for others and give. The problem is when you do and do and give and give and start feeling resentful. Again, you don't need to keep score, but you will **feel** the discomfort inside and that will be an indicator there is an imbalance you want to consider correcting. The feeling inside of the imbalance is a sign you are not providing you enough love or kindness. Instead of keeping score and getting stressed about that, or trying to get even by buying yourself something instead or having an affair, just tune in to your feelings and any resentment or discomfort building - that is the sign. When you are practicing conscious self-love it is easier to practice kindness without wanting/needed things in return (from others) because you are already taking good care of yourself! Then share your wants and needs, likes and dislikes with those you are in an adult relationship with. You can change things up at any time!

The Lens of Kindness

You must practice kindness toward others AND kindness to yourself (self-kindness) and both need to be in balance. An important life lesson is the Golden Rule. Do unto others as you'd have done to you. This is maybe taking on more meaning with our newly discussed projection and mirror idea (whereby everything you see in another-good/bad-is right there because of what you are within yourself).

If I am kind to you it is reflecting a kindness I hold for myself. If I am acting compassionate toward you it is because I have achieved an internal self-compassion state. If I am loving toward you and careful to not hurt you it is because I am those things to me! When we have a slip and we find we are not kind or loving to another (there is a good clue we need a little self-check in), and it is also a clue we need to make repartitions. We can own our mistakes, apologize for them, and fix them. We have the capacity to reflect on our actions and their results. We can see the inner workings of ourselves. Ask yourself: *How can I be better to others AND to myself?*

Measured kindness. So, to be kind to others we need to practice self-kindness. There is just no other way. Plus we need a balance of self-kindness and other-kindness. If doing a kindness for another takes something from you - that might be okay once in a while. However, when you are kind, kind, kind, giving, giving, giving to others and not to you-it will be impossible to not feel resentful. In that scenario you will likely also get mad at the other person, but he/she is not really the problem is he/she?

Even if another is not kind or giving to you, it is still possible to be kind to them and give to them if you have conscious self-love and are doing it for yourself. Do you see how the relationship with your other person (and their giving or kindness) is not even at issue? They may or may not be kind/giving in return (and hopefully they do and that YOU LET THEM). But really, if you are doing your thing and also taking good care of yourself, you are likely good, kind, and giving. It is when you are not doing those things for yourself (and not practicing conscious self-love) that we have a problem on our hands.

Sometimes to be the good/kind person you have to bring down the hammer! Sometimes the right thing to do is stand up for yourself or another, speak your truth, and let another suffer a natural/logical consequence. Being kind doesn't mean you are just always nice! Where was it written we can't be kind/thoughtful/helpful while at the same time kicking some asses of asses? I think women grew up thinking that! It is not true.

When we have compassion toward others, we have compassion for ourselves. It is in this balance, that your authentic behaviors can emerge. You are not here to take shit all your life because you want to be nice or have people like you. Sometimes being nice is standing up to the bullshit. Most of the time you must be nice to yourself first, or else all the kindness you are trying to give out is inauthentic. People can feel that and you get resentful. Please stop it.

I have to bring up boundaries here again and remind you when you are feeling like you want to set a boundary you are experiencing a mirrored clue for you - that you need more self-kindness, self-compassion, self-love, self-acceptance, and some self-something. Something is out of balance and it is on your end, not the other person's end. Is your measured compassion and kindness (the balanced kind) where you are kind to yourself first and in an equal manner? If not, that might mean saying no, not showing up somewhere, whatever. It does not require you to announce it and wait to get talked out of it, or made fun of about it (which sometimes can happens when you institute and share boundaries). When you practice conscious self-love, measured compassion, and kindness (where your self-kindness and compassion are implicit) your life becomes easier and you just end up taking care of yourself (boundary or not). You do this because you consciously and authentically love yourself.

Have compassion for yourself. Understand the rules of measured compassion/kindness where you matter as well. Realize your role is not to be the fixer, the nice guy, or fairy God mother. Sometimes you are handing out the karma (natural/logical consequence) to someone who needs a lesson. Sometimes you, an earth angel, is doing good by being strong, firm, and tough. Think about Glenda the Good Witch! That Wicked Witch of the West needed some natural and logical consequences delivered and that gorgeous Glenda was happy to dole it out. We all still really love her (maybe more). Taking care of yourself by loving yourself is key to being nice.

Being a decent human being. I hate that I have to write this section. *Dateline, 48 Hours*, prisons, murder, crime, child abuse!, molesting children!, animal abuse!, bullying, social media abuse, rape, assault, sex-trafficking, WTF! What is the problem in society right now where people are harming other people in this way? I don't really have an answer, but I think it is a problem with conscious self-love. Instead of harming other people, some people harm themselves with addiction, not respecting or taking care of their bodies, or respecting people's time and efforts in their relationships. I think this is because of a lack of self-love too. A lack of conscious self-love shows up when we treat ourselves or others poorly. It is just not possible to treat others with love and care when we don't feel that for ourselves. Remember the mirror. Everything we are seeing in one another is really a projection from us. Something we need to see.

Is it hard for you to find compassion and kindness for such things I wrote about at the beginning of this section? Does hearing about these things negatively influence your Lens for a little while? How can you muster forgiveness for such events? As I sit here today and write I am not in a perfect place to answer. I still monitor my news intake because sometimes it just gets too much. I think for right now I can say I forgive myself for being scared by and angry with the events and even the people. I forgive myself for judging people. I forgive myself for having a hard time understanding the good/bad balance. I am so hopeful about the positive effects of conscious self-love and do really believe when people start loving and accepting and having compassion for themselves more, we will be seeing a different newscast. I don't know how long it will take to get there, but I know. Have faith and believe we are on our way!

Be nice to yourself, others, your children, your loved ones, the people walking down the street. Smile at them. It is good for both of you. Your loved ones, and your children especially, are counting on you for your kindness. For until your children and relationship partners become conscious, their psyche is in your hands.

That you understand this makes you responsible - even if they don't get it yet. That you understand this makes it very likely you can change your world and the world at large! Demonstrate kind and loving behaviors toward yourself and others. Especially the children and animals :)

Chapter Five: Practicing Conscious Self-Love Daily DOs

"We always have a choice,

and if we love ourselves we choose love."

Don Miguel Ruiz

The Daily DOs to help you practice conscious self-love are behaviors, things to do, ways of acting daily to build up your conscious self-love growth process (sort of a supply tank, but I don't want you to think of this as something that changes from full and empty exactly). Because once you start practicing conscious self-love your tank becomes qualitatively different and your lenses change, so it is not really a matter of quantitative things to fill it up. It is more of an implicit love for yourself, which of course means doing things to take good care of you too!

When practicing conscious self-love, you are changed and you've activated a sort of self-love protection shield. In the beginning of this process, doing self-love behaviors/actions changes your relationship with yourself (on a behavioral level, but also works to chip away at our default filters and subconscious patterns of unworthiness, or not feeling deserving of love). Once you get to the point of no return - conscious self-love, then you still practice the daily behavior action plan of love and care in your behaviors and voice to yourself and others, but it is a normal practice, "a given."

One more thing, there is nothing to really DO to make you worthy of your or another's love. You are PERFECT as is, right now! These DOs help you to come to recognize, remember, and live at the much more fun state of love bliss... where you and your Beautiful Soul belong!

Practicing conscious self-love will replace your unconscious self-hate! Wouldn't it be great to have a positive automatic conditioned response to your daily on goings instead of your automatic inner critic (from your parental and environmental conditioning) where you comment on and judge your and others' every move? YES! That would be great!

Practicing conscious self-love (by simply becoming conscious of your self-love and intending to grow in self-love) is like stress proofing yourself to not react to cortisol when the sympathetic nervous system takes over. You are changed in such a good way. When you feel a twinge of discomfort (while you are practicing conscious self-love) you see in real time as it is happening. It is like you can see behind the clouded curtain. You realize: (1) we have a situation that could result in stress or a choice void of self-love, compassion, or gratitude, (2) instead you practice a self-loving Daily DO, and (3) you watch yourself return to relating to yourself more lovingly and kindly with more beautiful and adaptive lenses on.

Many of the Daily DOs of self-love behaviors are self-care and soul nurturing activities. Once you begin to increase loving kindness behaviors towards yourself and others, you will begin to see how rewarding it is. You just must keep it going and then they become automatic! Especially when you get over some of the humps of feeling like you don't deserve to feel good, take care of yourself, receive love, or have nice things. You get over these humps (conditioned patterns) by the things we discussed in the previous chapters: (1) your awareness of their origin, (2) your forgiveness/gratitude for that inappropriate conditioning, and (3) then your return to appreciating and loving your beautiful soul/authentic self.

I am presenting lots of things to consider trying or DOing. If you like them, good. If you don't like a certain one, or don't even want to read one of them, don't. These are things I tried and helped me. I can tell you what I've seen work, but you have to decide for yourself. How much should you do? You know yourself and what you like and how much time you have right now. You can trust yourself and your intuition here, but do commit and be motivated to start on the conscious self-love path. You are at a fork in the road and the self-hate side has nothing you want or need, but the self-love side is full of presents for you, your loved ones, and the world. Let's go there!

Some days, now that I look after myself, I wake up and intuitively think *oh gosh I should get a massage today*. Then, I go do that. In the past I would've put it on my never-ending to-do list and maybe gotten around to it that month. I am a priority now. Let's start this for you today. Even small behavior changes each day will make a big difference!

Sometimes during the day I think, *gosh I am getting triggered by one of my students*. In the past I would gloss over it, rue the day and the student, maybe get mad at myself for not speaking up, or react poorly to the student, and then chastise myself for not being kinder with my thoughts/behavior. This process might last for one or even more days. I don't do that anymore! I take some time for myself right then and there to think about what the challenge is trying to teach me. I am worth the short amount of time (or the long amount) I need in that moment to get myself feeling good again.

Perhaps the most important thing is realizing taking time for me is just as important as taking care of the things I have been charged with taking care of (job, children, volunteer work, me). Look at all the things in the parentheses and consider your list of charges. For me, I had so many things in the parentheses in years past. I was making my list of charges huge and for no reason, often without even being asked (and much to the chagrin of some of the charges ☺). I am happy now to have only me, my children, my relationships, and my job. I climbed out of a lot of butts and became a lot happier. I also added ME to my charges list and some days I am even first in the parentheses!

I also took back ME from other people's charges list - took back MY control. For a while I thought I wanted someone to take care of me. I thought I wanted this because of the severe emotional and physical neglect from my mother. I previously got mad at partners for not taking care of me well enough, BUT/AND I used to completely interfere with them taking care of me by my over caretaking of everyone, and refusing to receive their love. I projected, interfered, was confused, and then became resentful and wanted replacements. What feels best for me now is me taking care of myself!

It was time for me to take back control. It might be time for you to the same? It was time for me to let my loved ones take back their control for their lives. It might be time for you to let your loved ones do the same? The last thing we want is to be victims and live our lives based on the effects of other's careless mistakes and/or foster that in our loved ones. And the really really last thing we want is for our children to have to do that.

Our lives are ruled by our internal worlds. We have complete control over those even though it may not seem so right now. It is important we address the subconscious (maybe even daily) as well as our conscious thoughts. We address our subconscious by noticing our thoughts and feelings and becoming aware of why they are there (just becoming conscious of them and turning off your reactive and automatic pilot). We must do this because you can't smooth the outside and be loving towards others without changing the inside and becoming loving toward yourself. Let's get started with some activities!

In the previous chapter, I covered ways of being (adaptive lenses of life viewing). Maybe when you were reading about cultivating a lens of peace, forgiveness, gratitude, self-compassion, receiving love, and kindness and you liked the idea, but though, *how will I ever pull that off?* Let's go over some of the things you can DO to get good with your BE.

Doing your Daily BE of Protecting your Peace

The best way for me to protect my peace is by staying in the present moment (not ruminating about the past, or having anxiety about my future)**.** Practicing present moment awareness is also called mindfulness. Much research is mounting on the positive effects of practicing mindfulness!

Prioritize according to peace. Often we are thinking *How can I do more?* I used my driving in the car time to call people instead of enjoying the drive. When getting a pedicure I would read a magazine to stay up to date on Hollywood gossip instead of appreciating the sensations and kindness of another to pamper my feet. When we multi-task and don't prioritize peace we are not in the present moment and we are missing things – the juicy parts of life. I am suggesting you actually do less. Select the things you really want to do - hopefully the things you enjoy the most (make them a priority) and then really do them!

What can you do less of and how can we be focused on what is in front of us in the present moment? Even as I am wrapping up this chapter my son was home visiting for Thanksgiving. I had completely stopped working on the book, took a week off from work, and just kind of said, Jill you are last your list of priorities this week as I decided nothing was more important than spending quality time with my son I adore. I also was aware he needed some kid-type maintenance (he hadn't been home for several months) and I needed to help him as parents do. I took him to get a massage, haircut, acupuncture, doctor appointment, all the food he wanted, etc. In the past I might've been irritated by this never-ending list of activities for someone else, but it was really a joyful week. It was this way because I was aware of my priorities, that I would for sure not have time for my stuff, and could stay in the present moment, knowing I would be back to my activities next week. Missing my book writing or not getting myself a massage while he did -was all okay for me because it was important to take care of my child's needs AND I prepared for this by bringing the situation to my **self-awareness**. I also made a commitment to be present, available, and peaceful, and loving to him this whole visit. I also told myself he was the priority and this is how it would go.

I need to do things like that to stay present. If I was hoping to steal away some time to work on the book while he was home, I would not have been present, instead I would have been distracted looking for the moment when I could slip away. Seeing this for what it was and deciding to see and honor this helped me stop obsessing too. This was not a time for balanced give and take. It is not the child's responsibility to give to us. An option for me if I wanted/needed would have been for me to carve out some time for my conscious self-love activities, but in this case of a short visit I decided my provision of care to another was actually self-love for me! When he comes for two weeks for Christmas I will take some time to prioritize my needs in the form of receiving love from myself via activity. I will still keep my good lenses on and appreciate/acknowledge my efforts to provide good care of others. Before I practiced conscious self-love certainly none of that was authentically possible.

    I was just holding space for my girlfriend of decades. She doesn't have children, but is feeling so overwhelmed with work and after moving she is canceling her workouts, meditating time, time with friends, and church activities. I could see the wind out of her sails when I saw her. She was even feeling anxious and planning on a doctor visit because she thinks something is "wrong" with her. I listened and listened. I tried to resist making suggestions about how to solve her problems for her, although I had a lot of ideas. It was very easy for me to see there was too much icky stuff and not enough good stuff on her plate. My super sweet friend was being so hard on herself (about her decisions). She even said she wished she could go back in time to the day she found their dream house (because the move was just so stressful). She was not loving herself. She noted other mistakes, bad decisions, resentments toward others. Her self- and other- *resentments list* was long. She also recapped for me her *Mrs. Fix-It List*.

    She was making some good decisions about reducing her responsibilities (because there was just not enough time in the day!) but now felt so bad about cancelling on her friends and not going to church (things she enjoyed) to do even more at work (that was causing her stress). She was making things harder indeed. Now her body was feeling bad. She had an illness for the last 4 weeks and was going for blood work. When she was done venting (yes I made sure) I said what I thought was true. I only do this if I think the truth can be helpful, otherwise I might not mention it. I said, *Oh honey you are having much compassion for others and just not enough for you. Think about all you've been through. Please. Also, you are making such great strides to take care of yourself and eliminating things, which is ideal, but the stuff you are eliminating is the stuff you love and want to be doing.* She liked that. I could see her face relax as she took a deep breath. She asked me questions about her anxiety and processing those feelings. She seemed really interested to learn some researchers maintained anxiety is in your body for a reason - as a call to action (just like the other Seven Heavy Heroes from last chapter). We talked about being present, prioritizing differently – for peace, forgiving herself and her boss and others, and getting back to meditating. "Getting back to meditating" is lip service to people who have never done it. They are skeptical and don't see the value. I can say *get back to meditating* to a person who has done it and they get it.

I could see her subconscious patterns of not doing enough, doing something wrong, and not being worthy, but I didn't mention those things. In this case, what my good friend needed was to get some shit off her chest and change her immediate environment for some good stuff. She needed a little encouragement to take care of herself and love herself and feel worthy, a pat on the back for all her hard work, and permission to take care of herself because she certainly wasn't doing it (whatever the reason). There is time for peace and time for growth (growth where you work on the subconscious redo). Feeling good/happy/peace on a daily basis is the goal. You don't need to change your whole subconscious mind in one day, or even one, or ten years. If you can get to happy and peaceful a little bit each day – you are doing your "work" and there is nothing more you SHOULD be doing!

Self-awareness of where I am in this moment. This self-awareness step is crucial and really it is the "conscious" piece to any of the conscious-type things you want to cultivate (including conscious self-love!). Only in the present will I enjoy this precious time with my hilarious and fun son or sweet friend! I spent too much time missing those moments in the past by thinking/worrying about when I would get back to my to-do list: I should be vacuuming, what I should say next, or what I was missing (e.g., not cleaning something, a TV show, etc...).

This insight about where I have the tendency to "be" in my awareness AND advanced preparation of my understanding and conscious love/parenting goals toward him-helped me foster my self-love. When we give to others OR receive from others we grow a bit more in conscious self-love. It is important to see this in real time and even plan for it beforehand, so it doesn't slide by without happening, or us acknowledging. The last thing we want to do is miss someone's kindness to us. Or not appreciate/acknowledge just how loving we are being to others or ourselves. Those things should be the only real purpose of each day!

Knowing I would be back to work the following week and my prioritizing my son needs over my work, it was a non-issue. What's more, is seeing this scenario in advance, it didn't even have to be a win-lose, my son versus my happiness choice; it could be a win-win where I choose to spend time with my son instead of work (and feel good about it, not guilty!). I was doing us both good and I could appreciate and acknowledge these wonderful efforts. In that space I would completely enjoy and love to have this time be happy and harmonious instead of stressed, guilty, or irritated. It really was my choice. I went to bed each night that week knowing I chose well!

When I caught myself thinking about things on my shopping list, or when I would make the appetizers I said, *hey love, (me) let's get back to this moment*-and it worked! It is a nicer place to be with him and enjoying the time, rather than worrying about what I am not getting done by being present. What could be more important than that? Nothing, but we don't often realize that until the time has passed. Not anymore.

Catch and release activity. I call my activity to stay present and then to let go of the feeling/thought/behavior ...the catch and release. For this activity I do want to go in knowing my possible triggers, tendencies, modus operandi-this is your advanced prep of understanding. Say it in your head or even write it down.

For my other friend I helped her with her situation about advanced overwhelmed feelings (worrying) about how the holidays would go. I encouraged her to tell me the main concern (vent it out). She shared that her sometimes high maintenance daughter will be home from school for the weekend. She wanted most of all to enjoy the present moments and family fun. She wanted to laugh and experience joy and have harmonious relating. She knew she had the tendency to judge both her and her daughter and be a over-functioner and problem solver, but really did want to enjoy her company. I helped her reframe some of the venting for better outcomes. Her thinking her daughter is high maintenance is not helpful for her plan of peace. Her recognizing her daughter gets frustrated when she does everything for her interferes with her self-confidence is good to know. When you are done venting or sharing, and reframing unhelpful parts of the vent, then sum it up easily. For my friend, we arrived at: I want to be present in relating to my daughter and all family members this Thanksgiving week. I turned it into a prayer for her even, *Dear God, help me be present, especially in my interactions with loved ones and family*. She liked that! I also reminded her to acknowledge her efforts and even reward herself when she was able to do this. We love cheerleaders, why not be your own? This is the way we will reset the more challenging stimulus-response connections in your brain.

Set your intention to stay present. You can set your intention to stay present and this will be a great step in the right direction. When you do it, compliment/acknowledge your efforts. You can pray or affirm, *I pray/affirm all of my relationships are harmonious and I will take action when it is in my or another's best interest. Until then, I commit to being present, so I can know when it is time to take action.* Remember, joy and happiness occurs only in the present moment. The goal is to be connected to your present moment (where your authentic self lives) and to experience and then project your true self as often as possible.

When I see myself veer out of the present (you can learn to see yourself doing this in real time), I will **catch** myself. Tell myself *good catch*! I can see this distraction for what it is and that it is not consistent with my current goal. I smile at my distraction (fix it list, to-do list, obsessive list, rumination list, fantasizing, etc.) and ***release it***! I go back into this present moment where I share my love and attention with the human being in front of me (if I am with someone) or with myself if I am alone. Then I feel good for my good work!

The present moment is the only true place for happiness they say. In this present moment there is usually peace and joy. Even if not, the present moment is all we really have to work with, so if a challenging feeling comes up in the present moment the best thing to do is consider if it is there to teach you something or help you (*what are you trying to tell me fear/anger?!*). Do what you need to do to process it, then RELEASE!

Sometimes it was harder to release and return to the present even though I was committed, and that was okay too. Some things my son said would trigger me. Remember, a trigger is when something you encounter (internal or external) exerts a fear or discomfort for you. It is a real clue something subconscious is a foot! The trigger is good news because it helps us see the need to bring something from our unconscious, conscious for processing, release, and maybe even problem solving. For example, he is 21 and drinking and I am not a big fan of seeing him wasted. This might be true for all mothers, and with my dad and his alcoholism - this just freaks me out! I leave the present moment when I see him drunk, but now it has extended to when I see him grabbing a beer or anytime there is alcohol! This fear is my problem now. He is triggering it, but it is my problem, and a clue for me something from my subconscious is hoping to be processed.

When I leave this present moment I go back in time to thinking (worrying) about my dad, what I did wrong to my son to make him drink, and then worry about his future, and soon I have spun a lot of stress and have not been in the present moment for hours. I have conditioned this fear on my very own too and have associated my dad and my son for some reason (it is common, but not ideal obviously). We can miss a lot - not being in the present. In fact I think I missed a lot of clues about addiction. I was always providing guidance and lessons and information, but it was about what I wanted to spout on (something I just got worried about or triggered by), and not being sensitive to what was happening in the moment with another human who wanted/needed my love, attention, and presence. Because that was the one place I was not.

My **awareness-catch-release-reward** in this triggered situation has more to do with the understanding of my past challenges-*oh hey, this is reminding you of your dad situation, this is NOT that, this is different*. What is happening in this moment now. Oh, my son is ordering a beer. Okay, that is a normal activity for my 21-year-old son. There is no problem here. I caught it and I released it and got to just return to being present where it was not scary, and I feel good.

Pull out the triggers. What if he had 12 beers and was stumbling in? I have concerns. I might need to take action (by speaking up or helping with something and that will be okay too, but I won't recognize it if I am in triggered/reacting mode). Still, this situation is separate from my experiences with my father and it does no good for me to spin unneeded associations and more negative conditioning. I can't blend the two past and present situations, because then I won't be able to see what is best for me and this other person in this present situation.

Your trigger target can remind you of a parent, an ex, a current partner, your past. You are mad at your mother and you are projecting it onto your daughter! You think your mother is mad at you and you are projecting that on to your daughter. For a long time I was glad God gifted me with the boys. I thought I would be such a bad mom for a girl.

I thought I would had really messed up a girl. Truth is, having a girl would have likely taught me about how moms should treat their daughters and I would've recognized my mother's problems as hers (not mine) much sooner.

At any rate, make sure the person you are arguing with today is really the person you are mad at. If the interaction seems highly charged, or you are surprised at how you are reacting and can't seem to "control" your emotions/behaviors, you might be bringing the past into this present moment. When that happens, it is best to see it for what it is, and try even harder to return to the present moment. In the present moment you will see the difference, but this is difficult when you are not in the present moment and have a reactive unconscious ego mind running the show.

Daily Peace by Stopping Negative Self-Talk and Thoughts. You are saying mean things to yourself and thinking mean things about yourself (and others) because you internalized a harsh inner critic from your skewed understanding of other's projections of their self-hate on to you. These negative thoughts and words are interfering with your joy and possibly impacting your daily joy and bigger life outcomes. It is biology.

Thoughts change neurons (your brain chemicals). Your environment changes neurons too. Good thoughts make good neurons. Negative and hate thoughts create an explosion of bad neurotransmitters (more brain chemicals), these neurotransmitters influence your entire body. Your mind talks to your body.

Your **beliefs** also impact your body and mind chemicals. Your belief in healing is enough to actually heal you (the well-documented placebo effect)! Replace your negative self-talk and thoughts with positive self-talk and positive thoughts. Your body will change. Your soul with shift and you will be more in line with your True Self, your Divine self - the place in you where the Divine resides!! Embrace that and love it! Love who? YOU! You are Divine and you are the Divine.

It is the same thing. If you love God you have to love you ☺ If you believe in God you have to believe in you!

I found that, similar to staying in the present moment (being mindful), stopping negative self-talk and thoughts is most often a daily activity. Hopeless thoughts/words impact your nervous system negatively. Good thought make good neurons, we already covered that. Promise yourself....Today I will choose peaceful thoughts. I pray... today I chose peaceful thoughts!

When I first started my healing journey my therapist Dr. G would tell me repeatedly, "You keep saying, 'I AM' and then following it with something negative." He was right! I had subconsciously adopted my mother's criticisms of myself toward my very own self (........paging Dr. Freud). I had also adopted her dislike of each and every decision I would make and numerous other self-punishment techniques. I had really adopted her negative thought process of me (which was not really even about me). Plus, if I was saying it OUTLOUD I was saying it in my head way more (kind of like if you can see one mouse in your house you must have a lot more hiding!).

Dr. G would try to help me to understand this for more than a year and it seemed I couldn't stop saying the negative words about me out loud (it was my subconscious conditioning), or thinking them. My unconscious patterns of not being worthy, good enough, enough in general, doing something wrong, my mom liking others better than me, the list can go on.

Once I addressed some subconscious patterning and I could see myself deserving my love, it became easier to separate my mom's abuse from my reality, but it was a real conscious self-love effort. Becoming **aware** of the role of the subconscious in our daily abuses of myself was key for me. I am not sure why it took so long to figure that out for me. I have mentioned this to others and see them shift right sooner. I hope this book and other the things you've tried helped you with that awareness already!

Catch and refute activity. This activity to **identify** negative emotions thought/behaviors/words and then **refute** them, and then **replace** them is helpful. This activity gets easier and easier after you become self-aware of your triggers, subconscious tendencies, modus operandi, negative words to yourself, and negatudes (negative attitudes).

I can easily identify in real time when I said something to myself that was negative, hurtful, or not adaptive. I stop and think, *hey, I don't believe that about me,* or *hey that is something my mom used to say and she was wrong. I know she was just projecting her issues on to me. That comment she said about me, was not about me, I am going to refute it. I chose to replace it with......*it can be the opposite, something less hurtful, something positive. The only rule is it is not negative about you. It seems like this will take a long time. It will take less than a minute in the very beginning as you go through this dialogue with yourself. Over time it gets adopted as the automatic. I catch a thought, sort of laugh at the sheer ridiculousness of it now (I mean really how could I have held on to her telling me God didn't love me, or that I was responsible for my dad's heart attack, or that all the crying in the world wouldn't bring him back). What says that?? The evil step-mother lol? It is indeed ridiculous.

Negative thoughts are really *negative words* YOU are saying to yourself in your head. Negative thoughts/words are also very bad magnets and they collect more and more negative thoughts and even negative behaviors and outcomes. A negative snowball. Once you see them (it is normal if they pop in), you have the option of choosing not to attach to them (dwell on them or believe them), and just release them you are in a better place.

If you don't catch them, then you run on your negative auto-pilot. Catching them is great! If you can then release them and move on, that is amazing! If you keep coming back to them, then try and replace the thought with a more positive thought version for yourself.

Negative thoughts translate to negative belief patterns. This is the exact opposite of what we want. Epigenetics, the HEAL Documentary, Law of Attraction, the placebo effect, however you want to understand this undisputable reality.....your BELIEFs determine your health, wellness, and life. Don't mess around with not believing in the power of your beliefs. You are creating your reality and your future by the thoughts in your head. That is a fact!

Language in general. Words spoken out loud were once your internal self-talk. You said it in your head and now it is out loud. SO that means, **thoughts** are like **head words** (words you are saying to yourself in your head = thoughts). Words are powerful. Whether you are thinking them or saying them!

Shifting your language may result in a shift in outcomes (mental, physical, and tangible life things!). Not to freak you out, but people keep dying (famous people) who said they would die by 21 are literally dying by 21. This is heartbreaking. Stop saying that! Doctors, please stop telling people with your powerful words - they have 2 months to live. This is irresponsible and DOING harm (the opposite of your Hippocratic Oath) by limiting a belief in healing. How ridiculous. People die all the time without advanced warning. What you are really doing is interfering with the possibility for health and recovery. Please watch the HEAL Documentary, or read anything by Bruce Lipton (the Biology of Belief). Staying mindful of your language on a daily basis will protect your peace. Not letting others tell you negative things about yourself or your future is also within your True Self job description!

Something else we do and we need to stop doing - is our owning of bad stuff. I heard this idea from Marissa Peer on one of her YouTube talks. She said we take ownership of the bad stuff by using "my" instead of "the" when we complain about things. We say, my cellulite, my migraine, my mean mom, my forgetfulness. When we make statements like this (in our head or out loud) it is far harder to distance ourselves from them and from owning them (which is what we want). We want to say and have ownership of is good things! Instead of "my" migraine say "the" migraine. Instead of "my" cellulite say, "the" cellulite. Let's do the flip side too! My good posture, my healthy body, my lovely emotions. I also keep hearing your subconscious is always listening too. These are good reasons to use positive language from this moment on. ☺

Another catalyst for me stopping my negative self-talk was reading somewhere that your soul is always listening to the words you say. *My soul, oh gosh I didn't want to hurt her feelings* (we are always nicer to others, aren't we?). I named my soul Bridgette and put my plan of not allowing myself to talk bad about Bridgette forevermore. It worked! I also wouldn't let other's talk inappropriately to Bridgette, or take any crap in general. I LOVED Bridgette, my Beautiful Soul. If you need a little jump start to conscious self-love, consider starting with your soul and then after you get the hang of it, recognize you are your soul. Whenever I hear a friend or passerby say something negative about themselves, I stop and make a point to share my news.

There is a great free program by Christy Whitman called 30 Days of Watch your Words. If you have a problem with saying mean things to yourself (in your head, or out loud) please watch it on YouTube. Yesterday's was, stop saying "It is what it is." Replace it with, "It is what I choose to make it." I love that! Instead of saying I need to do something, say I get to do such and such, I choose to do, I want to do, I desire to do. Doesn't that sound much better and more powerful?

Stop daily worrying. This reminds me of another "lesson" I learned I want to share. Do you excel at worrying? Worry is holding in your head thoughts of what you DON'T want to happen! People low in self-love may worry so much because of their lack of belief in their ability to successfully navigate the future. We are learning the importance of BELIEF in all things!

Worry buster activity. You might already know this and be motivated to stop worrying, but you just can't (when practicing conscious self-love you will!). In the meantime let me share this philosophical shift that was very helpful for me.

Visualization is a proven technique to bring desired results. We can visualize good things and they may be more likely to come true. What do you think worry is? Oh my gosh, it is visualizing bad things, which may now be more likely to come true because of the worry?! I don't know if it is true, or mean to freak you out, but it helped snap me out of that recursive and unnecessary worrying habit I was trapped in during my time of self-dislike, so I present it for you as an example.

If I want something to happen I think about it and meditate on it, visualize it, give it energy. If there is something I don't want to happen I commit to not give it any energy. I see it in my head an unnecessary worry, and say, nope! Not going there. If there is really no need to plan for such a bad thing, why am I wasting my time thinking about it? Worrying makes you think you are doing something productive, but it is a total waste of time, and who knows if the energy you are investing in thinking/visualizing about it will make it actually become more real, or if you will search that out because it is in your mind's eye! At any rate, I try not to do it anymore.

Your life (you and all your stuff) is energy, that is science. The Universe works in energy. If you are sending out worry energy (and other negative energies - anger energy, victim energy), the similar type of energy is drawn to you (things to worry about, things to piss you off, more people to take advantage of you). It is not magic, it is just how it is.

Let's say you went to a party you really didn't want to go to and you were a real grump the whole time. Complaining about the food, decor, had a frown/scowl on your face, stood in the corner, AND no one talked to you. Hm. Yes, that party really sucked? OR did you make it suck by your negativity? What if you floated in with a SMILE on your face? Saw beauty in the decor, the hosts' attempts at creating a nice atmosphere for you, food for you. Complimented people, displayed gratitude, more smiling. This party would be amazing. Same party, different attitude. Your positudes (positive attitude) will result in more positive outcomes (others giving you them or you finding them)-period. You create your own reality – all day, every day. Why don't you create a good one for yourself!

Instead of a negative auto-pilot subconsciously driven Universal energy exchange, get clear about the lesson you are receiving, get clear about your negative thoughts, your worries. Or, *wow, I am so worried I won't get a job*, and you start visualizing you being broke, not making rent, losing your car. You look for clues to verify your visualization. You are investing a lot of energy here. This is an unwanted energy, so decide to stop doing it. Maybe there is a theme? *I keep finding losers, I will never find a good mate.* Instead of such defeating negative thoughts with no good ending -think, *Oh, I keep drawing in these people to take advantage of me, because I am focusing on all the stuff others did to me, like I am a victim in my own life. Oh, that is the lesson!* Once you learn your lessons (by being grateful for the lesson-or some part of it- and not getting triggered) and we FEEL differently about it, it will go. If all else fails get yourself a rubber band for your wrist and snap it every time you worry (here you learn to associate pain with worrying and chose to stop it!). That should help with that problem!

Daily Peace by Prayer. I took several Marianne Williamson courses and read most of her books. It was in her resources I learned about the idea of taking just 5 minutes each morning to pray, meditate, be at peace. Since I implemented her advice (I picked prayer) my days and years have gotten more peaceful, loving, kind, and joyful. At first I was doing the five minutes. Now I sit on my beautiful prayer chair in my beautiful prayer area for as long as I possibly can each day before my daily tasks take me away. I could pray all day in this spot I bet. On the days I can't pray right at the start of my day (before the news, email, to-do listing), the day is not as nice.

If you were going to do something to keep you busy in times of stress (a documented reason for worrying!) you might as well just replace worrying, biting your nails, pacing, etc., with praying. Praying is the exact opposite of and the antidote to worrying in my book. I am not going to apologize for talking about praying and God (I know it is not politically correct to talk of God/prayer, because we don't want to offend those non-believers or non-prayers), but good news; 80% of U.S adults believe in God and 77% pray (the majority 55%- pray daily!), so if I am offending anyone it is likely just a small group ☺

You can pray about anything and everything. Prayers can be phrased as the positive - the outcome you want! We don't have to worry about negative thoughts or negative words being thrusted into your subconscious mind or the universe. Your positive energy is intact! Also, because you are praying for things you want-your **belief** in the future (you remember the power of belief for all things) is intact! Plus, when you pray, you more easily see the miracles you are praying for! So, whether God, Angels, the Divine Order, the Law of Attraction, the power of belief, your thoughts, or your language is at play here....... the positive effects of prayer cannot be denied and should not be underestimated! Google research on prayer next time you are in a pickle and pull yourself out! Pray daily to protect your peace. Pray to pray more and notice how nice it is to believe in good things instead of bad ones! Reap the rewards of your personal self and world. Tell others! See my resources on prayer in the back of the book. Thank you!

Praying for others. After I became conscious about some of the things I was projecting to my kids and relationship partner I sort of freaked out. I thought I had made some big messes in my parenting. I worried, freaked out, worried, and freaked out, until......I started praying. It worked to calm me and my outcomes seriously improved.

Praying was such a helpful and beautiful endeavor for me. When I have a worry about a loved one, a pet, I just pray for them. At first I didn't know how to phrase my prayers. I found the beautiful book of prayers *Illuminata: A Return to Prayer* by Marianne Williamson so helpful with its lovely personal, family, and community prayers. The most helpful book for reframing my worries about my kids into helpful prayers was written by Doreen Virtue. Doreen's book, "The Care and Feeding of Indigo Children" sits on my prayer chair and I choose one of the several prayers throughout that book for my sons every day. What a peace (and I believe a lot of other things) saver.

At first I didn't feel like I was worthy to talk to God directly in prayer, maybe others had bad experiences with a formal religious activity. God is really different than church and the bad stuff going on there, or the difficult experiences we may have had. Still, I get it. For me it was easier to start talking to Angels ☺ then I worked up to God. I am not speaking for God here, but as I think I understand it, God loves me and you no matter what and completely unconditionally. Even if you haven't talked to him since grade school, or ever, or you've done something you are not proud of, that is very likely no problem for God ☐

Here is a good (sad but inspirational) story about the power of prayer. My beloved cat, Hobbes was diagnosed with untreatable cancer and given the prognosis of 3 weeks to live ("she won't make it another month" I believe were the exact words from the vet). I refused to believe that. I drove home from the vet with that cat in my lap and took her up to my bedroom (I had no prayer area yet) and got on my knees and asked God to give me three years instead of 3 weeks. I hadn't talked to God for a while before that day. I said the same prayer every day. I learned more about God and prayer. I had my beautiful God loving friend Vicki teach me it was okay to say out loud I loved God and was seeking his help. I became a lot less shy/embarrassed about my allegiance to God and the power of prayer as more time went on. Vicki arranged a weekly call between her and I and our pastor where we would pray together for Hobbes. Do you want to guess how long Hobbes lived after her diagnosis? Do you think the vet was right? My beautiful kitty passed exactly 2 years and 11 months and 23 days after her diagnosis. We were short of my prayed for three years by a week or two (and most likely because I gave her a new medicine the vet recommended). During these almost three years I had complete faith and for sure knew Hobbes would live for three years. Actually, the vet telling me my cat had three weeks to live might've spurred my super nuclear cat healing protocol, because I really don't like being told what is to be for me. I would say to the vet each visit, gosh can you believe this. This is God and the power of prayer you know. She would shrug.

My beautiful hair dresser friend had a similar situation with her mom being diagnosed with a brain tumor and given only a "short time to live" diagnosis. I told her, please say no to that! I created a prayer saying for her, told her to tell all her friends to say that prayer every day at 11 AM everyday (without even talking they just all say the prayer at that time wherever they were). She told me they did it! Friends from all over would write to her about the prayer, her mom was just overwhelmed by the love and support. Her mom had a spontaneous remission! These are just two things that happened to me!

I have told many others about the power of prayer and encouraged lots of other prayer circles. There is more information about the power of prayer (and prayer circles) on the Internet. If you feel like this is something you want to try I really strongly encourage you to try it! Please read the *Power of Eight*. Mother Meera says we can pray about anything and everything. No prayer is too small, too big, or too weird. Go ahead pray away!!

What should I ask for for me and others? You may be confused about whether you can pray for what you want - specific things, stuff, outcomes; or if you should surrender to what is given you (pray God's Will be Done). This may get really tricky when we wonder if it is too controlling to pray for specific things for our children or others. Can we really pray away the "lessons" we are being handed without working through them (please stop this pain)? Can we really pray for this house to sell when I am really learning a great lesson about patience? Can I pray my son finds a job right away so he doesn't get frustrated, or will this interfere with him finding his true calling? What should I ask for!?! This is an excellent question.

I was confused about what I should pray for until I read the most eloquent and masterful book by Elisa Morgan, *the Prayer Coin*. Spoiler alert, Elisa says both types of prayers are okay and we CAN ask for things we want! You can say something like I would like this or something even better - to cover that base of you never asking for enough stuff ☺ If you really want to surrender then say, I pray for your solving of this problem when I am ready.

People say all prayers are answered. It may not seem like the exact thing you asked for showed up. Sometimes what you are praying for is not even good enough for you and you get something better! If I don't get something I pray for, I think about why that would be. Soon after I think about it, or ask for clarity I realize the thing I was praying for would've resulted in something challenging, not worth it, or not as good as something I received.

If you don't know what you want, or what outcome would be best for you-then pray to find out. Or, just pray for the best thing to happen. Sometimes I pray for the best outcome for my soul and mind and body. If I pray to not experience something, I might miss a lesson (growth opportunity). If I pray there won't be a line at a story (you can pray for this), you might miss meeting a great person, so instead I stay open in the moment and aware (surrendered). I am constantly praying for my children and others, but again don't want to step on anyone's toes. One way to handle not interfering with other people with your praying is to say something like.... *under the Law of Divine Grace to help this person have the best outcome for their mind, body, heart and soul.* This is a tremendous gift to others, yourself, and humankind!

Let's say you are worried you won't find a job and it keeps popping in. You admitting you lack a job combined with your fear energy - will likely interfere with productive job getting behavior.

Instead, write out the prayer you want. *Please let me get a wonderful job that will be helpful for me and where I contribute.* Say this until you get your great job! It is coming. Prayer makes things happen! Your belief in good outcomes for yourself-because you love yourself-and you deserve great things will be so helpful! Believing you will get the job will help you be on the lookout and even more likely to take proactive steps. Therein lays the power of belief! And why prayer is so great!

My final prayer plug. Next time a worry pops in. See it. Switch it to the opposite and pray for that! Write it out! Say it in your head, say it out loud. Set a reminder on your phone and say it every day, or every hour. Google Novenas and try that for your prayer request. One challenging year I did several Novenas. They all worked out for me!

Daily Peace by Meditation. The Dali Lama said, "In order to save the world we must have a plan. But no plan will work unless we meditate" (A-Z Quotes, 2020).

I've loved meditation since childhood. I don't think I knew exactly what I was doing, but being still, deep thinking, and staying calm was my specialty, which was interesting because the environment was so chaotic (maybe that is why I found my calm). I took a history elective in college for fun and wound up with a really challenging class. The tenured professor called me, "a space cadet" early on. I was okay with that. To me it meant he saw my exterior as calm (I was the only non history major and student he didn't know, so a little out of my element-but apparently still holding it together). Exhibiting calm is good! I remember the first exam return day, he announced to the whole class "the space" got the highest grade and maybe there was something to being spacey! All the other students (the actual history majors) wanted to study with me and asked me my secret. Just a few years ago I was getting a heart test at the doctor and my pulse was 50. They kept taking it and asking "Wow what do you do to get your pulse so low, do you exercise?" I said I meditate. People appreciate calm.

It is far easier to have your head running amuck with uncontrollable thoughts of doom and gloom, so to be able to achieve a calm mind (which I guess can look like spaceyness on the outside), was something. I am not suggesting meditation is spacing out, it is not that. That was just the word my teacher used and I am using as an example. My look of "spaceyness" is really me effectively processing unhelpful thoughts, focusing on the positive, receiving insights (being quiet enough to hear them), displaying strength and resiliency in the face of numerous challenges, and being quiet enough to allow others to talk. Some say spacey, I say brilliant. ☺

I was called to teach a *stress and coping* class in my very early 20s while still in grad school, because no one wanted to teach that class. I took on that challenge and taught it for 20 years. At one point it was the most popular class in our psychology program. It was not because I was teaching it, but was because the information on meditation, mindfulness, the biology of belief, and coping with stress was being recognized by college students as pivotal. Thank goodness. When the baby boomers finally turn the world over to these young people I have a feeling we will see good things (If those lovely kids can make it that is). With all the problems we created for our kids and the societal issues (e.g., the negative effects of social media on mental health, and other things) impacting them, they really need our prayers and assistance.

There are now meditation studios in many communities and more and more people are changing their lives for the better with meditation and protecting their daily peace! You can download meditation apps to help you throughout your day. Please meditate. Please get calm. A calm mind translates to a calm body!

There are different meditation styles, practices, and traditions of meditation, but most practices will involve focused breathing, awareness, and self-regulation. People think meditation is so hard and seem to get nervous they won't be able to "control" their thoughts in meditation, but meditation doesn't ask that of you. In meditation you become focused and clear, because you gracefully experience the flow of thought in and then letting them go easily.

Mediators are more in control of what thoughts they want to attach to (by giving the good ones attention and importance) and letting the bad ones flow out. Meditation does not require you be in control of what pops in (your subconscious is in control of that!). BUT, Meditation can help you regain control over your thoughts because you practice easily letting thoughts go (just as easy as those automatic ones popped in), and/or you can choose to attend to the thoughts you want! I participated in a Practical Meditation Teacher Training with Ben Decker and of course I have never been the same since.

You can meditate at home, with or without tools (e.g., CD, app), go to a meditation studio, take a meditation course, or a multitude of other activities to start and maintain a mediation practice. Oprah and Deepak make it easy for us and created free meditation experiences throughout the year. Even though I know a lot about meditation (I mean I have that meditation teacher training certificate!) I do Oprah and Deepak's 21- Day Meditation Experience every time it comes out. It is FREE, amazing, and I learn more new and useful information each day. It is really outstanding. When I get the email invite for the session (just sign up via Deepak's website (chopracentermeditation.com), or Google "Oprah and Deepak meditation experience" I forward it to people I care about and pray they sign up.

Some people still think meditation is woo-woo. Wow, those people are out of the loop! The research is in and it is confirmed, meditation changes the brain in only good ways! The science behind meditation shows more than its calming and stress relieving effects. Indeed, meditation was shown to improve your cognitive and physical health (e.g., memory, learning, mental ability, emotion regulation, reduced blood pressure, and more positive emotions, stop the stress arousal response). Plus, the benefits are experienced almost immediately.

In my mind there is both purposeful meditation and quiet meditation. In my **purposeful meditation,** I know what I want or should do about something and I use this meditation time to give it energy. I start by breathing and getting calm and thinking about the good outcome I am looking for. I live in that place. I see, hear, smell all the things I want happening happen. When a thought comes in that is not consistent with my plan or vision I look at it, don't attach to it, and let it float out returning to my focused visualization.

I put my house up for sale last February. I thought it would sell right away and I would move to Arizona to get out of the cold. My house did not sell right away. It was June and I started getting a little nervous. My taxes were going to triple in September and I just wouldn't be able to afford the house. I was okay surrendering for the winter and spring and knew I was learning valuable lessons. I was okay praying for the "best outcome" for me and all related to the house transaction. Then when I got nervous, I started focusing my prayer more specifically, to just go ahead and sell it! I worked with one of my helpers who helped me develop a purposeful meditation for the house sale. First we unwound some of the issues related to this house not selling (it was my childhood home I recently moved back to renovate). Asking myself if I was really ready to let it go? I got conscious of that and some other facts (possible influences). Then I was instructed to visualize a nice couple coming up the walk for a house showing. It is the couple who would buy the house! I was to see them walking around loving it and them telling me, "We will take it!" I then visualized us signing the contract and them handing me the check. I did this. I wanted it and I needed it. My house sold within just a few weeks and I had the closing in September! This is an example of my purposeful guided meditation and visualization.

I also like use specific guided meditation tools for purposeful meditation application, such as CDs, or YouTube videos. You can Google your issue, sleep meditation, coping with anxiety, and you can enjoy a meditation with words as you follow the directions. Please check out my resources section, especially meditations by Michael Golzmane and Master John Douglas.

In my **quiet meditation** I may not know what I want to do about something, so I need an answer, or I don't have any issue at all and just want my mind quiet. When my mind is quiet (and my conscious mind focused on a mantra (repetitive phrase) or focused on being still, then the thoughts (from the Divine and from my subconscious or from the external environment) can come in. Some incoming thoughts may be an answer to a current question. Good. I can look at it and then let it float out and get quiet again. Then maybe another thought/idea may come in to my head and I can choose to let that one float out too. Sometimes there are no thoughts and my mind is just still. A still mind is not the desired state. The desired state is when thoughts come in you can chose to give them attention, or let them go. Meditation helps you realize you are in control of your thoughts. Even if the subconscious and ego make a challenging thought, you can learn to easily let it go. In quiet meditation you may use a mantra (sound, word, visual to help you focus - when a non quiet thought pops in you just return your awareness to your mantra).

If you have a peaceful mind and meditate, then you can practice deep healing for yourself and others. The Kirtan Kriya is a technique of meditation repeating the sounds (mantra) Sa-Ta-Na-Ma. It is easy to remember and do. This meditation technique has been shown effective for many mental and physical disorders! You can practice this meditation yourself!

In a different practice of Sat Nam Rasayan you enter a meditative state and you can see your and others' problems. You sit with the person, or the problem in this meditative-letting go state and you experience healing for yourself and the person you are sitting with. I learned about this practice in Los Angeles from an amazing woman, Hargopal. You walk in and take such a class at a meditation studio and you walk out with knowledge and practice in healing yourself and others, by being still with them. Please Google any topic that calls to you. My Sprit Guides love the Internet. I bet yours do too. Each of my Internet searches results in the exact and most helpful information I need at the moment.

We cannot leave this section until you promise to check out the amazing healing benefits of meditation as demonstrated by Dr. Joe Dispenza. Just following him on Instagram will be a game changer. If you were to attend one of his seminars - a life changer! He is a great medical doctor who has accumulated much research on the health and healing benefits of meditation, even people with devastating illnesses and just a little meditation. It is really amazing!

Meditation can help with pain and illness. Many people believe we can communicate with our physical body parts and even pain and illness through our conscious minds. People suggested we are likely to have these conversations when in a meditative state and your brain waves are supportive of such communications (like alpha or theta waves). Another way to communicate with our body issues is through affirmations. Louise Hay has a great book, *You can Heal Your Body*. In her book she presents an ailment, an insight about why it exists, and offers affirmations to say to help with the aliments.

Something else you may find interesting is something called Autogenic Training - developed by J.H. Schultz when he discovered you can direct your mind to make physiological changes in your body. If you say in your head, *"my left hand is heavy and warm, my left hand is heavy and warm"* while you are visualizing your left hand being heavy and warm (these are auto suggestions), and we then measure your left hand it will be warmer than your right hand. The auto suggestions usually center around feelings of warmth and heaviness and can be directed to parts in pain or body systems such as, "my heartbeat is calm and regular." I am telling you this so you know our thoughts and suggestions can influence our bodies.

Deepak Chopra said "if you want to know the condition of the body in the future look at the mind now." He was suggesting the importance of the mind in body health AND this is great news because we can use our minds now to make us feel better (now and in the future). He also said "a quiet mind now means a quiet body in the future." What if we cultivated an understanding of, or acceptance of, maybe love for ourselves (all parts of us including our illness or pain) and others? It is a radical idea, but this shift in acceptance of an illness was something Andrew Weil believed to be 1 of the 7 important strategies for spontaneous healing that returned his patients back to health.

People think meditation is hard. Basically, if you can breathe, you can meditate. I know this to be true because I see grumpy people dismiss (or not attach to) positive thoughts all day long. My advice is to do the opposite - not attach to negative thoughts and focus on the positive ones (purposeful meditation) or not attach to either negative or positive thoughts in lieu of a calm and still mind (quiet meditation). You can do it!

Breathing. Breathing is a very important conscious self-love activity. Believe it or not there is a correct and incorrect way to breathe. People who are stressed and frazzled are chest breathing in that moment (and/or are habitual chest breathers). This chest breathing interferes with oxygen flow in your lungs and exacerbates the stress response. In relaxation mode (through meditation, OR BREATHING in a controlled and slow manner) you breathe more deeply and your air flows through both the top and bottom of your lungs. Correct breathing (diaphragmatic breathing) involves you taking a breath in and pushing your stomach out and then when you exhale you push your stomach in. When I am doing the inhale I like to have my mouth closed and breath in through my nose, and when I breath out I do it from my mouth (this strategy helps me not get a sore throat at Soul Cycle too!).

You can become conscious of your breathing (and this gives the control of it back to you) and intentional (to stop this panic attack, to slow down, to connect with my higher self). When I was first learning correct breathing, I pictured my belly button as the air intaker. On the inhale filling up my stomach (you see your stomach push out). Then raise the air up to your upper lungs/chest, or just keep filling it up through your belly button. Then breath out slowly through your nose, watch your stomach push in.

Banana breath activity. For the banana breath activity I pretend my body is a banana (my feet are the bottom and my head the top of the banana). I breath in and see/feel/experience the air coming in through the banana bottom. The air is clean and pure and cleaning my bruised banana making it a beautiful yellow color as the healing air circulates upward. The air moves up the banana collecting the dark spots and healing me. The clean and healthy air is in the middle of the banana (my middle) and collects more dark spots, and then this one clean breath makes it to my heat the banana top. I hold the air at the top of my banana for about 5 seconds. Then I (my breath) rides down the banana with the air flowing out slowly and completely noticing how perfectly clean and clear my yellow healthy banana is! I rest at the very bottom and make sure every last drop of air is out of my lung, then I breath in again slowly going to up to the top of my banana. I do it again. I do it as long as I want. Be the banana ☐

Hammock breath activity. The hammock breath is where you visualize you are on a hammock or you are the actual hammock and as you breathe in and your body swings up the one way, you hold at the top for a few seconds, then you breathe out and swing completely back the other way – all the while letting the air out slowly. In this exercise the in-breath lasts the whole hammock swing one way; and the out-breath lasts the whole hammock swing the other way. Make sure you are on a lovely beach setting with the sun shining on you, the wonderful smell of sea air, and hear the waves and birds making happy sounds in the background.

Swing breath activity. Do you remember playing on swing sets when you were little? Try **the swing breath**. Imagine yourself swinging up to the sky to see your feet in the air. On this up swing, you breathe in. Stick at the top for a few seconds and hold your breath as you see the sky and touch the clouds. Slowly release your breath and let your air out as you float back up the other side. Hold your breath there and inhale as you move toward the sky again. I like to be on the high/sky part of the swing when the air is at the top of my head and when I am exhaling I am going down and slowly exhaling making sure every last sip of breath is out.

Body fix-it breath activity. I use my body fix-it breath for when I have some physical discomfort (e.g., pain, upset stomach, etc.). You could also do this for more serious health issues, maybe a thyroid problem, pancreas, etc. Imagine the organ doing the breathing. Breath clean and healing air into the organ where you collect up all the pain and problems. Hold it in and then release slowly, exhaling all the difficulty for that organ. This is a somatic breathing technique, which has shown great healing benefit.

I love pairing visuals with my breathing activities for relaxation. What if you threw in some pleasant smells or the feeling of the sun on your skin? What if you throw in an activity during the **swing breath** - where when you experience a thought you put it into a cloud and watch the cloud float out of the sky (mind) as a way of letting it go. **Now you are meditating**. Try it! Make up your own breath activity. What feels good to you?

There are so many wonderful and free breathing exercises for you. There is a one-minute panic attack buster, Breath of Fire, Breath like a Teapot!, The Dolphin Breath. So many! Please start implementing them daily to stay peaceful, calm, and healthy. When you catch yourself being out of self-love or engaging in unloving behaviors/word to yourself try a breathing activity. When you are doing your correct breathing put your shoulders back and open up your whole torso. Feel that relief! Let the love and air flow!

Affirmations. Affirmations were introduced in the section above about how research shows the mind directs the body through affirmation statements. Mind-to-body affirmations have been shown to make your body and it's parts physically healthy, raise your body temperature (autogenic training), and more. What if we use affirmations to help our mind. A mind-to-mind affirmation! *My mind is free of worry. My mind is calm and hopeful.* We can use affirmations for fostering conscious self-love. *My love for myself is strong and healthy.*

Please affirm and use positive statements about you, your soul, mental health, thoughts, feelings, and your subconscious. Say anything you want to be true and hope will eventually become your truth if it is not right now. *I am enough! I am worthy! I am making good choices! I am love! I am loveable! I matter! I deserve good things.* You say them now and really believe in them! Affirmations (similar to prayer) help you believe in a good outcome and positive future. Things that you affirm come true whether your mind tells your body or your mind tells your mind!

Louise Hay has affirmations for each body part, body system, and for mental health too. Check out her book, *You can Heal your Body*, or *You Can Heal Your Heart.* Louise believed in the power of affirmations and I do too. Remember, your soul, the universe, and your subconscious is always listening. Let's give them something good to talk about!

Talk about changing your energy, beliefs, and outcomes! Affirm what you think or know to be true (even if it is not true yet). Affirm what you want. Let these affirmations become your self-talk. Replace those unloving affirmations you so easily tell yourself and others about you, with good affirmations. The negative affirmations are like little curses. Let the positive affirmations flow through you, become you, and see what you draw to you! You are responsible for creating your own reality.

For so long I was affirming I didn't deserve love. I wasn't getting it. When I started affirming I was love, I was loveable, then I started to believe it and could see it in front of me (in a mirror because it came from me). There is no sense affirming negative things when we know the power of positive affirmations.

Why don't you hold in your head what you do want to happen in terms of visualization, prayers, or affirmations! Of course, it is your choice, and we are choosing love and kindness for ourselves and others now. Affirm it!

DOING your Daily BE of Self-Compassion, Receiving Love, and Kindness

We are making a plan to be conscious of times we are not receiving love, practicing self-compassion, and self-kindness. This is the way we will remove our negative subconscious programming.

That intention to recognize these times in order to make revisions is key. If you make this intention, you are more than half way there! I have been a kind and happy gal since I can remember. When young (like age 5) and I would hear an ambulance I would immediately pray the people in trouble would be okay. I would save all sorts of front yard rabbits, kittens, bugs, all of them. I would get so excited when people won on Wheel of Fortune! I just loved when others won or got new things I was so happy for other's victories. I just didn't understand why others weren't like that and some people (like my mom) were so envious of others and so self-obsessed. I hated it. To make sure I wasn't like that, I continued my joy for other's victories, but I went overboard, and forgot about myself (or forbade myself to focus on my victories at all). That is not the right answer either.

In the past when I would receive compliments I would say, *oh this old thing?* I am sure you said that too. It took a real conscious effort to say instead, *oh, well, thank you. I appreciate that.* We are taught to be humble and not prideful. I do agree with that, and we don't want to be boastful or arrogant, but we can accept compliments and nods of good works and approval, especially if they will help us grow in self-love!

Another old trick of mine was when I would receive something nice (a loving gift from another like a present or cupcake) I would immediately think of who I could give that to; as if I didn't deserve to receive a gift. It is nice to pass on the love, but I wasn't sitting with and receiving the love. That made it too hard for me to give love freely.

The outward flow of love (from you to another) is contingent upon your receipt of love. It is incumbent upon you to allow yourself to receive love from yourself and others, otherwise you won't be able to give freely. It is incumbent upon to you recognize when you are interfering with other's kindnesses to you and stop that. You can accept gifts, compliments, love, and kindness. You deserve all of them. Sit with these treats and let that joy wash over you. You will be more likely to pass it on (maybe not that exact gift you accepted, but a different one) in a more authentic way.

If we all woke up every day and decided today we would be careful, loving, and kind to ourselves and others, how could we have a bad day? If we made a mistake we owned it, apologized for it, fixed what we could. If we all minded our own business and didn't internalize other's projections, spoke up when it would be helpful, and otherwise reflected on our actions to develop self-awareness, always looking for ways to have more honor and care for ourselves and others- the world would be a wonderful place! We don't all do that yet and the world at large is not always so wonderful yet. Still, in our smaller scaled worlds, if we do these things we can make our worlds a kind place and this will eventually generalize. Until that time, there is a need for balance in all things, including, compassion, giving, and kindness, especially where you take your self-things into account.

Self-acceptance and unconditional positive regard. Remember from Chapter 4, the third part of compassion (realizing you and others as human and understanding mistakes are going to happen and there is no reason to condemn, blame, or otherwise feel resentment for such mistakes) reminds me of unconditional positive regard.

Unconditional positive regard is when you experience and practice acceptance for yourself or another while loving all parts of you unconditionally (not based on any condition). Actually, your love for yourself (or another) is not based on anything in this view. It is just yours to own no matter what. It is not like I love you less because you just messed up. It is not like I am going to abuse and berate myself because I made a mistake. I still love, care, accept, and treat myself, and you, with kindness period, regardless of foibles or good stuff, or any condition.

For sure it is easier to love cupcakes more than spinach, but you can still love and appreciate and hopefully see the good in both cupcakes and spinach. Deepak said on Instagram, "real self-acceptance, accepting your true self and living in the now is the goal. This is not where your ego self says things like: *I like me, my flaws and all* -it is even more than that." It would be good to accept your flaws, but we can take this a step further back and get to the real root of your lack of self-acceptance. This lack of self-acceptance lives in your subconscious until you chose to take action to make it conscious. This is where we need to be going (when you have time ☺).

You are hoping you have unconditional positive regard! You are hoping your relationship partners have it too! Well, good news, you can "condition" unconditional positive regard for yourself, children, and others! We do this by making it more than a point, but a daily practice to practice compassion for self and others (especially that all important 3rd part of the compassion recipe - it is impossible to be perfect and never make a mistake).

Your self-compassion comes first. Having compassion for other people in your head and heart is a very good thing to practice 24/7. However, **behaving** with compassion for others 24/7 in a currently uncompassionate world could get you killed. There is no one to benefit from that and the world will have lost a compassionate Earth Angel. I am not saying you shouldn't have compassion. Have all the compassion you can muster in your head. Behave with compassion when you can, but please, for the Love of God, if you are practicing compassion in your outward behaviors make sure you have compassion for yourself and balance the given-out compassion and/or use measured compassion.

Do you remember the sitcom Growing Pains from the 80s? I always think of that one Growing Pains episode where the nice Seaver family housed the homeless person. I had fantasies of doing that when I watched the show. I know my kids had such fantasies too. It makes sense if a person doesn't have a home, why can't they stay with us. I didn't understand when my mom said no, and I am sure my kids didn't understand when I said no. Well unfortunately, in the Growing Pains episode the homeless person robbed them. Saying no to housing people you don't know, even though you really want to be helpful, is an example of self-compassion.

There was still something compassionate the Seavers could've done to display their inner compassion and display their compassion for others (measured compassion). That year when my kids wanted to help the homeless we did other activities (sanctioned ones by experts who already figured it out). Us running in - like a bull in china shop - offering our home - might've turned out bad for us, the homeless person, and really lots of people in general, if word got out about how it doesn't pay to be nice.

Think of a different example. Some parents feel guilty about not spending time with their children. When their kid asks for money, they give them a lot of money (parent showing other-compassion). If the parent didn't take their self-compassion into consideration (in this case how they should be doing right by their kid by being sensitive to the kids current level of growth and self-control), the parent may keep giving and giving and saying no to things for themselves. Also, is throwing money at unsupervised children/teen (young adult under 28) even ever a good thing? No.

Please consider. Are you saying no when you need to? Are you allowing others to give to you? Are you receiving enough love and kindness to have balanced relationships (not with your kids though remember - they are not expected to give to you). This is the way to self-love without regret, remorse, hard feelings, and resentments (and getting hurt)! Are you interfering with your receipt of another adult's love toward you, because you are being too nice, giving, and compassionate? Consider that and make changes if so. Sometimes the best answer for everyone is *NO*, or *I need some more help, love, consideration.*

There are always consequences for your and other's actions. These consequences must be considered. Sometimes you are receiving the karma/compassion/love, sometimes you are giving it out, some interactions are just for fun, harmony, and enjoyment. Think about it, each of your actions has a reaction. It is best to consider your actions and not make too big of a mess. You always showing compassion to others (and not yourself) and you always being kind to others and putting them first is still making a mess. It is "nice" of you, but you are creating karmic imbalances that will likely need to be paid by you or the other person at some point (unless you are a nun).

Also, are you really even being "nice" just to be "nice" or are your intentions to be good, or to get people to like you? If so, the karma/compassion/love isn't good for either of you. Providing compassion and yet more compassion to others who misuse your kindness and understanding, creates an imbalance in your relationship with that person; which at some point needs to be balanced (by you or our friend karma). Kindness and more kindness to others who are cruel to you - creates an imbalance. Sometimes it is actually best to say no, mind your own business, and let the universal lesson be dealt out.

One thing I am sure of, it is always best to practice balanced giving/receiving, and balanced compassion for others/compassion for self, especially to foster self-love growth. Practicing a balance of self-other compassion will make making choices much easier (if you have a difficulty making choices). Plus, when making decisions from a place of self-compassion you will make choices that are consistent with your authentic desires and have far less resentment seep in to your relationship. Your relationship partner will be much happier in the relationship without your resentment toward them. So you are really helping others with your practice of conscious self-compassion and self-love!

The most helpful thing for me about self-compassion, and compassion in general, was learning about the third part, that it is okay to make mistakes, everyone makes them and I needed to stop judging myself (and others) so harshly. I didn't need to be on the lookout for missteps and slip ups from myself and others. That even if there was a slip up, that it would be okay. That recognition was hugely helpful! I hope you can embrace that third and most important aspect of compassion, especially as it relates to YOU!

Cast out judgment. How in the world are we going to stop judging ourselves and others? Well, the answer is to cultivate your conscious self-love. Once you love and accept yourself, you will love and accept others. Until that happens, you will be judging from the moment you get up until the moment you go to bed.

We judge because we feel bad about ourselves most likely based on our conditioning and what is currently in our subconscious mind. We chastise or complain about others to make us feel good (which is the exact opposite of what we should be doing/feeling). I think this problem starts early. It is set up by our school and sports programs, based on competition, and/or a view of limited resources. It is also an undesirable trait passed down in families; whereby you likely saw it right before your eyes. You can tell yourself or others that you have "high standards" for your kids, or that your judging words are "motivating" you or your children. But such words are fear based and it is difficult to be encouraging from that perspective. We can have far more authentic successes and much more enjoyable life experiences if we are kind and accepting of ourselves and others instead of being harsh, critical, judgmental, and fixing everything to be "perfect."

The perfectionist. People with very high standards for themselves or others are referred to as perfectionists. Perfectionists have a lot of negative internal stuff going on. Their self-talk can be highly critical, very judgmental. They may be doing this to motivate themselves and on some level it might look like it is working, but there are much better ways with fewer negative side effects.

Parents who are perfectionists (and hard on themselves) create some challenging life experiences for their children. First, their inauthentic responses to the child's imperfect attempts at school projects, coloring, you name, it are obvious to the child even though the parent thinks not. Kids see their parents attempts at "doctoring up" assignments, dishes in the dishwasher, art projects. Kids see parents saying, good job, but you know what would even be better... Children can see right through this. What children take away is - they are not good enough.

The perfectionists' feedback and correcting on things all throughout life (the art project, homework, bed making, essay, selected college classes, job, what their boss said, feedback on their mate, etc.) can undermine healthy growth and personal feelings of mastery.

I would say it is okay to have high standards (expectations) for yourself, but don't judge others who don't do it in your perfect way. Just because you are doing it this way doesn't mean it is the right way (or the only way). I like having the belief you will succeed, but belief is one thing and perfectionism is a different thing! If your self-talk is critical and you are beating yourself up when things aren't perfect, or go your way, then I think we have a little problem of self-love and self-acceptance on our hands.

Catch yourself the next time you are being hyper-critical (standing in judgment) of yourself or another. How does that feel? Is it a good feeling inside? If not, you can see it for what it is, refute it or talk yourself out of thinking that is the norm. Then always be cognizant of the third component of self-compassion - where you see the kinder and gentler and more accepting part of all human behavior and tell yourself it is okay to not be perfect, to be kind to yourself instead, to enjoy activities instead, to motivate yourself with love not fear.

What if when we are in perfectionist mode, we consider loosening up and practicing more conscious self-love, especially as related to self-compassion. Then you could stop obsessing about being perfect, judging yourself when you are not perfect, and projecting that on to your loved ones (no one could ever live up to those standards though). This is better than your children adopting the perfectionist mindset themselves (by your modeling). Especially if the kids are not be interested in being perfect. If that is the case, they may just end up thinking they are a loser.

In our society it will be next to impossible to grow up with your self-love intact, so it will be next to impossible to not judge others in order to feel better about yourself. Your day is an ego-ruled, judging, expecting, comparing, and resentful mess. It is so hard to be happy and have joy when everyone you are looking at - has something so wrong with them (remember a projection of your own self).

Then, it is far easier to blame our lack of joy on another, our environment, our current circumstance, boss, partner. The more we blame, the more we reduce our power and the more victim energy we put out. The more we judge ourselves the more we judge others and more resentment we accrue.

The obvious answer to self-and other judgment, is self-and other-acceptance. Self-compassion. Accept all parts, regardless of condition, but most importantly requisite in compassion there is the realization that we are human and not being perfect is simply part of the deal. Unconditional self-acceptance, unconditional self-love, unconditional love for others. It is okay to practice conscious self-love. It is okay to accept ourselves, our behaviors, and our choices (hopefully they are all legal and good for society), no matter what they are. Catch yourself doing it and stop it.

Self-compassion for your blunders. Remember the third aspect of compassion. Everyone makes mistakes. Big ones, little ones, mistakes, mistakes, mistakes. Oops! No one is perfect. That is the human part. Sometimes our blunders are cute. Sometimes they are not!

Most of our "blunders" are just normal life events and we are judging ourselves too harshly. When you make an actual blunder, or when you judge yourself harshly for something, catch it. Instead of just catching your blunder, "oh I am so stupid." Catch that reaction. "Hey, stop saying you are stupid, everyone makes mistakes. It is easy to see why I made that one." Be on your side for once. What would you say to a friend who made that exact blunder? Say that!

See it (the blunder) and thank goodness for you catching your too harsh response. This is an opportunity to show yourself compassion and understanding for being human and making a regular mistake. This is not the end of the world. Tomorrow is another day and you just learned a valuable lesson from this experience. Use the lesson to write tomorrow's story a little differently – with self-love and kindness toward yourself.

What if you joined each moment in its perfection. The moment is perfect, you are perfect, this other person is perfect. Most people are out in the world doing the best they can from their understanding of the world and themselves. If we think about that before judging, or condemning we can get to a better place. This can apply to you too. Give yourself a break, Dear!

Judge Buster Activities. When I become aware I am comparing, judging, myself or another. I immediately say, hey, Jill honey, what are you feeling threatened about? Why are you comparing yourself here? I stop and assess this judgment. I know that what I am judging this person on reflects a lack on my own experiences.

My friend was going to a fancy party. She was feeling not great about her weight at the time. She said she was mad at herself for gaining weight and nothing looked good on her and was just not excited about going, etc. (the negative loop). Then she said, well I do know when I look around and compare myself to all the other wives I am not the fattest or ugliest, so I shouldn't care. She was not feeling worthy and projected this on to the other potential women at the future event by suggesting they wouldn't look good. Judging yourself, projecting, and then judging others is not an example of showing yourself self-love. I stopped her and said, oh Dear, you are so beautiful inside and out and you always look great! You don't even need to compare yourself to the other wives because your husband adores you and is so proud of you (which was the truth). I was able to stop her judging (which I know she then feels bad about later) because she is my very good friend and we have a **no judging pact**.

You can set up a **no judging pact** with a person you know (maybe one you talk to a lot) and each of you point out when you hear the other person judging themselves or another. It is easier for another person to see it. Making a commitment to be accepting of yourself and others is such a beautiful step in the conscious self-love direction.

Once you start giving yourself a few breaks, supports, nods, acknowledgements, acceptance passes; the easier and more common it will be for you to relate to yourself better, stop projecting, and start giving others some slack by not judging their and complaining about their every move. This won't make you start slacking, it will make you happier! Remember, the third component of compassion and self-compassion (about knowing we are all human and being human means mistakes will be unavoidable). The first and most important thing to do to stop judging life, is to just start accepting yourself and loving yourself. Once you treat yourself less harshly you will automatically be kinder to others. Everyone is doing their best given their current circumstances and understanding of what is what (even you!). Help people see different things if you want them to grow.

Another's blunders. Well, I think the second thing we can do to have more other-compassion is to **shift from expecting things** to being **curious about how things WILL turn out.** The next thing is to always hold that third step in your heart (all people will make mistakes). Just like you will like mercy and deserve to ask for mercy, so too will other people deserve mercy. The more you understand this for yourself, the more you will understand and apply this to your loved ones and others.

Sometimes judging things is our way of staying safe. Maybe, *He looks scary. She is too pretty to hang around with. I think he is crazy.* Judging as a form of heuristics (categorizing to make your understanding easier) is something that could be helpful, but look at the quality of these judgments. It would be far better to think more in terms of, *hm... he is using drugs? I don't think I would like to date someone who does that...* In that example, we are giving you back your power, not judging another. Moreover, when you authentically accept your likes and dislikes you feel empowered to create your environment around them. It is far better to find out what is for you, or not for you based on your preferences than to judge others. Judging feels weird and you may not know where exactly your discomfort is coming from, but may be because YOU are so judgy (and not even because of the other person's flaws - and we know a lot about those already because of our projections). When all else fails and you cannot muster compassion for this jerk standing in front of you, picture them as a baby. It is hard to be mad at babies :)

Practicing MEASURED self-compassion in the context of other's blunders you are involved in. Now what are we going to do if there is a self-other compassion imbalance and you are demonstrating compassion for others and not yourself? We are going to have you stop that pronto!

Let's say your partner cheated on you (or some other big thing that was offensive to you). That will always be your partner's misstep. Sure there were relationship problems, but it is no reason to disrespect you, put your well-being at risk, and/or otherwise treat you very poorly. You are mad. Then you remember them as a baby. You start forgiving them, saying well, you weren't great in the relationship and start taking on the blame for why they cheated, or treated you poorly. What would you tell your friend here - you would tell them to stop that. You are having too much compassion for the other, and not enough for yourself!

Maybe you don't have compassion for them and you are mad as hell. How could they hurt you like this! You remember they didn't purposefully try and hurt you (hopefully!), but they were acting out of their lack of self-love and you were in the direct path of it. How can you have compassion/forgiveness here for both of you? Try mustering it in a measured way. Too much compassion for him/her might make you forgive him, take him back, and spend the next 20 years in hell wondering/checking if he is cheating on you again. Compassion for only you would be, that's it, you crossed my boundary, you are outta here!! What about a measured compassion approach. Well, the cheating wasn't about me, still I don't like when people can't control themselves in the context of a committed relationship. He is doing his best and I have compassion for him and this problem is stemming from his inner problems. Then you can practice measured self-compassion.

I can see a measured compassion approach going one of two ways (maybe you can think of more). Way #1: Your self-talk looks like this: *He shouldn't have done that, still, I have compassion for myself, know that I will dislike greatly not being able to trust him. I don't want to be in this situation.* OR Way #2 Your self-talk looks like this: *He shouldn't have done that, still, I have compassion for myself, know that I will dislike not being with him, he is begging forgiveness and promising to not do anything like that again. I believe I can trust him again if he agrees to work on the issues, and I do want to be in this situation.*

Having measured compassion means taking your own likes and dislikes into consideration too. There is no right/wrong answer about what to do if someone cheats on you (or if you cheat on someone), or any other thing from the list of how we hurt others when we are not practicing self-love. The best answer though is to show compassion to others AND also yourself in a measured manner. Who knows how it will shake out. You have to decide your preferences and then make choices about actions. It is confusing if you don't take time to consider your needs.

Loving You and Your Great Choices. If you think you are bad at decisions, can't make choices, immediately get buyers' remorse after any decision, check-in with 12 people before deciding the color of your hat today, then this section might be helpful for you.

To make choices you must connect with your inner truth detector. This is your soul, your inner self, your True Self. Not your ego-self, which contains (or is the result of) all of the conditioning. We want your choice maker to be your true, calm, non-reactive, self-compassionate, soul self. This self feels very little pressure to make hasty decisions. This self asks for more time if you just don't know the decision to make just yet. This self has your current needs and desires in mind when confronted with a choice. This self has the power to express these needs/desires, and even say "no" when a choice comes up that doesn't feel good/right/in your best interest. Have you seen this self lately?

Choice questions. A good way to help yourself make choices it to take that moment and ask yourself some questions. You ask a question in the form of thoughts, but then listen for how your body answers. You might need a little space and quiet for this activity. Let's say your boss asks you to work on Sunday.

Ask yourself....What do I want to do? Do I want to do this? or that? Is it consistent with what I like? These are nice litmus-test questions to help you make choices. When I ask these questions and my stomach feels knotty, or my thoughts run amuck, or I start making fists with my hands I know my body and inner self would prefer that I said NO to the request! In the past I would not ask myself the questions, not listen to my body and would just always do what others wanted. Years later I would take the step of asking the questions, know I didn't want to do something, feel it in my body and STILL say yes to such requests. How could I have done that! Now I ask my questions and do what I want for myself. I deserve to take care of my own needs. I am practicing conscious self-love. I am much happier and far less busy!

BUT, what if you don't even know what you like/dislike? It's been so long (or maybe never) that your opinions about things mattered, or that anything was about you. Gosh I am so sorry about that. I was there for years! I had such a problem making decisions because my inner compassion for my true self was just so quiet and my mind was filled with too much noise (ego messages, the conditioning that I was bad at decisions, that I didn't deserve good outcomes, etc.). I had the subconscious pattern of always doing something wrong. My true-self, and good at decision making compass was broken indeed!

We can't let our egos run the show and talk us out of what we think/know is right! That is why it is so important to take that moment. Clear your head. Ask your questions, but let your body answer not your mind. What do you want to do? Which option is most consistent with your likes, your values? Which choice brings you more love, joy, and the lighter path? Empower yourself when making choices by thinking of what would be good for you then sharing that with the person giving you the choice.

When I was getting to this place of good decision making I started by having one rule.... Don't make anything harder. This rule worked for me for a long time and it was a good rule when I needed it. I am much better with decisions now and expressing my choice. If I don't get a body reaction to right away, I ask for more time. If I have a choice and my body screams out the answer- I go with it. If I am calm and see the good in both options, I like to really check in and evaluate what I want to do. I do this because in the past I would get resentful easily and have chooser's remorse constantly.

Lots of times this was because I answered too fast (and it was always yes because I wanted everyone to love me and send me love coins). I learned I am a person who really does need to take my time with decisions. That is okay! Anytime I feel pressured to make a choice (by another person!, or by me being in a hurry to snap something up) I know for sure my/or their ego is at the control tower. Ego choices aren't the best ones. Talk about making things harder I was making things harder for myself and my loved ones for years all because of a lack of self-love and my punishment patterns because I didn't deserve a happy life. I am glad I stopped that!

One more important thing I learned was that I didn't have to announce all my choices. Just as all of your thoughts don't need to be expressed (and shouldn't), not all of your choices (or plans) need to be expressed (and shouldn't). Once I made a choice and announced it I felt bad changing my mind, which we shouldn't because that is always our right!

Practice choice questions with yourself activity. Next time you have a choice to make, stop, become present. Think about your heart and stomach area. Present your choice thought to that area. Do I want pancakes or blueberries. See if you get a gut feeling. A gut feeling is when your body helps you make a decision. What is your body/gut telling you to do? What would feel the lightest, best, most helpful thing for yourself right now. Can you feel it? If you can then your choice is made!. Now how are you going to act on that choice (especially if it will disappoint someone else). You can always do what you want. You might just need some practice putting your needs first, or disappointing a person. To get comfortable with this strategy practice it for small choices, daily choices. Have your mind ask your body a question and then do what your body says. If you make this a habit when the big choices come around you will have even more practice and belief in your good decision making!

Practice choice questions with your friends activity. When someone asks for advice, don't tell them what to do, instead ask them your special questions so they can ponder and you can see their wheels working. What do you want to do? Do you want to do that? Is it consistent with what you like?

Empower others when making choices? or being asked for assistance with choices? Remember it is best to only make choices for yourself. Even when someone asks for advice about a choice - the best way to answer is with these empowering questions. You can share what you would do, but encourage other's self-determinations. Maybe you can help them to express their choice to the person they need to express to. That would be very helpful, especially if they have trouble speaking up for themselves and their truth. You can do this in a compassionate way.

Likes/dislikes/*oh hell no* - list activities. As a fan of lists I encourage you to make all of these lists. Clarifying your likes and dislikes and *oh hell no's* from time to time is good for you! These things can change over time and it is good to check in to know where you stand. Sometimes we like things because another liked them and we adopted that feeling about the thing. It is okay to change your mind, and it is essential that the things that are on your lists are in their spots because YOU feel this way about them.

The lists have great applications. If you are frequently bombarded with choices from others you can refer to your lists and then respond accordingly. Such listing activities are also helpful if you have a hard time with decisions, or immediately regret them. Check in with yourself more regularly- especially after you are not happy with a choice. You can return to your list for verification, *oh hey yea, that was a good choice, I don't like scary movies! Well Done!*

Other self-love (self-compassion and self-kindness) promoting activities. When someone doesn't give you the love you desire it is a sign of their emotional pain. When someone treats you poorly it is a projection of their emotional pain. Whenever another person is involved, we can be subject to challenging stimuli. Practicing conscious self-love will help you see this reality and separate from other's projections of their pain on to you. It will help you make good choices about partners in general and decisions about on goings in all relationships. **Remember the more you love yourself, the greater your ability to give love to others and to feel their love to you!**

Unzip your heart activity. When I am upset, starting to loop a negative thought, or start acting like a rescuer, or victim, feeling resentment, grudgy, or get into list mode - I stop and think about my actual heart. I picture myself unzipping my heart and letting my love out! Not the red anatomically correct one, but a beautiful golden bubble heart in the middle of my chest. There is a zipper on it. I unzip the zipper and gold energy and other beautiful things like starts and sparkles flow out of my heart. My heart is open and I am feeling warm and gold loving energy all around my body and in my body. I fill my heart with love for myself! I can put other things into my gold heart bubble. I put my cat in my gold love bubble and surround this little kitty in love. My love is filling her with joy. My love is repairing her and she is loving herself. She is sending her adorable love back to me! I can put a small version of me in my love bubble and do the same things. We (me and who is in my love bubble) are together in this gold and sparkly heart of love sitting in my chest. We are sending love to others. We are so full of love we are only able to receive love in. I breathe in this beautiful gift of love!!

Open your heart chakra activity. The heart chakra is in the middle of your body and when it is closed or blocked you stop the love from coming in and going out. This stops your ability to feel peace and be happy in relationships (even good ones!). I think about my heart chakra (or my actual heart) and imagine it. I see it in my mind's eye.

My heart chakra is green! It looks like a green plate in my chest. If I am thinking about opening my heart chakra I start spinning the green chakra plate slowly to open it. While I am opening it I see the little or big problems of the day there. They are like little peas. I can visualize all the little pea sized problems in the heart chakra plate and I imagine them floating out as I see them one by one. They are happy to go. They didn't want to be there. After I imagine my heart chakra opening I see my gold bubble heart and feel joy. An open Heart Chakra is important in loving yourself and others without conditions or judgments. Loving yourself without judgment or conditions is essential for peace.

Sometimes when I am sitting with someone who is upset (or even talking to them by phone) or holding my vomiting cat with a hair ball. I just take my mind off the situation for a minute and unzip my heart and see the person or cat surrounded by my love. I see it repairing and calming them. I can do this for myself too!

You can also unzip your heart and share how you are feeling with another person. Sometimes you don't even need words. If I am feeling really great and I open my heart I send it out and I can see like the heat transfer or something (I am not on drugs lol). Emotions are contagious! I remember this, and purposely try to spread the good ones. Sometimes when I could be irritated by my list of errands, instead I get present and open my heart before I walk in to Walgreens and Jewel. I smile at the people, I see my heart filled with joy spilling on to everyone. I was supposed to be there today to unzip my heart and send the love out.

Mirror Work activity. Louise Hay developed a brilliant and easy exercise to foster self-love. The exercise requires you and a mirror and no one else! You are to look lovingly in your eyes in the mirror and say over and over that you (actually say your name) love you. Jill, I love you. I love you. Jill, I love you! When I do this I feel the love from my heart to my subconscious. It must be something about the eye as the window to the soul?

There are positive physical changes in your body when you smile. I try to always have on a smile. I am usually happy. The facial cue of smiling sends happy signals to your brain. Sometimes when in public I look around and no one is smiling! Why not? One of the easiest things to do is go out and just smile at people. What if you smiled at yourself when doing your mirror work! Try that. Please Google more about Louise Hay and Mirror Work.

Picture work activity. I do "picture work" when I am irritated with a person. I get my favorite picture of them and stare into their eyes for a good 5 minutes while breathing in a calm and relaxed way. I am smiling when I am doing this and remembering something really good or funny about this person. I am grateful for this person and our relationship in this moment of peace with their picture. When the time is up I thank them for being my loved one. I pray that we forgive each other and our relationship is in full repair. This helps me feel good about me being angry (self-compassion) and helps me feel compassion for them (the balance!).

Love letter to yourself activity. When I wasn't getting the love letters I wanted from admirers (lol) I started writing them to myself! You can write a note to you at the end of a day celebrating your accomplishments and wins with yourself on your calendar, or in your journal! You can write a love letter to yourself in the morning to have a nice day! You can write a more formal page-long letter, weekly, monthly, or even when something big goes right or wrong. You sharing your love, acceptance, acknowledgement, and appreciation with the one person who actually sees all you do and knows your deep and important thoughts (you) will provide much joy, help develop your conscious self-love, and will make your previous bids for attention a thing of the past.

Loving Kindness Activity. There is a Buddhist practice called Metta where you offer love to yourself and others; whereby you are practicing a type of loving-kindness. The act of you offering love to others helps others AND increases your love for yourself. It is a beautiful and easy breezy activity to practice whereby you just offer love to others and yourself through repeating a statement as you go down your list of loved and not so loved ones. You say something like....*May I be happy, healthy, and liberated for the highest good. May Bob be happy, healthy,* *and liberated for the highest good. May Jan be happy, healthy, and liberated for the highest good.*

When you do a Loving Kindness activity like this you are sending unconditional love yourself and others. Sometimes when I do this for a person in my life then end up calling me or texting me (like they must be feeling it on some level). Researchers revealed there are actual health benefits of Loving Kindness practices, including good physical health, reduced pain, reduced inflammation, reduced stress, self-compassion and acceptance, and even longevity.

Let's try a Loving Kindness Body Meditation for ourselves right now! (adapted from an assignment I submitted in my meditation teacher training class with Benjamin Decker)

In this mediation we will go deep and access unconditional love and compassion for ourselves and our body parts first and then we gradually expand the field of unconditional love to our families, social and professional circles, and beyond to all living beings.

Anyone who enters your thoughts during the meditation can receive your compassion and love. It is an exercise to see all things with compassion and love. It is important in the world today to be loving and compassionate. The more you practice this the better our world will be.

When your mind wanders away from the experience of Loving Kindness - you will notice this wandered - just gently direct your attention back to the Loving Kindness meditation allowing everything else to be as it is. I invite you to gently close your eyes and bring your awareness to the experience of your breath.

Take a few gentle, deep breaths, settling in and becoming very present.

As you inhale, feel the sensation of loving kindness fill your body.

Say in your head. *"May I be happy, healthy, and liberated for the highest good."*

Focus on your legs now. Notice any tension in your legs as you inhale and then exhale the leg tension out the bottom of your legs and into the ground now say, *"May my legs be happy, healthy, and liberated for the highest good."*

Focus on your torso now. Notice any tension in your torso (stomach, chest, ribs, back) as you inhale and then exhale the torso tension trough your back and into the ground now say, *"May my stomach, chest, ribs, back, and internal organs be happy, healthy, and liberated for the highest good."*

Focus on your head now. Notice any tension in your forehead, face, neck, back of head, stiffness as you inhale and then exhale all head tension through the back of your head into the floor and say, *"May my whole head be happy, healthy, and liberated for the highest good."*

Focus on your shoulders, arms, hands, and fingers as you inhale, and then exhale and say, *"May my shoulders, arms, hand, and fingers be happy, healthy, and liberated for the highest good."*

Now I want you to go to your pain part, your illness part. Take a few breaths in and out offer loving kindness to the part of your body in discomfort. Smile at the part, breath in, exhale feel compassion toward the part. Breath in and say, *"May my _____ be happy, healthy, and liberated for the highest good."*

Let's stay here again and do the same thing two more times - you can stay on the same area, or move around to a different area. Smile at the part, breath in, exhale feel compassion toward the part. Breath in and say, *"May my _____ be happy, healthy, and liberated for the highest good."*

Once again, stay here or move to a new part and smile at the part, breathe in, exhale feel compassion toward the part. Breath in and say, *"May my _____ be happy, healthy, and liberated for the highest good."*

From the inside out look at and feel your whole body as one now. See you laying there healthy and full of love and kindness for your body, Say to your body, "May you be happy, healthy, and liberated for the highest good."

Invite to your mind all the people you love dearly, seeing them filled with unlimited loving kindness, silently say, *"May you be happy, healthy, and liberated for the highest good."*

Notice any changes in your body and breath trough them. Try to allow the only movement in the body to be the breath and the heartbeat.

Now think of your friends, colleagues, coworkers, saying to them: *"May you be happy, healthy, and liberated for the highest good."*

Bring to mind strangers, public figures, and to those with whom you have difficulty. Breathe through any resistance, visualize them healthy and happy, sending them loving kindness, *"May you be happy, healthy, and liberated for the highest good."*

Think of all the people all over the world. Think of all the animals all over the world. Think of all the plants, oceans, rivers, valleys, and mountains all over the world, *"May you be happy, healthy, and liberated for the highest good."*

Think of all the planets, stars, and beings for out in the universe, in all directions. Repeat the mantra for them all.

Now come back to your body. Again see yourself as healthy and happy, all parts relaxed and loved, *"May I be happy, healthy, and liberated for the highest good."* Say that three times and rest in stillness for a few more breaths.

Combine this activity with the photo activity. As you look at the picture send love (by saying the mantra - may she be happy, healthy, and liberated for their highest good! - and feeling it transmit) to each member in the picture. You could do this for all kinds of people in photos!

Saying no and boundaries. We talked about boundaries. In truth I don't think arranging your environment to not get triggered by a person, event, experience, or setting is ideal for me now, but there definitely was a time. For me now I see there is likely value in all experiences on some level. Still, I understand why boundaries need to be set. I've set them in the past.

My main problem came in when I announced them, so I am not a fan of stated boundaries. Please have them in your head (like your *oh hell no* list). For me personally, I've been mocked for them, and in my stages of low or no self-love I continued on with relationships after people pushed the boundary with a bit less respect for myself. If you are not going to follow through on your stated boundary (which is a tough one when you don't have self-love) you will end up with a lot more boundary pushing and a lot less respect from those jokers. For those two reasons I am not a fan of **stated** boundaries. I know others really like them. You will have to decide for yourself. Here is some information you might find helpful.

Consider who you can announce a boundary to. Many a time I would tell my mother "*…stop talking about me that way in front of my son, stop that or I will leave,* or *I don't want to talk about how you think I am a bad mom on each phone call or I will hang up, stop bringing up my husband's affair please or I will leave.*" It was like requests to a toddler (i.e., the more I asked her to stop, the more she did them)! Boundaries to her (someone low in self-love and happy to mess with me) were not only ineffective, but were eliciting the exact opposite behavior toward me. Plus I was giving her the ammunition about what would be bothersome to me. For these people I am not a fan of stating boundaries. Boundary stating might be effective with people high in self-love and/or with no personality disorders, but please don't be discouraged if you tried boundaries and they didn't work as you thought they might.

Whereas sharing your boundary is not essential, the ability to say no and mean it is! Your "boundary" is really just you determining what it is you want to do, or not do, and then doing it or not. It doesn't have to be stated on a scroll, emailed, rehashed, or shared with 5 friends before being sent. There should be no confusion, hemming or hawing, "but you crossed my boundary." How about, *"Ouch, I am hanging up now."* I started implementing that one and my mom seemed to understand real quick why I was hanging up. It wasn't passive-aggressive, it was that I wasn't going to be treated how I didn't want to be treated, and didn't need to explain it, argue about it, or create an even larger mess with it.

I had a few boundaries or rules in my head and gave myself permission to say no, and/or just walk away from her when I wanted. It didn't matter to me if she didn't see my point of view; she was not going to, why should that be my goal? My goal was to take care of myself. I don't need to state that, or get permission for that - from anyone. You can get up and out, say no, do whatever you want at any time without narrating out loud the thought process behind it. You love and respect yourself.

Can we learn about ourselves by our boundaries? Yes! When I get the feeling I should set a boundary, instead of saying it out loud, or blaming it on the other for making me choose like this (or for whatever they are doing); I turn my attention inward and think about why I am feeling this way (e.g., disrespected, put out, taken advantage of, having a hard time expressing my needs/wants/values). I take this twinge to see what is going on in me. This is usually hugely important information from my subconscious mind!

Let's say work is asking you to take an unscheduled shift to cover for a different employee. I take a moment and check in with myself. *Oh, I am feeling overwhelmed, and reminded of the lack of appreciation when taking on the last extra shift, and more overwhelm. I really don't want to do this. The only person who can fix this is me. The last time I was so mad at the job for making me do this, but wait, did they "make" me do it? They asked me. If they asked me I had every right to say no thank you. I didn't. Why? I was scared I would get fired. I was scared they wouldn't like me or think I am not a good employee.* Go down the list. Since they "asked me," this meant it wasn't mandatory. *They asked me and it is my responsibility to say what I want.*

Anyone and everyone can ask you for things. You will have little control of that in life. You have control about your thoughts about such requests and your responses to requests. Become conscious and aware of what you want to do and then do that. This consistency in your wants and behaviors add up to more time being your authentic self. Then when you make good strides like this, acknowledge and appreciate your good works/efforts!

Maybe the boundary you set should be with you. Maybe feeling like you need to set the boundary is your trigger for growth. Instead of telling others to treat you better, or getting mad at others for making requests to you, how about you treat yourself better.

You can, walk away when someone disrespects you. Ask for more time when given an invitation. Check in with what you want to do. Listen for the Divine whisper about your choices. Feel free to say no. Feel free to say yes. Feel free to be you! Uncover your authentic-self desires and then express them. When you start accepting yourself and loving yourself it will be impossible for others not to. If they don't it is really not your problem.

Now it is much easier for me to see when others are not respecting me and the time I would allow this to go on would be almost nil. If the person is important to you (also your choice) you can decide how you want to respond. If you are bothered by it and you keep thinking about it, implement your measured (balanced) self-compassion along with the other-compassion you are holding for that person. Just because you have insight (her abuse of me was a projection of her self-hate) and compassion (she was likely mistreated the same way by her parents), doesn't mean you need to ignore your self-compassion and allow her to treat you disrespectfully.

It is also fine to have more self-compassion than other-compassion, or measured compassion as you are repairing and growing in your conscious self-love. You can look forward to a balanced and measured compassion when you are ready! The world and you will be better if you are doing what you can to feel good, especially as you are growing in self-love.

Start With No Activity. If you have a hard time saying no and are feeling a lot of resentment for people and irritation about all the things you are doing for others - try this activity. When given a choice about something you think will make your life a little harder and you want to think about it, just start with no. The request for more time is sometimes awkward (even though it is completely our right). Calling to cancel makes us ending up feeling bad. Instead of doing either of those things, just go ahead and start with no. If you end up deciding you want to do it, you can change that decision and the inviter will likely be even happier than if you said yes in the first place! If you decide you don't want to do it, good, you already said no. If you start with no, you don't have to lie, you just say, *"Oh I am so sorry I can't."* That's it! What if they respond with *"Why not? what else is happening?* etc...) You respond.. *"I just can't."* You can keep saying that until they stop asking you. If they keep badgering you (they might if you were a big yes-person before) you have my permission to smile and walk away.

Being your true self. Being true to yourself is exquisite. It requires no advanced preparation! You don't even have to remember anything (facts or details so you don't get caught in a lie). You just go in being you! PERFECT You! Happy You! Loving You! You are a Role Model of Peace! You inspire others by demonstrating your self-love, self-acceptance, self-kindness, and self-compassion! Your True Self is one with the Divine and you are protected, but also free to be you! You are surrounded by your love inside and out and that is truly all you need!

If we woke up committed to feeling good and taking care of our bodies, using healing words, took action on our responsibilities, let others take care of theirs-how would the world look? Do you do this now? Can you do this now? You can change your focus of attention at any time. You can regroup and go for what you like and find pleasurable. Figure it out and share it. When you lead from conscious self-love it is far easier to have measured compassion for yourself and others and take balanced actions that are consistent with your true and authentic self.

DOING your Daily BE of Gratitude

"When you arise in the morning, think of what a precious privilege it is to be alive. To breath, to think, to enjoy, to love." - Marcus Aurelius. We don't need to talk a lot about the benefits of gratitude as you know them! Let's just start practicing more gratitude today!

Scale of Gratitude Activity. What if we are not feeling grateful. How do we shift out of lack feelings, or feelings of annoyance and get grateful? I like to practice my magic Scale of Gratitude. I see myself starting to get annoyed with someone/something, or I am irritated, I am feeling like I am about to complain about something; about to break my peace, grace, humility plan. I close my eyes and make a scale situation with my hands (like the old-fashioned weight balance scale). I put the thought taking me to negative town on my left scale hand and I put something I am grateful for on my right scale hand. I look at the thing I am grateful for. I really look at it. I feel it. I smile at it. I feel the weights move and I see the gratitude side moving down because it is heavy/beautiful/and peaceful. I watch the other thing on the left (I forgot what it was now) floating up and away because my heart and I chose to be grateful in the present moment.

In this moment of gratitude there is peace, grace, love, and happiness. I move on with that image of being grateful and present in my mind. I can also use this magic scale when I have a choice between two good things. I close my eyes put each thing on one hand sit for a moment and let my body decide. When I open my eyes one hand is always lower!

Happy Place Activity. Another practice for gratitude (and the present moment) is a visualization called the Happy Place. Everyone has one, you make it! The happy place changes your thoughts immediately, accesses the present moment, and makes you happy! Let's develop your Happy Place now and then you can go to it whenever you want (just not while driving :)

To establish your **Happy Place** lay down and get comfortable. Close your eyes and slow and steady your breathing. Now drift off to a mental scene inside your mind. It could be the beach, a mountain top, a grassy field, a warm and beautiful couch in a nice cabin, laying in the sun, in a pyramid. What place do you want to drift off to, where you would be happy right now? Once there get even more comfortable. Breathe. Now engage your visual sense (still with your eyes closed-in your mind's eye) what can you see. If you are at the beach maybe you see the water, the beautiful sand, a gorgeous bird. If you are on your couch in a cabin maybe you see a beautiful fire in the fireplace. Look to your left, look to your right, build your happy place. Then think about what you hear in your Happy Place. I hear seagulls, the waves crashing, the wood crackling. What do you smell? Maybe flowers, the ocean air, coconut suntan oil ☺. What do you feel? Maybe the sun touching your skin, the breeze on your hair, the heat from the fire. You are happy. You are at peace. You feel loved and cherished here. You are grateful for this place, this moment, for your imagination, your soul. You can go to this place whenever you want and you are grateful for that. You promise to come back soon and you do! You are grateful you are taking such good care of yourself.

Gratitude List Activity. My life also got a lot less blamey, judgy, and resenty after I implemented **gratitude lists**. You can have a long list you keep near your work computer, short list in your kitchen, on your phone. Have the list in places where you are likely to get stressed or irritated.

Maybe you have a photo that causes joy whenever you look at it- it triggers a good memory (finally a happy trigger, right!). Take this **gratitude trigger** and make copies to place around you, carry in your purse, focus on before you go to bed, or upon waking up. Find more pictures like this and place them around your main spots. Smile when you see them, feel joy in your heart. Relive the experience or moment. Feel the love. Unzip your heart and feel the gratitude and love flow out from your heart to your head. See it surrounding you and then floating you up to the sky in a gratitude ball of sparkling gold love liquid. You rise up in the sky in this gratitude love bubble! Can you feel it!

Three things you are GRATEFUL for today. My best friend and I were both overwhelmed and irritated at the same time a few years ago. We started texting each other a gratitude text each night of three things we were grateful for that day. Some days we would be so exhausted the list wouldn't get out until the morning. The cool thing about that was that whenever the list came through, the other responded with theirs and there was this happiness and love party. So many times I was grateful that a great thing happened to her. We always commented on the other's three first and our joy for them in their life. Then we shared ours. It is nice to have a few people who will be happy for you when something good happens. Not everyone is like that. Find at least one and feel free to share your good news as well as bad news.

What if you don't feel like sharing your good stuff, or your friend is going through a thing right now and you would feel bad sharing all this great stuff, I understand that, but don't think for your friend! Getting her or him to focus on the positive and the good things happening right now (even for you) really may be the thing she needs! If you really, really don't have a person to work on a gratitude list with you can start a list in a gratitude journal, or make a **gratitude calendar**. I have seen people write on their regular calendar three things they were grateful for that day. I have also seen gratitude calendars you can buy with specific gratitude things to practice on certain days. If you have a problem mustering gratitude right now, such a tool might really be helpful. Instead of a *thank you note* to a friend, write a *gratitude note*. You can also write *thank you notes* and *gratitude notes* to yourself!

This one is from my friend you should follow on Instagram, Mariaa (@mariaa_Healing_Light). She said to name one thing you are grateful for the most today. Focus on that word for 15 seconds. FEEL gratitude and love in your heart and it will raise your vibration so much! She suggested we practice this every day with a different thing and vibrate high! If you are still having a hard time finding one thing then maybe Google kittens! ☺

Gratitude/Meditation Activity: Open Eye/Mindful Observation Meditation. Let's try this (adapted from another meditation assignment I submitted in my mediation teacher training). In this meditation you gently rest your awareness on the object you've chosen to mindfully observe (pick something around the room, painting, dim light, candle, nail on the wall, anything will work). When your eyes wander away from the gazing point, notice that your eyes wandered, and direct your gaze back to the gazing point. Allowing everything to be as it is - just for the duration of the meditation. You will become aware of a thought that arises in your mind, you can observe it, but breath through them, let it go, and return focus to the gazing point. This technique of mindful observation builds mind focusing skills and letting thoughts pass through without getting attached to them.

You will also come to be **grateful** for the things you are gazing on. Look at them to represent joy and peace and love. Change the objects so you view more and more items this way. If you do this activity when doing the dishes or making your bed or cleaning something (and look at the instrument with love and joy and appreciation) you can see how easy it is **to be grateful for even everyday items** and even things we don't particularly love. If you pair a peace thought or a love thought with a neutral stimulus (remember Pavlov) then that item will soon come to represent peace and joy. We do this automatically with kittens and fuzzy things. Why did we initially pick that up? We set up that stimulus-response connection! You can now set up a bunch of new ones. I find peace and joy in so many of my regular daily objects!!

You can take this new skill of Open Eye/Mindful Observation in order to **Hold Space** for yourself or another into the real world (more on this in the next chapter!). You can try to be to be extra present with your friends and family today. Make eye contact, give them your full present moment attention. If you notice your mind wandering, and you are coming up with solutions, and judgments (instead of just listening-which is the goal), witness those thoughts, breath, let them go, and return to making eye contact.

Because you know how to do Open Eye/Mindful Observation meditation you will be able to sit with and look at another person and see and hear them (that is really the whole point of holding space!). If you experience an upsetting triggering thought about your life while holding space, or if you have an irresistible urge to solve a person's problem (interfering with your bearing witness and holding space), this meditation will have you practiced at witnessing your own thoughts without attaching, letting them pass, and then returning to your gift of holding space for another. It is normal for those thoughts to pop in even when you are holding space, but the goal is to see them for what they are (just thoughts) and then let go of them. You can come back to them later, or maybe not at all.

If you find this is really difficult with a particular person (maybe one who reminds you of someone) and you are just really having a hard time being present for a particular loved one or friend (or a few :) you can practice before you see them - try looking into the eyes of a picture of them for 5-10 minutes. Gaze on their eyes, notice what comes to mind, breath through, let go, and get back to the gaze. If you had a hard time dismissing some of the thoughts or are still thinking about them after the 5 minutes try journaling them to get them out of your head and onto paper :)

DOING your Daily BE of Forgiveness

Some forgiveness activities that might be helpful are forgiveness lists and journaling. **Journaling** is an excellent activity for mental health, emotion processing, awareness making, consciousness development, and developing your self-love. You can get a notebook at the store, use your phone, your computer, all formats will work! The idea is to get the thought/feeling/emotion/irritation/judgment/resentment out of your head and into some other receptacle. Maybe have one page for each of those things in your journal (e.g., current irritations lol). If you don't remove those things from your head they will just sit there in your noggin, guiding your daily behaviors, seeping down into the subconscious, interfering with your joy, and otherwise spoiling a very nice day.

When I have a thought rolling around up there and it keeps interfering with anything I just stop what I am doing and go jot it down. Get it outta there! Then I return to my activity. I challenge you to try this. Most of the time, once out of my head and on paper I am relieved of the thought or feeling or irritation. Some things I keep returning to, and I keep writing down facts/emotions/venting about it to my journal. I can ask myself those good questions for problem solving after I vent things out and write down the answer. The one thing that is certain is the process of journaling affords growth and freedom from otherwise trapped and unproductive recursive negative thoughts rolling around in your head.

If you prefer to talk to someone to vent out your feelings, or distracting thoughts in your head then do that! What if the thoughts you are having are about the person you usually talk to! Then journal. My mom would always call me to complain about me! On the one hand, good for her for trying to get it out of her head lol. On the other, I must have told her 80 times, *look, I am not the one you should be saying this too. Please gossip about me and complain about me to your friends or literally any other person if you must. I am sick of hearing about what a loser you think I am.* Obviously that boundary setting was not effective.

I don't know if this ever happened to you, or if you have been so mad at someone you couldn't control yourself and you lost it. Just yelled at them, made up stuff, had that argument with them (the one you had been practicing in your head, jotting down notes about). You finally do it. You got in every last word you wanted to. Well, how do you feel. Did that explosion solve your problem? Are you guys in a better place now? Hum. I don't know that just never worked for me and I ended up feeling so bad after (didn't fall asleep easy that day after my mess). Let's make an agreement to stop those things. When deciding what to speak try to live by the rule: Is it the truth? Is it kind? Is it necessary? Not all thoughts need to be shared with another human (some can and should be saved for your journal!). This is indeed the reason why we have paper and pens! One more note, if you don't want to be on everyone's irrigations list, then tell people hard things (about themselves, or in general) when they are ready for it (the law of good timing!); or maybe not even at all (remember the rule: Is it True? Kind? Necessary?). You got this!

Forgiveness List Activities. You can have a forgiveness list in your journal for yourself and/or others. You can have a **self-forgiveness list**. Let's say your inner critic is out of control. You become aware you are berating yourself with your thoughts. Run over to your self-forgiveness journal and tell on yourself! *I am mad at myself for not saying NO to my boss today!* Vent it all out. *That jerk asked me for this and made it seem like I didn't even have a choice. Do I really even have a choice? OH, I am so mad I am still even at that job!* Then forgive yourself. *Oh, Jill you are so kind hearted. I forgive you for saying yes. I* *forgive you for not putting your needs first in this situation. You are doing the best you can. I love you.*

If you are keeping an **other's-forgiveness list** you will write other people's names and the things you are forgiving them for. Who do you need to forgive, what did they do, and how it will help YOU by forgiving them, you could have all of those columns.

Richard, you are a complete dick and I hate working for you!!!! I am quitting just as soon as I possibly can!! Now forgive him. *I forgive you for asking another "favor" from me. I realize you are doing your job and what is likely your best in this situation. I forgive you and I wish you well. Now I am sending out my resumes to other, more ethical companies. I forgive myself for not doing this sooner. I forgive myself for not speaking up when you are rude to me. I am doing the best that I can with this situation, I see it is time to change the situation!*

We talked about sometimes not wanting to forgive others. We also said sometimes the best DO action in forgiving others is to decide, it is just not my place to forgive him/her for that. I can have compassion for him/her and me, or another (measured compassion) and full well choose to just forgive myself in the context of not forgiving this other person. That is okay. In this case, in your journal jot down what they did that you are not ready to forgive. Get it all out. Then in a column next to it, write two times more things you can forgive yourself for, related to that situation. Then end with some compassion for yourself. That should do it!

Your forgiveness lists can be from today, last month, last year, when you were 10 years old. You can have all your lists compiled in a 250-page notebook with all of the pages filled. You can go back and insert forgiveness to any event or situation - towards yourself or another. Often the things (others or ourselves) we need to forgive are not even the main problem; mostly it is our thoughts about the situation/event that exacerbates suffering. Often times we are keeping stories alive when they can and should be let go.

Interestingly and notably, you cannot go back to change an event, BUT you are completely responsible for your thoughts/feelings/emotions about it and you can forgive these things in the actual moment, or go back and forgive your thoughts/feelings/emotions from the past!

What if you are mad at God or you feel there is a super-duper shameful thing you need to be forgiven for. Well, you can ask for forgiveness for yourself for that too. You can go to a church and talk to a priest, talk to a friend, therapist, you can write in your journal with words, there is the Atonement prayer for peace in *A Course in Miracles Text.* Nothing is off limits when it comes to DOing forgiveness. Go ahead and ask for it. You deserve it.

Forgiveness exploration. If you are not ready to forgive yourself or another, then maybe you can ask yourself why that is. Is there some anger that still needs processing, some other reason? Listen to your True and Authentic Self when you ask such important questions and answer yourself from within to move to greater place of self-awareness and self-love. The process of asking the questions and hearing the answers, because you deserve to know and treat yourself well, has to do with conscious self-love.

You can ask God to forgive you and you can ask God to help you forgive yourself. Praying for forgiveness (or asking for forgiveness in a prayer session) is a beautiful, soul nurturing activity. A Course in Miracles refers to such an act (asking for forgiveness) as Atonement. This important text (see Page 90 for the Atonement prayer) suggests you know when you need to ask for Atonement because your peace is disrupted. The way to fix that disruption of peace is to request more peace, say goodbye to guilt, and receive the gift of reparations from the Holy Spirit and God.

Another way to make forgiveness more likely is to not take things personally. If you process other's poor choices and bad behavior with that third part of the compassion definition (knowing we are all human and mistakes are unavoidable) we can look at foibles with curiosity and even forgiveness.

In Chapter One when I said, Don Miguel Ruiz said, "Don't take anything personally. Even when a situation seems so personal, even if others insult you directly, it has nothing to do with you. Their point of view and opinion come from all the programming they received growing up." Ah-ha!!! Now, please let me finish this important quote about what we are to do with this information now. He finished this quote by saying, "When you take things personally, you feel offended and your reaction is to defend your beliefs and create conflict. You make something big out of something so little because you have the need to be right and make everybody else wrong."

What is the lesson here? We spend so much time in reaction to others and condemning others, we are missing very important lessons and teaching moments, that if we just received the first time we would be happier and healthier. The answer is less reaction, more reflection, more forgiveness; this leads to more positive action for ourselves. Moreover, because most people's behaviors are just projections of their own heart; it is quite likely we are being triggered completely unnecessarily. Unless we look at the trigger as a mirror for our issues (reflection) and make use of the lesson. These poor people are ignorant. We can forgive them.

Each morning as I work on this manuscript I get a little help from the universe in the form of an interesting Instagram post. Today's post was from a lovely lady who advertises herself a coach available for helping people on Instagram. Today I was reminded that even helping professionals may be lacking in, or confused about conscious self-love. This lovely lady posted a video of her sobbing and sobbing and sharing an experience, trying to teach us about self-love. Someone had said something mean to her and it triggered her and really just shut her down, and she was crying she said for more than a day. Now I am not suggesting emotions aren't good, or we shouldn't express them! I am not saying we should be robots and let others give us interfere with us experiencing or expressing emotions! Maybe you remember my mom telling me to "stop crying because all of the crying in the world wouldn't bring my dad back" (2 days after his death when I was 15) - obviously that is not what we are going for; but this other end of the spectrum (out of control blubbering to teach us a lesson about self-love) suggests a misunderstanding about self-love.

When practicing conscious self-love, we recognize other people's missteps (even ones directed at us) as a likely projection of some problem they were having. We strive to show compassion for ourselves and the others, and we believe everyone is doing their best, see the lesson for ourselves if there is one, and then forgive and moved on. Almost none of these things were being practiced by the coach who was teaching us about "self-love." I have a hard time with "experts" giving out misinformation.

She spent some time sharing how she could see the growth potential and did some self-exploration about why and realized her inner child was hurt and she had to take her hand and comfort her and then it didn't really matter because she knows she loves herself (saying through her sobs and unmatching facial expressions) and that we all should love ourselves because we are Divine and that is our right. But she just kept crying and crying.

It was uncomfortable to watch and I just wanted to right back to console her and say, *oh my goodness please it will be okay*. So, I have compassion and love her yes, and I am happy she is getting real with her feelings yes, but here is my problem. She was trying to teach us about self-love, and that everything is okay, when it was clearly not. She was saying it is important to be strong, but in a complete mixed-message manner, and she is an expert-a person who is paid to help you. She has a coaching practice and she is helping other people from her place of reference, which seemed a little fragile. Not that such people need to be perfect, but remember you can't give away what you don't have. If you are attending coaching with this woman for self-love or compassion it might not work.

I also got the feeling she was suggesting the other person (who said something mean to her) was at fault for having been so mean to her and starting to vilianize the person. I noticed her followers were jumping in to also condemn the person who upset her. We all do this (get people to climb aboard our victim/hate train). This is not the right way though. Such retelling of the story, laughing, or seeming to feel better when others hate on people who are mean to us makes it linger, brings more people in, and grows hate instead of love.

With conscious self-love you see in the moment the person trying to hurt you is not able to hurt you and not actually even looking at you (they are projecting what they are feeling). You would recognize it for what it was (their ignorance) and most likely not be so upset (your ego is reacting). Then when you practice conscious self-love you would have compassion for that ass (it is true people are jerks sometimes) "trying" to hurt you.

You wouldn't put them on blast or condemn people and accept hate-spewing guests to your pity party to foster this hate circle. It must have reminded her of her childhood and I don't think she revisited that place for self-awareness yet. I just don't know if she is going to get to the juicy self-love place she was trying to sell to others without some changes herself. Practicing conscious self-love would've taken the sting out of the comment, resulting in no negative thought/emotion reaction, and no condemning of a most likely innocent (in spiritual terms) soul - acting out of their unexplored, unconscious and conditioned reality.

When we are high in self-love we know that a negative comment (even by a friend) is - remember - say it with me - NOT EVEN ABOUT ME. You know there is nothing wrong with crying and the feeling of things deeply of course, but we need to be strong too and think about the cycle of negativity we are accustomed to. That is not exactly where we want to be - right? That is not where I want to be - I guess that is my frame of reference. Sobbing like that will interfere with us seeing clearly the lesson. Although it looked like the comment triggered some deep insight about her inner child, and this seems desirable possibly, given all the coaches working on inner child things, but I think the lesson was she still didn't love herself enough to see the reality of the comment and her true Divine nature. When you are in love with yourself you are rather impervious to negative comments. You are able to see if there is feedback to put to good use and then discard the rest. You don't spend three days in your bed because a good friend made an offhanded comment (that wasn't even about you). I hope I am not being harsh. I feel like it is time for us all to take the reins back and not allow others to throw us into such a tizzy.

We spent a lot of time in child mode, but we are adults now (all people over 18-28 reading this), things don't happen to us for us to react to like that. The fixing of the inner child doesn't need to take years. If you read the previous chapters it is possible you just fixed yours. We can move on! I don't know how long we want to go on about the details and living there in that vulnerable state. I can go back to my childhood memories now, but they are uncharged, they don't control me, or even upset me. Today (and most all days) I choose to make that story just something from my past that made me a hell of a strong person today. Strong enough to see the fragility and beauty of life. Strong enough to see I cannot control what others do to me; BUT I can control what I make of it in my head and heart, and then what I chose to do with that information. For me, most everything (good and bad now) is just a constant reminder to love myself and others.

Forgiving your subconscious stories. Your past is part of your story (subconscious or conscious) and it may be hard to let it go. But it really needs to happen so you can get on with giving your special gifts to the world (likely cultivated by your inner child experiences). Let's agree to love ourselves, forgive the story, and stop connecting to this story.

Are you really willing to forgive your story and let it go? There is a term in psychology called secondary gain, used most often in physical illnesses. Secondary gain occurs when an illness provides something rewarding, like attention, soup, not having to work or go to school. These rewards can actually work to perpetuate the illness (either consciously or subconsciously).

I feel like the subconscious story (especially negative ones) might be providing some secondary gain, possibly. It is perhaps the case that the story provides a little excuse to be wounded, to not feel great, to not be perfect, to not help others today, to make you stay Cinderella (victim) instead of the fairy godmother (hero). For me, I think there was something enticing about being in the victim mode. Did I like it when others felt sorry for me? Did it make me feel appreciated, give me a little attention? Maybe now that they knew this context (I was so nice and I was so wronged by another) the people would understand why I was a little odd? Or maybe they would now be nice to me?? Getting real with my unwillingness to let go of the story and the good things that came from people feeling sorry for me was helpful! I realized that the story wasn't the good thing about me!, the good thing about me- was ME!

I forgave the story, I forgave me for wanting to hold on to the story. I forgave me for making the story important, for letting it impact my current life. I chose to forgive myself for hanging on to my story and wanting to hang on to it. I forgave myself for wanting people to feel sorry for me. I forgave myself for wanting people to like me so much and attend to me, that I was willing to be a good girl and put my needs to grow and heal last on my list. I forgave myself because I didn't even become aware of the study until my 30s. I forgave myself for misunderstanding the purpose of the story. I became grateful for the story itself even! The story holds very little power over me now. Even when I call up story details for this book they float right back out of my head as I am done writing about them. Forgiving my story took its power away and helped me move on.

Subconscious Re-do Visualization Activity. We can use visualization for remodeling in our subconscious! Think about who messed with your self-love (if there is more than one, just take it one person/situation at a time). Maybe it was your parent, mate, friend, teacher, someone who hurt you, someone who messed with your self-love, the cheerleading tryout, the swim team situation (you are aware of this now). It was not great. Sometimes you think how you would be different if it was. This fantasizing is NOT really a moot point because we can go in and visualize that relationship/situation differently.

Researchers demonstrated visualizing (even things from the past) elicits a very real physiological response in our body, whereby you can change all sorts of things! If you visualize a lemon - sniff it, hold it in your hand, cut it, pick out the seeds, and raise it up to your mouth, can you feel your salivary glands getting ready! Your body changes when you visualize! Go ahead visualize your mom, mate, friend, the swim team, etc. happy and full of self-love. They are behaving kindly to themselves AND to you. You see her/them providing you the care and kindness that you would have received if she/they loved themselves. If it is too hard to see their face/voice then replace it with your current face and look at the young version of you.

Let's stop here for a minute and really go there. Hug this child. What is happening right now that you can redo? What should have been said? What does it feel like to hear helpful words instead of harmful ones? Close your eyes. Imagine and visualize the kindness inside you, this feeling of contentment inside you, and even the ease with this person/place/thing.

How do you feel? Why can't this be the story you pack away? It can! Let's rewrite the story where you love yourself and understand other's behaviors were/are not about your, but reflect their lack of self-love. You might cut your parent some slack or you might not. Either way you are the hero and you are loved, understood, adored, and fantastic. Jot some things down about this now.

Let's write all future stories with this plan to have them turn out great too! Cheryl Richardson said, "If you are going to make up stories in your head about people and circumstances, please make them love stories with happy endings." She noted, "We all make up stories, every hour of every day." Why not start making them turn out better?! I remember my youngest son's favorite book had a non-happy ending and it would always make us both cry (not super fun to read every night). I started skipping the last page and made up an alternate ending. I even wrote it out with words and we both drew a picture to represent the happy way the book should've ended. This certainly did the trick. That lovely son is 21 now and he showed me a note he took from a special training he is in. He wrote, *You can rewrite the pages of your story/book.* Wow, this brought me back to when he was 3 and made me believe. Once you change your story your daily choices become more adaptive too.

You can change your story daily. It may take daily reminders to remember to stay present, aware of the story for just what it is, and to undo some things in your subconscious. Remember your subconscious is always listening to your spoken words and even sees the words you are reading right now! I see you subconscious! Take that! ha.

It took a bit of work on my end to understand that narcissistic mother pattern I was exposed to (a bit of more work to depersonalize from it, and shake off the narcy quite honestly). But I stuck with it and just knew it was essential to my happiness. When we hate ourselves, our main mission each day is to find others who hate us too (and/or behave in a way that makes them hate us!). When we love ourselves our main mission each day is to wake up happy, spend time with those who also authentically cherish our company, and spread that love and joy to the world. When we hold a negative subconscious story in a place of priority, instead of forgiveness, we are walking around hating ourselves and looking for others to hate us too. It is time for a change!

Affirmations to undo subconscious patterns. I think there is a tendency for children of narcys and maybe alcoholics and other personality/substance disorders to **overcorrect**; this can be subconscious too. Wow, we for sure don't want to be narcy. We may see some narcy behaviors popping out of ourselves sometimes. Then we freak out and overcorrect and return to being a martyr and mom of the year. We harshly judge our neighbor who has a gym membership *"are you kidding me, she can't work out at home, her poor kids?"* is really a projection of your sadness/envy for not being able to leave the house without the group in tow, and an overcorrection.

The **narcy child overcorrection problem** results in much people pleasing, codependency, enmeshment behavior, and a whole lot of crazy for everyone. I would bring gifts to all people (friends, hair stylist, neighbor) all the time when we would get together. You might think, wow, she is so thoughtful. The gifts were very thoughtful and I spent a lot of time figuring out what each person would like, and I really thought this was just because I was a nice gal; but honestly now I think I did this because my subconscious was oozing *you are not good enough on your own.* I had to buy people's affection with gifts (like my mom's). When tipping I always gave more than the 20% because again, these poor people had to deal with me. I was so happy to smooth out my ***not good enough* subconscious pattern**! I ended up saving a lot of money, realized people like and appreciate me for just who I am, and if I (my authentic self) wants to give a thoughtful gift I do, but it is not mandatory. I hope you like me, but I don't need you to, because I love myself.

A great tool to smooth out and redo subconscious patterns are affirmations. My first work with narcy affirmations came via the wonderful website: *Dauthersofnarcissticmothers.com*. Danu Morigan the website creator and author has so many resources for children of narcissistic parents. I signed up for the lovely email resource where you receive frequent notes you by email (if you just sign up I believe it is free!) where you inner mother is saying something nice about you! Today's note: "My lovely Jill, I am proud of you. So proud. The way you keep going despite it all. You are a hero. I love you, Mom." They go for a year. I am on my third year of receiving these notes from Danu. These affirming, redoing messages really made a dent on my subconscious pattern of narcy mom, taught me about the gift of and importance of receiving, and was significant for my conscious self-love and growth.

Making sense of your story and smoothing out the subconscious patterns (by awareness, and tools to repattern) you can see the value of the story, be grateful for it, and start a new one today. This new story is going to be way better. I used to carry that old story book on a pedestal and think it was so important in who I was or could be. That story book held me back from loving myself and my life. That story book sits on a shelf in my house and I haven't looked at it for a long time. I don't need to. I moved on.

Changing stories where we are victims is also essential for enlightenment. I just saw a brilliant Instagram post by Deepak where he noted, "the key to enlightenment is to never be okay being the victim." The only way we are going to get out of victim mode is to pull that story out of the subconscious and change the story.

We have the ability to learn to be strong in relationships (people will be nice and people will be neutral and people will be mean - that is just the reality). We can watch people (and ourselves) with these new eyes of understanding about projection. Go ahead and just try and get triggered when you know that the person trying to put you down is ignorant and just projecting their woe on to you. You sure do get a lot of good information about their woes.

Remember we don't want to live in a subconscious reaction cycle. We want to calmly process our input and lessons as interesting information-not something to fly off the handle about, take personally, and react to. When you do it this way you won't be able to recognize the helpful nuggets (maybe there is some constructive criticism that could be helpful there), or see the lesson - as we are too busy writing the response email and showing 5 friends what we wrote and talking about what happened. That is not the way to growth.

It could be the case that the story is so deeply engraved in your subconscious you may need help uncovering it and removing the patterns too. I know both of these things were true for me. Please see my resources section for subconscious reworking helpers.

The Daily Do of Self-Care

An important daily DO for life and your conscious self-love growth is self-care. You can call this taking care of yourself if you prefer. To develop our conscious self-love we need to care for ourselves. There is no one else to do it.

Don't believe the myth that another person - your soul mate - is going to take care of you, or put your pieces back together (my gosh I see that meme all the time!). It is YOU who is going to take care of yourself. If you refuse this assignment and abandon yourself you will be unhappy, search for outside people and things, give your power away, and most certainly not achieve the level of care you desire.

If you expect others to take care of you, this unrealistic expectation will lead to resentment and broken dreams. Now, having said that, I realize children growing up without conscious parents will not automatically know how to take care of themselves and practice conscious self-love, so we need reparations. It is okay that you are just right now realizing it is you who should take care of you. I didn't figure that out until later in my journey.

Why don't we want to take care of ourselves? Some parents didn't provide care for their kids. Some parents made children feel they didn't deserve care. Some parents were too busy, working, narcissistic, addicted, ill, etc. Some parents did so much that children grew up thinking that other people WERE supposed to take care of them and handed their power away.

Around age 35 I realized I was completely dehydrated and had been for maybe most of my life. I saw some information we are to drink as many ounces as half our weight each day (if you weigh 140lbs you should drink 70 ounces of water). I thought, oh my gosh I can go a whole day with just one cup of coffee in the morning and a pop at night. What a shock. I started drinking more liquids and water and I immediately felt better. Then I remembered some things. There were no beverages at my house when I grew up. No one was bringing me drinks or telling me to drink anything. You read about my mother's neglect, but I didn't know about it when I was a child! When my brother lived at the house, or he came to visit after he moved out my mother would buy his favorite Coke, but any other time there was just butter and some other things in the fridge! No juice, milk, or other beverages! That my brother only deserved the special pops (I was not allowed to touch it) and that there were no drinks for me suggested my self-care was not important. In high school I remember other children eating and having money for lunch, but I just didn't. I was hungry and the subconscious story of not being worthy of care was starting to stick. This was outside of my awareness until that day when I was 35! Up until that time I just thought I was supposed to take care of others, others were supposed to take care of me - but they didn't do their job right. Then I picked bad partners who were so selfish (like my mom), so I didn't get stuff, and that is how life should go.

I remember going to people's (my mom's friend's) houses when I was young and them asking me if I wanted a drink. I would be so thirsty and my mom would always answer, *oh no she doesn't want anything*. I carried on this lack of even basic self-care in high school or later when visiting with my friends just always said no thank you. In high school I dated a boy who took me to Taco Bell every single time we were together (his friend worked there and gave him free food). Every time he would ask me, what would you like? I pretended I just ate or had something to drink. I didn't even know how to receive a free food item.

When I became a parent I realized my children needed beverages and did a good job taking care of them (providing for their food and safety for sure), but still not me. I remember one day I was with my son visiting a friend's house (he was around 8) and someone asked him if he wanted a drink and he said "no." I knew he was thirsty. I knew at that moment he was saying no because I always (and was still at that time) saying *no thank you*! I stepped in and got him a drink, but I could see the problem now. How sad for both he and I! Both moms causing some harm (regardless of my good intention). Interestingly I would always have sufficient pop at my house for the kids and guests, like way too much and would always ask my kids if other people offered them drinks (that should have been a clue if I had explored it!).

Can't I just get someone else to do this for me? Please? For so long I was really looking for a partner to take care of me. I was looking for that because my mom was so deficient in loving me and herself and so unconscious in her parenting that I thought I missed out. I was thinking she was at fault and to blame, but what really happened was I abandoned myself! I was making her responsible for my feelings and self-worth. My fix for that was finding a different person to take care of me. Maybe you are so busy taking care of others (you think you don't deserve to be first on your list) you think it would just be easier to not take care of you, or to get someone else to do it. Neither of these things will work though.

I changed things about ME to get my mom (and others) to like me and care for me. I could get things I wanted sometimes by being nice, responsible, taking care of others, anticipating their needs, and giving. But I was doing these things to get good feedback and stuff (and care). This is how I learned to behave and over-function. Self-abandonment happens when we make others responsible for our feelings, care, and self-love supply. When I saw I wouldn't get good stuff from her I tried harder and harder. When it didn't work I just moved on to a new relationship partner.

I should have given up and recognized I should provide my own care, but instead I looked for another person to sub in. I know my mom was an extreme case, but I think this happens when all parents (and people) love with conditions. We as people are never able to live up to the (unrealistic and projected) conditions of others and WE end up feeling unworthy of love (and care!). I really didn't understand it until the notion of the self-abandonment (making another responsible for your feelings/care) became clear. Once that is front and center we can decide to regroup. You need to understand you deserve to be taken care of! You can even be grateful for the past experiences of not being taken care of by another, because now you have the supreme ability to do it for yourself, which is highly rewarding! Only YOU have to do it!

Something helpful for me was having a friend who was good at self-care. This friend I love unconditionally (since the beginning of our relationship) and instead of judging her for practicing self-care (which could be common considering projection), I was impressed by her! This one friend taught me a lot about how things are supposed to work. If you didn't have such an experience growing up then find a friend or some information to help you. This friend knew my mom and actually went out of her way to be helpful to me. One time she had my sons and I over for dinner and I saw on her dinner table she had glasses of water for all the diners. I never did that, but implemented it right after. She taught me about getting my nails done, massages, and treating yourself to nice things when you can. I found other activities that I enjoyed too.

When I was teaching my *stress and coping* class to the college students I had them do a 20 pleasurable activities list. I would walk around the class. There were always a few students who had just a few activities they enjoyed listed on their paper. This was upsetting to me the first time I saw it (because I could relate and how sad!). I rewrote the class activity on the spot. I said, oh, let's actually number 1-20 on the paper. We need to fill in all 20. I said if you are having trouble coming up with ideas that is okay! I had us go around the room and everyone would share one of theirs and the others could add it to their list. We did this until everyone had 20 activities they liked. It was a beautiful moment! I refined the activity over the years, but it is always the case that some people just have a few things when we begin. I feel like I know why that is, and you may be reading this thinking about why you only can identify 3 pleasurable activities you like, but I am telling you right now that you need all 20! AND you need to practice self-care (taking care of yourself) on a daily basis, for you AND your loved ones. Anita Moorjani wrote on Instagram, "If you're going to relax in a bathtub for an hour, you may think that it doesn't serve anyone else for you to do that. In the big picture, it does because you've become a better version of yourself. You brightening your own light benefits everyone around you." WOW! Exactly! When I am practicing my conscious self-care I am nicer, less bitter, more generous, more encouraging, and spreading a lot more joy than just taking care of the others! When I get to be a snappy turtle it is my sign it is time for a something from my list!

20 Pleasures Activity. Please sit down. Get a piece of paper and number on it 1-20 (or write in this book margin). Please write down 20 activities you find enjoyable. When you come up for air then add more. Then add more. If you have more than 20, great! If you don't have 20, then you need to contact some friends and ask them for theirs and expand your list. Once you have at least 20 then organize them into three categories: **Daily, Weekly, Monthly**. You will want some from each category. You will then schedule the activities. At least one of the Daily Activities each day, at least one of the Weekly Activities a week, and at least one of the Monthly Activities per month. I suggest actually penning/typing into your calendar, planner.

The level of care you desire is something to explore within. It is not something a past person assigned to you. Maybe you heard you were too needy, or too independent. It is possibly you were coming across that way, or the person telling you that was projecting on to you. Your level of care may also vary throughout the year, month, week, day. All levels are appropriate at all times. When we rely on ourselves to provide our very own self-care then we - the only person who can fulfill our needs (especially for love) does so and we are happy and glowing from the inside out and we are ready to take our nourished souls on the road without complaints, striving, resentment, blame, and confusion.

I chaired (served as the chairperson of a dissertation committee) more than 100 dissertations. As a dissertation chair I work with a student from project inception to teach them how to conduct a research project. When the project is completed and they write their 200+ page dissertation I run the dissertation defense. This is a highly charged stressful situation. At the end I always ask the student how they will celebrate getting their PhD and encourage them to do so! I remember my (this will hopefully be my last sad story lol) defense and graduation were both nothing to speak of, because as I think about it now I was expecting others to make a big deal out of it. My mom actually cancelled the graduation luncheon I planned because I gave my sons candy to sit through the long graduation ceremony. Before the candy problem she was yelling at me about my driving - she would have picked any fight to make sure there was no celebration of me. I published two books and two CDs before this one and always was curious why no one I loved (or who I thought loved me) said boo about my accomplishments. No one ever even offered to take me out to dinner. I am wrapping up this manuscript in a completely different place and I (just like I hope for my dissertation students) will make a big deal about my accomplishment, because I deserve that. It is really not up to anyone else anyway.

Pleasure activities versus self-care. I believe there is a lot of confusion about self-care. When you think of self-care you may think of things from your pleasure activities list; including things like, baths, manicure, massage. Yes, yes, yes. Some self-care things may feel good, pleasurable, and be rewarding. Some self-care things like eating healthy, drinking water, exercising (the basics we all must do for ourselves) may not be that fun, but they are still considered self-care activities. Your basics are your non-negotiables. Are you drinking enough water?

Self-care is also going to the doctor (a basic) when you have a pain and/or for a check-up or scheduled test, going to the dentist, getting your roots done. Not buying the cute dress because it is just too expensive is sometimes self-care because you are making sound financial decisions (basic self-care). Taking good care of yourself and making good choices for you is caring for yourself in a positive manner. I like to think there are two categories of self-care (pleasurable things like massages) and not as pleasurable self-care things (eating well, or going to the doctor). It is likely best to have both types represented on your self-care to-do list!

The motivation/intention and manner behind the self-care activity also seems to be important. Working out to lose weight to look good for others (albeit healthy and a great idea to lose weight) is other-focused. Working out by punishing yourself with an hour long work out on a tread climber huffing and puffing hating it doesn't seem like self-care. Actually the former is likely a self-punishment and the latter is more about earning your love coins from outside. These motivations are the opposite of self-love and self-care. Do you see what I mean?

Self-care when you are high in self-love is a kind, uplifting, a gentle hug of joy/bliss delivered to you in this moment because you deserve to be well taken care of, and you make good choices for your health and happiness. You get your nails done - not because you won't look like a slouch at work, or because all your friends do it and you won't fit in (external); it is because you love pretty colors and enjoy looking at your hands throughout the day and seeing these nice treats on your fingers (internal). You eat a healthy salad because you love the way you feel afterward, not because you have to lose 10 pounds by Friday. See the difference? I mean getting your nails done, eating healthy, exercising for whatever the reason are likely good for you in absolute terms - sure, but if you don't feel it is nourishing your soul and you have some responsibility to do it, then we are erasing some of the fun "self-care" parts of the activity. Let's get clear on that so we can add some enjoyable (and soul nourishing) self-care activities to your day.

Go through the list of all your self-care activities and think of the motivation behind them. It may be treating yourself to something nice from a store that you will find joy with and appreciate and wear with pride (self-care), but what if it is "retail therapy" that you turn to after a disappointment, that you really can't afford, that you then feel guilty about - oh I should take that back, I don't deserve it, plus my credit cards are worse now (self-hate). Can you see both sides like that?

I much prefer meditation and ballet to yoga and telling me to do yoga will make me feel annoyed. Also, I ask myself: *"Are you going to yoga to get the Jennifer Aniston body (you might want to try spinning instead actually)? Are you going to yoga because you want to tell your friends you went to yoga? Are you going because you know you should do it because people keep telling you that is what you should do when on a spiritual growth path?"* Get clear on it. Yoga is most likely good for you, but is it an official self-care activity for you personally? What is your belief about it and motivation behind it that is important? Why are you doing this activity? Is it because you just really feel enjoyment by doing it (like a big hug around you)? That is enjoyable self-care. If you are you doing it to escape some feeling, or to self-medicate something, or for someone else, or for something else (like you know you "should" do it), then it may it is not "self-care."

Maybe you are doing restorative yoga to heal something right now. Good for you and this is a "healing" activity. This insight is important and valuable because you most certainly can have healing things on your daily self-care plan, but you also need pleasurable self-care things too! You need these self-care activities to really nourish your soul and help you realize you deserve good treatment. Me getting my favorite sushi roll from my favorite place is such a treat. I float out of there in a love bubble. I feel cherished. I would prefer a Swedish massage over a deep tissue massage any day. I would like a foot massage and that would be a treat and I would walk out feeling I took very good care of myself that day. For me, taking the time to meditate is not a chore or a responsibility, but a gift (pleasure). When I am done I feel loved. Maybe you find meditation frustrating and you having to do it is more of a chore. The feeling at the end is important for me ☺ How about you? What do you do that makes you feel like you are in a love bubble?

What if identifying positive self-care things is harder then it seems it should be?! I would think then that you need to check in with your insides to get an idea about what is nourishing to you. Not something your mom used to give you (ice cream to solve problems, so you have ice cream on this list). It is more of sitting with yourself and visualizing you being happy, joyful, content. Close your eyes and go there. What are you doing? Look around, what do you see? What do you hear? What is touching your skin? Is your main feeling contentment and freedom and joy? Stay there and collect all the details so you can recreate this in your real world. Stay there until you find a place/activity that offers you this comfort. No one is taking you there - you are taking yourself there. Where are you? What are you doing? You can do this exercise over and over to generate a nice list of possible self-care activities.

You deserve (and need) to have several self-care activities on your schedule each day. Try one day where you schedule and then do 1, 2, or 3 such activities. How do you feel at the end of that day? Do you see how much better you are at your job or more conscious with your parenting? There is only one person responsible for your self-care. You. Still, when you don't tend to your self-care your others will be negatively impacted - make no mistake about that.

Let's write down some self-care activities you do now and brainstorm some others. You can record your motivation for doing them. Put a "P" by it if it is a pleasurable and uplifting activity, or a "G" by it if it less fun and considered "good" for you. You can try them out. You will like some self-care activities and not like others. Once you figure out which is which, you can make an effort to balance them out. Then add BOTH of them into your day! Schedule these things too and make sure you are balancing the Ps and Gs. Be sure to reward yourself for doing both, but especially the Gs!

Even days when you are super busy working or taking care of others, you must find some time for yourself and your care, both types pleasure/uplifting and good for you! Actually you're *on the job self-care* (you still taking good care of you while you are doing your job and/or taking care of others) is essential to fulfill your job requirements with joy and no resentment.

Current "S-C" activities   Motivation for activity (P/G)

_____   _____

_____   _____

_____   _____

Possible new S-C activities   Motivation for activity (P/G)

_____   _____

Self-care and judgment. For me, I do like getting my nails done because of the pretty colors and smooth edges. I love sitting in prayer (not because I should be doing it), but because I love talking to my Heaven team and praying for people - it's fun to me. I sometime prefer staying home to going out because I truly enjoy and feel nourished by spending time with my pets. I also like watching sitcoms because I love to laugh - laughing makes my insides warm and smiling feels so great to me. For a long time I felt embarrassed to tell people I loved TV and sitcoms, that I wasn't doing something educational, that I prefer to laugh when watching TV and movies and really enjoy *Friends* reruns. ☺ I am not ashamed of, or apologizing anymore for my personal preferences or discovered joy activities to anyone (self-love).

If someone were to shame me or make fun of me, or secretly or openly judge me for loving something "beneath them" (or beneath who I am supposed to be to them), I may feel their judging, and hear their ribbing, but I won't hold on to it, or allow it to impact me at all (self-love). If anything it will make me want to help them to grow in their self-love, because to project those things onto me suggests they likely have a problem.

Self-care and guilt. Now I know I said no one is responsible for your pleasurable activities and self-care, but in healthy relationships, your partner encourages your self-care without making you feel guilty about it. He/she may help you plan it, watch the kids, move things in the schedule, bring you brochures (but it is really your responsibility to see to it). If you want your partner to do these things for you then you can ask for them, or start providing these things to them. The best way to get what you want is to start giving it out!

What if you are in a relationship with someone low in self-love (especially a narcissist). For the most part, they won't like you taking time for yourself, or understand it (because they don't think they are worthy) and they may try and make you feel guilty for taking good care of yourself. This is not about you. It is a projection of them feeling as if they don't deserve good care, so they project that on to you. In this situation the answer is for you to continue on with your self-care with no guilt. It is my hope you will not get angry, or irritated, but may see the situation for what it is and explore it. You might be able to see their unworthy pattern and bring it to their attention. This helping of another is secondary to you forging ahead with your self-care and not feeling guilty about it.

Any messages such as you, *you are getting another massage?, or your nails again,?* are a projection of your partner not feeling deserving of self-care. This should not upset you now because you are not taking it personally. Instead you approach with measured compassion (with compassion for both him/her AND you). A measured compassioned response to something like this would be, *"Oh, I would love you to support and encourage my self-care activities. I look forward to them, save money for them, and they make me happy. Do you think you might benefit from some of those activities too? I give you permission and encouragement to care for yourself in such a way. Thank you for your feedback. Love you!"* It only takes one to break the resentment cycle remember.

Get back to looking for the good in this friend, instead of focusing on their misinformed and ignorant comment about your self-care plan. These little ignorant comments make you feel like you don't deserve to take care of yourself! They are little tests to get you to finally address them with self-love for yourself! You do deserve the care and the love! The comment doesn't bother you now. You realize it is a reflection of another's lack of self-love. You aren't mad, you don't need to tell three of your friends why your partner is such an ass. Really encourage some self-care activities for that partner/friend. Remember what you first liked about them. Shift your attention to the positive. It will be so beneficial for both of you!

To Do or Be, that is the Question

There is a lot of duality with this question and the messages (sometimes platitudes) can cause quite a bit of confusion. It did for me, that is for sure. We know about free will and we are to make choices and do things, but we also hear we are to surrender and let God (things happen for a reason). Not surrendering, sometimes we get in our own way, and sometimes the greatest things happen when we just let them be. Do we pick our partner or let our soul mate find us? Should I be alone or go out? Should I lower the price of my house for sale, or just surrender and wait for the perfect buyer to come along? Am I supposed to just be or just do it?

When we lead with our spun-out thoughts (our ego) and not our heart/soul we sometimes look back with regret. Just who is in charge here, and what are we supposed to do?! My favorite answer to this duality and question I struggled with for so long came from a DailyOM course of Mother Mary channeled through Danielle Gibbons. In the course I heard Danielle who channeled Mother Mary share the most eloquent insight and I won't ever forget it. She of course used the word God, but you can use Universe, the Spirit, your Spirit Animal, Heaven, the Divine, you know what you call your Source manifestation. Anyway, Mother Mary said, "We (God/Heaven/the Divine) sets it up for us and then we choose." It will be up to us and no choice is ever better than another (because of the lessons). Also, the Divine has no skin in the game other than us being full of our self-love, acceptance, forgiveness, and joy. Beautiful right - there it is - the answer about free will and how the Divine is involved. This shared insight changed many things for me. We have choices and the Divine supports each one. It is up to us to figure out what is right for us to choose. We can't even ever choose wrong, because there is no wrong - all choices are perfect in the present moment and if the outcome is something we are not fond of - then what a valuable lesson for next time and even for others vicariously. What a gift! Another gift - choices made in self-love are much better (e.g., healthier, wealthier, wise) than choices made from a lack of love. Always choose the option bringing you more love!

About your choice of To Be or To Do, from what I've learned, in general, and for me - If you do, do, do too much and don't just Be - we will have a problem. If you be, be, be, and don't Do- you have less of a problem existentially, but may have a bit of a problem as a member of society.

I believe on both the self-love and spiritual awakening paths (or if these two paths are merged for you) I can say with confidence that you will for sure need to spend time just BEing - to get come to understand the good stuff. I also think there is a time to BE and a time to DO. Figuring out which time it is may be the lesson of the lifetime!! I also know that you might feel like you need permission to just BE and for that reason I am giving it to you right now. The first time I heard this in my life (from Dr. G) was really one of my very best days!

When "DO" motivations come from the ego. I just watched a beautiful video from one of my favorite conscious influencers and heard something that triggered me, so I needed to explore it. It bothered me because I think these messages about improving from the outside are leading people down an incorrect path, which actually postponed my growth for years. The post was about how we need to take one step toward our dreams. I like dreams, sure. But I was triggered on this day I think because I am writing this book section and needed to say something. This post reminded me of so many Instagram posts and platitudes about how to stay motivated, keep busy seeking that dream, don't give up moving toward that dream, reaching for the sky, taking a positive step in the right direction. All of these statements (and now sadly about 75% of my Instagram I just realized) are so bossy and about DOING when sometimes we need to get quiet and have permission to rest and BE. For me, I was avoiding all of life and my problems and my subconscious story (which was running the show) by my obsessive DOing. I was exhausted and running in circles seeking but not finding. You can move toward your dreams at any time, but do take the time to be with yourself to figure out your dream.

I feel as if I may have mentioned this before in this book, but your happiness, love of life, love of relationship is not happening from you taking steps toward your dream/fantasy career or person. Please, continue to work on your dreams, but do sit with your dream for a bit and find its origin. Make sure it is your dream for your soul (not ego), and not about any external conditioning forcing us to change, DO, grow, and remodel something that suggests something is clearly wrong with us, making us seek, and is not working.

A good litmus test is to take a moment and try to ascertain where the motivation for your current activity or choice is coming from. Are you doing things to get recognition, so others will like you, to win approval, good grades, lots of money, to make you happy? Okay. Are you doing these things to make up for something you think is wrong with you? That is less okay. There is nothing wrong with you. You are perfect, you are beautiful, you will learn to love yourself more and you will be free to take steps how you want. There are no rules to these steps (no one knows more than you do - especially about your life!) and no one really ever said the steps need to go toward any specific direction. That you have a dream about what you want to change in a relationship or job is good, but you need to decipher where the dream is coming from. If you love cats and feel called to help the cats of the world- okay! Sub in oceans, homeless people, people with addictions, other things like that. If you see your friend helping and she got an award for it and that's why you want to do it, that is an okay motivation, but this is not the conscious self-love stuff we are talking about. In fact, that you are seeking acknowledgement is more of a projection about something lacking in your self-love and a better action for you would be to shore up your conscious self-love stuff.

Discomfort is the sign (not the end). When we are uncomfortable we try to change something outside of ourselves, but that is not the right way. Discomfort is the sign you need to go inward, listen to your soul and figure something out about how you relate to yourself. You need to determine whether or not the discomfort is coming from your ego telling you to do something to distract you from loving yourself.

The ego is usually telling you something is wrong and in need of fixing, but your soul is helping you to love yourself, life, and others. Do you want a different partner because you don't feel appreciated? This is an ego need. You don't need a new partner you need to appreciate yourself. Do you want a different partner because yours doesn't love you enough? This is confusion caused by ego (suggests you need to grow in self-love). Do you want a different job because they don't recognize your efforts enough? This is ego need for recognition (means you need to honor your very own worth and efforts).

Seeking the new partner or job and taking steps in that direction will NOT solve these problems. If I were you, I would cultivate conscious self-love. I believe love for yourself, life, and others is the inside that needs to get right. Once this happens everything on the outside shores up for you almost automatically!

Some people like to be DOing, having big plans, and others prefer to be comfortable and confident in BEing, and sometimes it changes. If you feel like you are already doing so much, feel tired, feel like running away, feel resentful, feel overwhelmed in daily life, feel like you just cannot take one more stupid request from work, your family, even your friends I would say right now you can put your air mask on, remove some things from your plate and start BEING instead of DOING. If this sounds more sound to you than taking on more (but different) things to do, then let me be the one to encourage you to BE in your moment, be kind to yourself.

If we do too much (for others or ourselves or work) then it is harder to hear our soul trying to get our attention (that can be the cause of the discomfort). Time is a limited resource. The more I did externally, (with work or helping others) the less actual time I had to BE (and take care of myself); which was the very thing I needed to do.

If you are having confusion or discomfort, I encourage you to take a little time out for yourself and check in. You might need some time to just be with yourself, asking yourself things and listening for your answers. Check in before you make a choice and stop doing what others want you to do. Make choices for the moment and what you are feeling - even if they are only perfect for the moment. The moments add up to a beautiful life, but be sure you relate to yourself with kindness and self-acceptance as you move about your day, and especially as you review past life decisions - they were perfect too!

There is so much to be said for the BEing phase - where we get happy in the moment of silence, where we take it easy on ourselves and nurture our soul and maybe inner child, where we learn about our soul, where we cultivate kindness, compassion, and love for our self - this is, I believe, requisite for raising your consciousness. Without it, I don't know if it is possible.

Do Get Help from Others

It is important to tell you that much of this work on clearing your past and clearing your present can be achieved by yourself - by going within, but there is also reason to believe another person (likely a professional) will be of utmost assistance in this journey (especially if you are feeling stuck, too much discomfort, suffering, or simply want some assistance). We are here to help one another.

Please don't feel you have to solve all problems or have to be "strong," or an island. Sometimes the strongest thing you can do is request assistance. My only personal suggestion is you seek assistance from a human who possesses self-love. ☺ This is not one of those necessary-sufficient situations for me, I feel it is essential. In fact, I feel like the well-intentioned humans who assist other's on their path, but don't achieve the desired results for the client may be because of deficits in providers' self-love.

Remember you can't give away what you don't have. You can't really teach or be a way-shower of something you don't possess either. That is motivation to get all of the beautiful helpers of the world growing in self-love to show others the way.

On the other hand, we can all be helpful to one another, self-love or not, if we do more holding space and helping others become aware, accepting, and forgiving of themselves. We step out of the doing mode to "fix" the others and just sit with them as they are and accept them and help them grow in love.

Psychological therapy. I want to tell you about my favorite therapy. It is from a Humanistic perspective and is called, Client-

Centered Therapy, developed by Carl Rogers. This therapy was introduced in the 1950s (a humanistic psychology therapy) and the job of the therapist is to offer a non-judgmental stance toward the client, whereby the therapist **offers unconditional positive regard** to get the client to feel accepted and supported from their insides. It is really a beautiful approach to help people be comfortable and love themselves. This Humanistic approach is different from other more directive therapies (e.g., Freud's Psychoanalysis, Beck's Cognitive Therapy, Ellis' Rational Emotive Therapy, Linehan's Dialectical Behavioral Therapy). I sure do like all of these other examples, but for me, Humanism is the one.

In Carl Roger's Client Centered Therapy the goal is to get people good with (and accepting and loving their being - just like what we are talking about here - conscious self-love! You might expect me to say something like - without being comfortable and loving and approving of your being, then all of the doing will be incorrect efforts to DO things to get that love (which is actually in you and you don't have to DO anything to get). Once you are comfortable with and understand that BEING is just as important (maybe more so) than your doing, you can work on doing things. But, we really need to tend to your center of you - and your self-love first. That is my opinion. That is where I am coming from. If you feel like this is something that is resonating, tell your coach/friend/partner and see what happens. If they don't get it, find a different person to talk with about it, or talk to yourself ☺ or journal (you talking to the paper). I feel like if we can get good inside, then we are free to explore the things we want to shine up on the outside. If we don't do it this way I think we will be back to the drawing board - even after time and money spent shining things up.

The thing with therapists (and I think one reason for the explosion in coaching) is that each therapist is different and certainly some are better than others, and some may not be good at all. Lots of therapists are even leaving the profession to do coaching. Nothing about the helping system is ideal as of yet. From my frame of reference, and from having friends and people tell me their challenging therapist/coach stories, I can tell you how important it is to do a little research to find your fit. If something doesn't feel right trust yourself. My best friend did her research to look up specialties to try and find good therapists for her daughters with anxiety and depression. My friend said at the anxiety therapist appointment explained the therapist was a nervous wreck, clearly on some medicine for anxiety, but still fumbling and just very nervous. Her appointment with the depression specialist didn't go better and she told me this therapist also seemed to be heavily medicated and very low in energy. She gave up with both and is now very happy with an Executive Functioning Coach for her child's ADHD management. I am sharing this because we (as a profession) missed out on helping two young girls because of a poor fit and a failed therapeutic relationship. We need to do better in terms of healing. Anyway, the good therapist/coach will be in the know about such truth and not claim to have all your answers.

If what I am saying (about lack of self-love) is resonating with you, do yourself a favor and find a Rogerian therapist or positive psychology practitioner to try out. We can all agree though that accepting oneself and loving oneself more might be a great place to start - so I prefer Rogerian therapy in this case (where you know you are lacking in self-love) even more than cognitive behavioral therapy.

We've all heard the great efficacy rates for cognitive behavioral therapy, but it is not a win all the time or forever. Can you guess why I think that is? It is because we can change our thoughts to be more adaptive all day long, but if we don't know why or feel like we deserve to be happy and loved we can lose steam - especially because there is homework in CBT. Some people lacking in self-love might not even do it because they believe they aren't worth it, or don't even deserve to be happy. My second favorite therapy is Dialectical Behavior Therapy (DBT), which combines CBT and mindfulness! This is getting closer, because when we become mindful and quiet in our head we are led to a place of comfort with our being. DBT has higher success rates than CBT in many studies and I believe this is the reason. When children are hurting themselves I recommend DBT and Client-Centered Therapy. I say this because conscious self-love and approval to begin seems like a buffer and cure for all things to come!

Coaches? I see a lot of coaching now offered for personal problems and motivation. I want to support all people helping others, but I want to offer a bit of context I think may be important. Again, when I think of a coach (say a team sports coach) I think of a motivator type person who gets you to achieve some goal - a doing. I think this is okay if you need that! I tried some coaching before I was ready (I didn't know what I needing coaching on). There are coaches for the lotus petals - the doing of and accomplishing of external things. I didn't need help with that.

At the outset of my spiritual journey, (not the path of self-love yet) I knew I needed a little help. I had my PhD in developmental psychology and I had my LPC (license in professional counseling) but something was for sure missing (spiritual Jill was emerging and science Jill needed to take a seat for a second). I enlisted a coach/change agent who seemed to know something spiritually that I did not. In retrospect the experience was helpful, but during it, it was difficult for me. I am sure coaching/coaches are helpful. In fact, I want to say how wonderful it is we have so many coaches today! I have never seen a more beautiful group of people just trying to do their best to help the world and its people (they probably like animals too!). It is more than a step in the right direction! With anything though, we need to use discernment in selecting coaches and it will be most helpful if you know what you need coaching on.

During my three-month coaching experience I constantly felt as if I was in need of improvement, or that I was doing something wrong/not good enough. I believed I should be doing more more more - my great life purpose - get my values in line, do this, write me a review, do that. It was constant and I was in flux - a real *fix-it mode*. This was the exact opposite of what I needed. My coach likely didn't know that, mostly because I didn't know that! I finally figured it out on one of our last calls when every time she spoke there was this loud and offensive buzzing noise from the phone drowning her out, but not on my end when I spoke. For some reason that was a real moment for me and in my head I was thinking, I bet this is a message *it is time to listen to your heart and not these outside words now.* I accepted my gift gracefully. I then decided coaching wasn't for me, but that isn't right answer either.

As with most things, there is the duality of information to be both understood and integrated. On the one hand, what a beautiful gift there are more people available to help you on your journey. I believe assistance in all forms is positive and certainly don't want to interfere with anyone's helpful coaching business. Still, my coaching experience for me was too challenging and not what I needed at the time and I didn't really know how to reconcile it. I later heard something lovely from @Warrenzinger via Instagram - who also had a lack of luck with his coaching experiences (but he is a coach now!). He noted the coaching directions he received were from the place of where the coach was and their journey/experiences. He said he found more than 99% of coaches are teaching a method called "perspective coaching;" whereby a problem is intellectualized and it seems like a shared lingo but has very little healing effects (unless the coachee is in the same place or perspective of the coach).

I actually could relate to that (because I do therapy like that! we all do) and believed my coach was sharing what she thought would be helpful, but it was not exactly right for me. What a great way to understand this situation and a good lesson for you in making sure you select a coach/therapist with a similar perspective to what you need (even what you think you need or intuit if you don't know), and then check in over time to make sure the relationship is still working for you.

Remember the only person who really knows what you need is YOU. Still we need a little assistance! How do we reconcile this conundrum of needing help? You realize that *...here is a great person* *offering to help but they are coming from their experiences and really not mine. Given their experience... will they be able to help me?*

When you do that and seek a coaching or other therapeutic relationship (with that goal in mind) you may have a much better experience. I could've said to my coach, *hey um, what I really need is permission to take a break, nurture my wounds so I can get over them, and just love myself and all my parts.* I didn't do that, because I didn't know. The perfect coach/therapist for me would have been one who pointed that out (like Dr. G did!). But what if someone wanted to be doing more because that is what they really authentically wanted, then telling them to BE would be just as frustrating. What I am saying is - a sensitive (and client-dependent) practice should be offered by therapists and coaches. By sensitive I mean the helper asks questions about how they can help without assuming they know the one method (their method/plan) will be the perfect fix-it mode. Indeed, thinking people are broken and needing fixing is a most common example of a lack of conscious self-love.

In coaching, therapy, and all professional relationships like this - it will be the one place you want to play tennis with someone who is better than you. What "better" means is relative, completely about you, and should be explored if you are feeling uncomfortable, or that something is just not quite right in your therapeutic relationship. For me, better meant high in self-love, self-acceptance, and self-forgiveness - a resentment free zone. I later came to see why Dr. G was so helpful to me was because he was in that zone. I don't think that lovely lady coach was there yet herself (which is indeed the norm in our society) and her motivational advice to do more didn't help me at that time.

I thought it important to share this context with you because you are encouraged to seek help in your journey. It is most likely essential! I believe when you (finally) reach out for help you have come to a very important access point. If you do have a bad experience and give up on that help all together at this reach out point - then that is harmful - we missed an opportunity.

Because on that experience, and a few others, I implemented a 3-Chances Rule. This 3-Chances Rule can work for therapists, coaches, doctors, even yoga studios. I will spare you the details of my love-hate yoga relating. Just know Time 1 of my yoga experience was a disaster that almost led me away from it completely. Time 2 was better, but it took a Time 3 to decide some parts of yoga delivered in a certain way are helpful for me. My friend and her daughter found their Executive Coach on Time 3 and her daughter really benefitted. When you have an intuition you need assistance, try out Provide 1. If you are happy stick there. If not, try Provider 2 and then Provider 3 if needed. Don't give up!

How much can we really rely on others for our repairs. Let's discuss some of the things to take action on - for the inside repairs. The conscious self-love work you do (amount and type) will depend on the depth of your lack of self-love situation and your personal interests.

When I teach my *stress and coping class* I have students take a quiz about whether they prefer physical or mental activities for stress management (there is a quiz for this!). It is so important to understand that when someone comes in for help you cannot offer an approach they are not comfortable with, because you may miss an important opportunity to access their health. I don't want that to happen to you with your mental health professional or coach. Get clear on what you need and then find your person to help - not the other way around.

Professional therapist, coach, or friend, everyone needs someone to **hold space** for them. This is actually the most helpful part of the therapeutic/coaching experience I believe. You need to vent and explore your feelings. If your coach/therapist/friend is glossing over that part too quickly (getting you to shine up your petals) kindly ask to take a step back. Tell your coach, friend, partner what you need and see what happens. You have every right to be heard and validated. No one else is going to see to this for you - please take care of this for yourself. Your soul really just wants to talk to you. I am all for you including a third party, but make sure it is a helper and not a distraction. You must be sure they are coming from their very own place of self-acceptance, self-forgiveness, and self-love.

As a rule, please make sure the person you are seeking assistance from is in possession of the things you are seeking assistance with. This is one scenario where "fake it till you make it" won't be effective. I think one reason some therapists and coaches go in to this field is because they are compassionate. We will want to make sure they are practicing self-compassion too though. If you want to learn how to love and accept yourself, you will need to learn this from someone who does that. In therapy you do want to play with people at a higher level then you (especially with the situation you are striving to address).

One thing we can surely agree about is, you are the expert of you. Try that on and connect with it. You know what you need. For so many years I had been searching for and trying to fix, "my problem." I kept thinking other's held my answers and sought out all sorts of assistance. The most important thing my psychologist Dr. G said to me after years of knowing him (and I can still picture us laughing hysterically after he said it) was, Dr. G: *Jill, do you want to know what I think your problem is....* Me: *Oh my goodness, yes, please tell me!!!* Dr. G: *Your problem is you think you have a problem, but you don't have any problem, and that is the problem.* That was a real turning point for me!

The *Other* Helpers. I tried psychological counseling and had a wonderful experience with my psychologist Dr. G! I tried coaching and did learn things, but I was upset about the experience for a while after (I do now see my growth because of it). My main breakthroughs came from the reprogramming of my unconscious patterns and my automatic, subconscious, pilot I had running my show for too long. It is unlikely a coach or therapist will be able to help you with that. This is the reason for this section of my book! What was most helpful to me in my self-love journey were my "soulapists" I like to call them.

The Other Helpers category is a group of people you might not find in your yellow pages under therapist. They are helpful people, but when you tell your friends about them, your friends will have opinions and may think you have lost your marbles. I have seen this. I know who I can talk about Angels with. I know who can handle me telling them that I will pray for them. I know who I can tell about my spiritual group. Some people outwardly make fun of me! It used to bother me. I have also seen these same friends ask me for my Other Helpers' numbers when a challenging situation overcame and call me later to share good results.

In our spirit of non-judging and acceptance I will be sharing new information and if you like it great, if you don't that is okay too. Still, the people most helpful to me in developing conscious self-love, awareness, and smoothing my subconscious patterns and stepping away from my story were those from the Other Helpers category.

Something I recently learned about was a type of trauma called moral injury. Moral injury results in deep feelings of shame, grief, meaninglessness, remorse, and a violation of moral beliefs. Researchers believe soldiers may have this and doctors too (I can have compassion for doctors too!). Experts reported moral injury or moral trauma is high in any group with a high suicide rate who just can't respond to traditional psychological treatment. Boy I sure wonder if our beautiful-souled young people addicted to drugs and dying by suicide all over the world are experiencing this deep-seated soul trauma.

I would presume - that in order to fix soul trauma you would need more of a soul repair type provider. There is spiritual therapy and other resonance repatterning therapies that dive in to your subconscious mind and meet you at the soul level for your repairs. I believe these are the providers to address the increases in moral injury in our world. Next time someone tells you about their soul repair experience be sure to have an open mind.

I also believe this Other Helper category is the one to change the landscape of our world. Spiritual therapy and others practicing soul repair (that I know of) suggest self-love is the cornerstone. It will be interesting to see what unfolds. Do know that when you pay attention to practicing conscious self-love, you are reaching your soul level; it is just what your soul has been waiting for. ☺ Do know that by you reading this book all the way to here means you are doing your part to make this world a better place! Thank you! Be sure to check out my Other Helpers and Subconscious Repair section in the Resources section of this book.

A Day in the Life of Practicing Conscious Self-Love. We will leave this chapter with a daily plan example of practicing conscious self-love. My goal is to **wake up happy**, live through the day happy, and then go to bed happy. Most of the days I do this and I love all parts of my day. I used to plan, my day to get everything done without time to breath or for any self-care. Most days back then I felt overwhelmed, like there was never enough time, and I hated everything. What changed was my attitude. I am doing the same things for the most part, but I feel much better about the tasks I chose (the ones that I "get" to do instead of "have" to do). ☺ I look forward to the tasks and being present during them (not rushing to get them over with to catch up to the next task). Then during the task I am singing and humming and extracting the joy associated with the task and me being present! What a gift! The joy is in the participating!! Not the accomplishing even! Accomplishing is good, but it fades and only remains in the past (where we don't want to be).

For me, my self-care starts right away. Before I get out of bed I do a Healing Spectrums Method Self-Healing activity taught by Thomas Gates (www.thomasgates.com). I pursued advanced training in this Method and will do a healing activity on a friend or family member during the day. My brother, Jack (yes that is really his name!) swears by doing his stretches even before he gets out of bed. You could do stretches, name something you are grateful for, think about how you can be a role model of peace or grace today. Feel a happy thought about the day. Get excited. What do you GET to do today?! Think about one of your great qualities and appreciate the gift that it is and that you are! Promise to (and actually think of something) you will do for yourself today from your self-care lists (both P and G)! You already have it on your day planner! This is all before I leave my bed!

Soon after I am out of bed do my praying. I pray for my loved ones too and hope that helps me think happy thoughts for them too! Because I am a helper, my self-care is also serving others (it just makes me feel good now - not for coins, but because it brings me joy). It is important for me to take my time in the morning to send helpful texts, emails, resources, and notes to my loved ones. I need to have freedom in my morning schedule for this self-care activity. My current job affords me that freedom. I like to play as a librarian. I connect people with helpful sources and information. If I don't get to do this in the morning I feel like I didn't take care of myself. My friend's daughter is depressed, so I will hold space for her in a phone call, pray for her, send her a prayer or some helpful information I know about.

During the day let's say a **worry** pops in. I just immediately turn the worry into the opposite and pray for that. I feel better. Prayer also helps me dispel resentment and irritations. If I can't get my mind off of the worry I might do a guided mediation. You may have these on your phone, but if not, check out YouTube. Google your *problem of the day*: Worry about money meditation. Can't fall back asleep meditation. Staying calm in a stressful situation meditation. Something interesting is, although there is so much more stress in the world today, there are a lot of great meditations/guided visualizations for you to help you!

Let's say I notice myself **getting resentful** about something. As soon as I hear the words......that jerk.... start to flow around my head I immediately stop it. Resentment made me bitchy, judgy, and grumpy for too many years to let this stick there. I will look at this with **curiosity** and for the clues about how I need to love myself more. I am usually over-functioning (still- can you believe that!). Yes, I made the dinner and am doing the dishes and no one said thank you. Hm. Well, I didn't ask for help, I didn't say I would like feedback, or appreciation, I am mad at myself for not doing those things and projecting them onto my loved ones! Stop that. Maybe I should ask for those things, and/or maybe I should just feel those feelings for myself and reward myself with my internal praise and a pat on the back! It was nice to make a healthy meal AND I clean it up. I feel good about it! The only thing better than a compliment from another person, is a compliment from myself! Well done! Another resentment buster (after I explore the feeling of resentment to see if there is a message for me) is I just flip it to gratitude. Yes, I am irritated I have to do the dishes too, BUT wasn't it great when he helped me put all the decorations away and clean up after the party? I didn't expect him to do that. He is so nice. Remember when you need help again, just ask.

You can feel good about this and remember the balance. People are not mind readers, but you also don't rely on people for your self-love. There is that balance we are talking about! At this point if I am not done with the issue (you will know this because it doesn't leave your head and it is your clue to give it a little more thought) I might pray that I understand the message of me feeling resentment. Am I doing too much? Am I interfering with allowing others the gift of giving to me? I pray that the relationship between me and my loved one is filled with positive communication, understanding, and love. It sure beats the hell outta bitching about them in my head the rest of the night (for both of us!). Maybe words of affirmation are one of my love languages? Read that book about Love Languages with your partner. Share about what you both want and need. Pray for more helpful thinking (even if it is for you to stop feeling sour). It just takes one to break the resentment cycle and shine lighter and love to the relationship. This makes the other person even more accepting of themselves and loving to you! Gifts for everyone!

I do my job (the thing I get paid for). I can do some *on the job self-care* even during my work day too. For example each hour of work I take a break to get away from my desk, get some water/snack, step outside, look at nature, move around. Just because you are working does not mean you can't be kind to yourself. If there is a problem at work I try to resolve it right away and in the most balanced kind and compassionate way (I take my needs into consideration too).

Some "P" self-care activities for me right now are meditation, exercise, eating healthy, consciousness raising activities, and smoothing out subconscious leftovers. I am learning new methods to help others (and myself) like Feldenkrais, the Alexander technique, and neuromovement. I practice the Healing Spectrums Method daily. I am learning to play the harp and I attend Soul Cycle classes each week. Something I just started is combining meditation and exercise. I am on a elliptical machine (I am good at this, can close my eyes, and don't really need to be paying attention to not fall or get hurt) and I add in a meditation in my headphones, close my eyes and let go. Only try that if you are not worried about falling. I listen to a daily meditation CDs on Karmic Repair by Master John Douglas (masterangels.org) around 3 o'clock and will maybe do another one from his collection later in the day. I will most likely work on my conscious raising and will listen to or read information by Michael Golzmane (clearandconnect.com). Michael has many free activities on YouTube that are always helpful. If something specific pops up, and I know how to deal with it, I will do so. If I don't I will try and find out in the spirit of love and care. Some "G" activities this month is to get my roots colored (I don't love this because it hurts and it is always cold) and to go for a doctor check up. I will reward myself with a P self-care activity after both of the Gs.

I will be PRESENT most of the day! I will look at all my activities as "getting" to do them. I will be careful with my language. I won't say I can't do something, or claim as my own anything bad (my headache - no). I will hold space for myself and as many people as I can in a day. I will send encouraging and inspirational messages to my loved ones and try to be kind, cheerful, and grateful to all people I encounter. I will SMILE at almost everyone I see. When I make a mistake I will own it right away and apologize, then fix what I need to, then gracefully move on because I know no one is perfect and I was doing my best. When I see that play out for others I will try and remind all parties of the same. This makes sleeping at night and falling asleep very easy. When I was causing messes when I was not conscious and/or just worrying about anything and everything sleeping (and falling asleep) was harder. My peace, gratitude, forgiveness, compassion, and kindness mode through my day resolved any sleeping problems.

When I go to bed I do another Healing Spectrums Activity, pray, maybe put on a meditation or Friends in the background and float to resting land. My motto right now is: be happy, be kind, be understanding, be in love with life, yourself, your loved ones, and neighbors. Be careful with yourself and others. Be respectful to nature and animals. Reflect on your actions and results. Ask how you can be better. No judgments on yourself or others, just keep perfecting your journey in line with your true self/soul.

All of these beautiful things are made possible through the lenses in this chapter. The lenses are what we need to practice conscious self-love. Once you are practicing that everything becomes better. You are reading this book because you realize, or have awareness about something very important in your and your families' story.

Keep going! You are doing great! Keep being the best you can be. There is love for you everywhere! Especially inside of you ☺

"You are loved just for being who you are, just for existing. You don't have to do anything to earn it. Your shortcomings, your lack of self-esteem, physical perfection, or social and economic success – none of that matters. No one can take this love away from you, and it will always be here."
Ram Dass

Chapter Six: Helping Others See Their Worth

"When we tap into the feeling of being unconditionally loved,

we're able to begin to unconditionally love ourselves, others,

and we want to share that expansive, loving feeling

as much as we can, as often as we can."

Anita Moorjani

To help others it is not really about telling them stuff (although we will discuss some things). The most helpful thing you can do to help others is to get YOU right in your head and for YOU to be in a state of your own personal conscious self-love when you interact with all people. I hope you are sitting down for the rest of this chapter.

Life Purpose

Understanding your life purpose is important, but I want to take some pressure off of you right at the outset of this chapter. Many are seeking their *life purpose.* You have heard of this, you have uttered this phrase many times. You bought books, took a master class, paid a coach to find out yours. People have been telling you have/need a purpose, and have been telling you it is something specific, and you need to figure it out or you will be unhappy, and you are worried you are going to not figure it out, or get it wrong.

People are spending a bunch of cash on this unicorn (me included!). For many people this takes years, frustration, and some even die without thinking they found it. I circled back around and around again on my purpose unicorn. Every time I thought I found it, it poofed right out of my hands because I wasn't happy doing it, or things didn't work out (of course I interpreted that as a sign). Then one day I heard a talk by Matt Kahn and it all made sense to me! I paused, replayed, wrote notes about his brilliant message, which was essentially this: There should be no controversy about what your life purpose is. You might think about what job you want, or what hobbies you want to pursue, but your job/hobbies/relationship are NOT your purpose. **Your purpose is to love yourself and others.** You may be charged with teaching others how to do that (say your children or other humans in one capacity or another). You will have a job doing something you enjoy and are passionate about (hopefully), but that is not your purpose. Your purpose is to begin to love yourself as God loves you and love others as God loves others. If you are going to do anything to help others in the terms of service, then please understand it will not really matter what service you are providing; other than you are helping the person to love and accept themselves more (that is the purpose). I remembered Marianne Williamson said something similar and others too. It was just that on this particular day I was ready to understand the message and graduate from my purpose seeking and never finding! I think it was because I was practicing conscious self-love!

This life purpose is much better and greater, isn't it! We do our life purpose by giving love, modeling love, and we heal other's by teaching them to harness their own self-love. We take on different roles in our communities in the form of our career and jobs. We behave in that job with self-love when we are answering phones (receptionist), or replacing a hip (doctor). All jobs are equal in terms of filling your purpose if you do them with love. Your "purpose" (our life purpose) is to love ourselves enough to be a mirror of love to all who see us. We might ponder how to live out and express this life purpose in the form of our day to day activities, volunteer/paid work, interactions with others, and that is okay, but everyone's purpose is the same. How you express this purpose of giving love is your gift to the world. You can help decide how to express this purpose by the gifts you've been given and what feels right to you at the time, and it may change throughout your life!

I have heard the terms small life purpose and big life purpose and I don't agree with that. You might've heard that too, a small purpose would be you stick close to home and effect a small group. A big life purpose would be to affect masses with a book or podcast, some grand world size scale action. Whether your career is to positively affect one person or 5,000 - all are special, none are special - from The Course in Miracles ☺ You could be a best-selling author helping millions of people, or you could be that person's mother, or the friend who supported the author during a time of crises. I don't think there are different size life purposes. All purposes are equal in terms of gifts to the world!

My best friend has been the most amazing parent to her two beautiful daughters and reading tutor to a small number of lucky children in her community. She always listened to her instincts. She decided it was important to stay home and raise her girls (and what a gift that was to them - especially how she did it!) and do the part-time tutoring (even though school district after school district would recruit her each year for reading specialist work). She only doubted herself because of some present-day mis-conditioning, but she held firm in her beliefs and answered her calling as she felt intuitively guided. Would you think she is doing a small purpose? NO! She and I know, and her daughters know, and the hundreds of children she helped feel good about themselves to read know, and now you know - She lived her very big and grand life purpose! Also who knows what her students/children will go on to do! When we love ourselves we trust ourselves and love our decisions. I am so glad she made those decisions and I want to support you on listening to your intuition/soul/insides when you have something to decide. We don't have to listen to those who don't understand what is going on inside of us ☺ Just in case you needed to hear that.

For many years I sought coaching for seeking (out of lack) my life purpose. Only until I grew in conscious self-love did I realize a few things. The first thing was that I didn't need career or life purpose coaching! I am not saying you don't, but what I needed was some help with self-love. No coach really caught on to that. I was a successful professor at a university (I won awards) with publications, two meditation CDs, I was good. I also always considered myself a helper/teacher and I was doing literally that. How could this not be my purpose? My job was okay, but I kept thinking I should be Doing MORE, or a different purpose.

That needing to do more discomfort was the clue for me! The clue that something was off. What was off was that I was doing a fine job at my job, but not a good job loving myself. I really wasn't doing my actual purpose of loving myself. I was not teaching my children how to love themselves. I might've been teaching my students how to have compassion and grow and was able to muster it in that capacity, but for me and my main people - no.

This discomfort was my soul call! I tried to enlist some help, but I was not in my right mind to select the right people to help me in the beginning (I thought I had a problem with my career choice!). Also, those people I selected couldn't even help me with what I needed (to love myself more) because, as I previously stated, your love must come from the inside. Moreover, this help I was seeking was actually taking me away from growing in conscious self-love and had me down rabbit holes such as I needed a new partner, job, more goals, more respect with the kids, etc. The coaches were good to talk to and I am sure they think they were helpful in getting me to a certain place regarding the paths they thought important; however, what I really needed was someone to just tell me I was OKAY! I was good! Love yourself.

Loving your job. I work a full-time job. It took a while to find a job that was consistent with my likes and values. I resisted a lot and took jobs inconsistent with those things when I was not practicing conscious self-love. Taking jobs you don't like and staying in them when you are unhappy is a classic example of unmeasured compassion (compassion for others and not for you), and feeling unworthy. You deserve to be happy in your job. If you are not you find one that is consistent with your likes and values. Period.

My philosophy for work was, I work to make money to live. For me, my job didn't have to be a source of fulfillment. I could have hobbies and volunteering for that. I needed my job to be enjoyable, allow me freedom to do my other things, and not be too stressful. I have been a "helper" since the beginning, but it was not essential that my job job for money was that. Indeed in our society the "helper" jobs don't seem like the real money makers. I have also observed that the nice people in these jobs are less likely to practice their self-compassion and get unhappy in their work more frequently. I hope both of these things change soon!

When I was searching for my "perfect" job I thought back to the happiest time of working in my life. It was in high school, a summer job at a bakery. Okay, it is true there was a lot of whipped cream there, but I realized what I loved was that I started at noon and worked until five every day, and enjoyed a relaxed morning. That time from waking up until noon was golden! I decided I needed a job where I could set my own schedule (freedom), or at least not work until noon so I could have my soul nourished before I left the house. I was not good at saying no or work boundaries, so I would need a job where I wouldn't feel obligated to accept additional assignments. I needed a job where I helped people, and was ethical. Helpers often have so much compassion for others they stay in jobs they don't like and completely ignoring their needs. Every job I had like that was a dread. Also, in each of these jobs I got burned out, and/or it was too hard over time to keep oozing other compassion, when I was practicing no self-compassion. The balance was off. I thought I was hiding this discrepancy, but I am sure it was palpable to those I was working for and with. This is not a way to help others. For me, I needed a work from home job where I could set my own schedule AND in a kind environment with an ethical company AND where I practiced self-compassion and conscious self-love. I found a job that met most of list criteria. They did keep asking me for more and more though, with no increased compensation. Why do companies do that? It is so ridiculous. At first, I kept saying yes yes and was getting burnt out (no self-compassion) and I was starting to hate this job too. Then I started saying no. Practicing my conscious self-love. I didn't receive my full 3-point evaluation, I received a 2 - most likely for saying no and practicing my balanced compassion/kindness, but I was okay with that even if it was a little irritating. I wondered how many other really good jobs I interfered with because of my over functioning and unwillingness to practice self-compassion, or knowing my needs and attending to them, or my lack of practicing conscious self-love. This isn't only a personal problem.

I listen to many people tell me their job woes and I can usually intuit their problems are because the environment is not a vibratory match for them (they are nice and caring and the place of employment is not), or there is not a lot of freedom in their schedule to tend to the things that really matter to them, or they are away from their home just too much, and there is a limited opportunity to express their creativity. This problem of mismatched values/vibe/work rhythm preference, and creativity causes discomfort for a person. The discomfort manifests in different ways.

The discomfort is a gift to help you find a more personally suitable job! Your purpose is not to do for others in your work and you to be unhappy. This will not help you fulfill your purpose of loving yourself, or helping others love themselves. When you hate or even dislike your job you come home at the end of a work day and do neither of your actual life purposes (loving yourself and family). You don't need to leave your job if you can find other outlets to do the things that do make you happy (your job affords freedom in scheduling or not all of your time). Personally suitable means you figure out and determine your preferences and values and then find a good fitting job (that makes you happy most of the time) because you deserve it and you love yourself and take good care of yourself. Maybe you work full time as an accountant, but volunteer in the afternoons at an animal shelter. Maybe you work in grants management at a homeless shelter. Maybe you work in advertising for a company you feel is a good ethical and vibrational match for you. Maybe you do have a podcast or are a life coach. To help you decide if a job for money is personally suitable, you need to interview the company on your job interview (just as they are interviewing you). You are really doing them the big favor of working for them. You are the prize. You also need to know you deserve to be happy and even if you interviewed them, but decide you don't like this job now that you are in it, you can and should make a change. I don't know how many people I hear tell me they hate hate hate their job. When I suggest they send out a resume or explore a different employment opportunity I am met with so much resistance. Why do people not want to correct situations that are making them miserable? Oh, is it because their subconscious program of not deserving to be happy is running 95% of their day and they are not practicing conscious self-love. Yes, that's right. If you find yourself very unhappy at your job, but need money to survive as we all do, start sending out resumes (and collect your lesson of the discomfort being there because you need to love yourself more). If something happens on your job and it is abusive or just too toxic, and you are like, *oh hell no*, then leave it right then and send resumes from your home. Take care of yourself in this way! You deserve it! I would say we should teach this to the children, but I feel like they are the ones teaching this to us ☺ Have you noticed that? Thanks kids!

A final note about jobs. I work with some people who are so afraid to speak up for things because they fear they will get fired. I have seen this irrational fear by others at my place of employment. My observations about people getting fired or getting laid off is ….getting fired is a special gift from the universe because you weren't going to do anything about a bogus situation for yourself. This is not the end of the world, in fact you just got a total lucky break! Hopefully you can now get unemployment/severance and get paid while you do yourself a favor and find a more suitable job for yourself! This time you interview them, because you are the prize! To think you will never have another job, or another job you like is similar to thinking you will never find love again after a break up. A trick of your subconscious mind to keep you small and sad. Practicing conscious self-love is the panacea!

Helping Children Love Themselves

Talk about your life purpose. If you have kids - what could be a more important life purpose than to raise those kids loving themselves? Nothing. Having your children leave your home with their self-love intact is your life purpose.

It is not enough to love the stuffing out of our kids. That's good and Thank You, but your job/purpose is TEACH THEM TO LOVE THEMSELVES!! You can't make your children have certain feelings. You shouldn't talk them out of feelings or deny or invalidate their feelings. What we are going for here is where we do NO HARM in fostering their practice of conscious self-love. Where we practice conscious parenting, unconditional love (not love with conditions), and model us practicing conscious self-love.

As we discussed, parents are not practicing conscious parenting yet. I believe this is because parents are not practicing conscious self-love. So as a whole, parents are not really getting this job/their parenting purpose right just yet. Parents are NOT encouraging self-love, self-acceptance, and self-compassion. We talked about how parents can interfere with launching and a kid's self-efficacy. Parenting is a delicate, crucial, and special job to help a child love their very own person. The reward for such a miraculous accomplishment is not devotion from your child, it is more of a personal soul victory for your job well done (the award is given to you by you, not any other person, not a trophy or mug).

It is essential our children love themselves if we want them to make good choices about their bodies, relationships, and life. Ben Franklin said, "Nothing is of more importance for the public wellbeing, than to form and train up youth in wisdom and virtue." I will add self-love to the list!

The first step in the process of helping children love themselves is to cultivate conscious self-love for yourself and becoming conscious in your parenting. Remember we can't give away what we don't have. If you are not relating toward yourself with love, acceptance, and compassion; then you will be judging and fixing and interfering with your children's growth by giving off a confusing vibe about their worthiness. I could stop this section right here. But, there is too much conditioning and unconscious parenting we received (it was not our fault we don't know this), so I need to share some more information. If you were not ready to practice more love for yourself (practice conscious self-love), then do it for the children!

Your parenting JOB. Talking about working at a job consistent with your life purpose! You must realize your main and most important job in this life is raising the children you decided to have. And raising them to be in receipt of self-love.

We must also agree that the nature of the parent-child relationship is to be one sided. It is less of a give/take relationship and more a giver/apprenticeship type. It is the parent's role/responsibility to provide for and train the child to the best of their ability. Parents should not have expectations their child is to be their friend, counselor, confidante, *old soul* companion, mini me, mini me redo, or in most any way contribute significantly to this relationship of adult-child, especially when they are under 25. Your children are not here to give you approval, work for you, help you, serve as a buffer in your marital relationship, or as a buffer between you and your other children. Children are actually not even here to give you love. You as the parent are here to give that to yourself and to them.

Your job as their parent is to raise them kindly, appropriately, safely, hopefully encouraging the growth and development of their bodies, minds, souls, and spirits. You still get things from your parent-child relationship though. Dr. Shefali says, "gifts from your kids are they teach you to be in the present moment, help you shed your identify about yourself, and your worth, they teach you to laugh, play, and evolve" (those are amazing gifts - a balanced relationship indeed).

Far too often parents have unrealistic (inappropriate) expectations for their children. Expecting more from your child will set you both up for failure and resentment and likely interfere with your child's self-love. Just so we are clear on that!

When I was in graduate school for my PhD in Developmental Psychology (around age 21) I was one of the grad students allowed to teach full classes. My mentor even referred me to teach at a different university! It was a big deal and the class I was awarded was called Parenting. I was experienced in teaching research methods, not parenting. I was 21 and not even a parent. I thought kids' tongues came in around age 3 (that is a joke my editor let me keep in). Anyway, I accepted the class late. The text was already ordered and it was an amazing life changer for me. If you get a chance please read, "*Peoplemaking*," by Virgina Satir. Wow. If everyone read that book and Dr. Tsabury's *Conscious Parenting* book, the world in 5-20 years would be miraculous. Can we please start handing those books out at the DMV?

Dr. Satir thought children were unique beings coming into the world of adult unique beings. The adult is to be like a gardener. To be a good gardener means to see your unique and beautiful seed and tend to them. You tend to them by figuring out the light and nourishment your seed needs to thrive. Gardeners don't control the seed or tell them what to do. They listen to them, are present with them, see their gifts and encourage maximum growth on their terms. Gardeners (parents) should use their listening/observational skills with far less judgment and control, so we can be sensitive to what is going on with them.

Dr. Satir believed if families created more peaceful child experiences that a more peaceful world would ensue! She noted that the skill of conflict resolution is learned in families, and then the child takes that skill into the world. If children are taught they matter, are worthy, feelings are validated, how to deal with conflict appropriately (instead of with blame, resentment, violence) then we are setting up a good world. Remember the world is just adults who were once children.

As a gardeners we are to be delighted in what our new seeds bring us on their terms. We are to honor them. We shouldn't introduce unrealistic expectations (based on our lack of self-love or achievements). We shouldn't take their reins and try to control them, or make them "better." Gardeners get excited about all the new possibilities and opportunities. They have patience, trust, belief, and faith (without judging or ruling the show). They know if the right conditions are present they will encourage the growth of their special and unique seed/gift. We are so busy with things that don't matter and getting people to conform to our stuff (our unexplored and unconscious stuff!!!) we are not doing the basic gardening work.

Gardeners who shift from being a controller to empowered (even in the winter) will get their miracles. Interestingly and I forgot this part, Dr. Satir believed we can change our self-attitudes at any time! Great news! She also said, when we get more present and we see ourselves and our children as the miracles we all are, and listen to each other, and respond to each other by sharing feelings, it will help the seeds unpack even brighter with even more beautiful connections.

One more gem from Dr. Satir (but please do watch at least one YouTube with her) is her belief in the function of anger. She said anger is your anger is a clue something is OUT OF ORDER. We need anger and we can articulate it. Try saying: *"I feel angry about xx."* - instead of, *" You are a huge asshole.* One is owning a feeling with an I message, and the other is a declarative and shaming statement. Such a shaming statement will not lead to positive relating or problem solving. If you aren't comfortable sharing what you are angry about, try some inner bonding (where you experience your anger and you talk to yourself about what you are angry about). It is okay to be angry. It is best to take a moment to work through your anger in a peaceful manner with kindness, compassion, forgiveness, and even gratitude for yourself and others. We can teach this to the children. ☺

What did your mother do to you? lol There was a joke in the 80s that we blamed everything bad on moms. Then it became politically incorrect to blame mothers. I will go out on a limb and be politically and politely incorrect here and share the truth as I understand it. I know I said previously we are all on our sovereign journeys and soul paths. We exist with a few special people to us on the journey. When we are children we don't really have a choice and we exist with and need our parents to provide for our care. Then later, we take over our care taking. Friends and relationship partners influence use (but we can pick those and control parts of the relationships) and it is really mostly up to us. How we will do this is based on what is in our subconscious mind (the imprints from parents to their child in childhood, I am talking birth to 18). It is impossible to think the parent is not responsible for their actions toward the child and the results. It is impossible to think these actions don't influence a child's subconscious mind's development.

Although it is (or should be) incumbent on the parents to do no harm, as we have learned throughout this book, it is not what is happening in the world. Most adults had difficult experiences, experience self-hate, and are running in auto-pilot with their unexplored subconscious minds. How can we even expect young people with no reality testing to behave appropriately with the parental harm being delivered. We just can't. I took us off the hook from our parent's unconscious parenting and its effects on us; now it is our turn to help our children with the same. If we catch things in time they might not need to reparent themselves!

We have a responsibility and should intend to get it right for our kids. It is not the case they are here to provide for us. It is the exact opposite and how well we do this can and WILL impact how they relate to themselves, others, their starting point of conscious self-love, or self-hate; and what is in their subconscious mind. There is no point in arguing this. There are no exceptions to this fact. I know you didn't intend for a child to become an addict and no one is blaming you. That is not why I am writing this. I am writing this to be real and let us all know it takes more than good intentions to raise a healthy kid. Let's please love ourselves enough to see its effect on our children. At first I was going to write this book for 18-20-year olds because I thought that was the best way to tackle parent's unconscious parenting and diffuse the situation right when the kid reaches adulthood. Now I see all the problems of kids 13-20 (they are dying!) and decided we all need to get real here and accept some responsibility for the problems; realize it is okay to see our role, AND make reparations now. Why not?

As a rule is it likely the case that good children have good parents, "bad" kids likely experienced some serious parenting missteps (but it is never too late), and great kids had great parents? What do you think? There are resilient kids who didn't have great moms who figured out how to give themselves love on their own. Can rogue situations in a child's life can be traced back to parenting missteps (even if not directly caused by the parent, maybe a lack of protection by the parent/ a distraction, unconscious parenting, or inattention to the matter)? I am asking you.

Maybe I can take the sting out of it by saying, I don't think we do it purposely, but when we parent with unresolved negative subconscious patterns, we are not practicing conscious parenting, and we don't love ourselves (or model how to do it). As a consequence, we can be implicated in our children's messes, no matter their age. If we are NOT loving and accepting them (or ourselves yet), and/or tending to their garden with the good stuff; then we have contributed to their issues. Period. Sorry.

Again we are not looking to blame here, but I keep coming across examples of parents just not seeing the connection. I am writing it to help us have some awareness and take appropriate responsibility and steps for correction. Plus, it is likely politically more correct to take some responsibility for this now and do something different for the children. When I mention blame it is more of an esoteric blame (I am not blaming anything on you personally) if that makes us feel better, or blame for the early childhood environment (as the DSM does). Also, some messes actually make children stronger. Let's agree if you made a mess, let's not blame yourself or feel guilty. Let's just use that as a great example for your kid to be greater because now you are approaching things a lot differently. Talk about making a kid stronger. Pointing out your parenting mistakes is huge. Who better to help a child put that into context and the child sees the parent taking some responsibility. Huge! This might actually be the difference whereby some kids go on to get strong (and practice conscious self-love) and why some choose the escape route. Until a child becomes conscious of the environmental conditional and considers correcting things, then we can agree that bad parenting behaviors are likely to cause bad child behaviors.

As I mentioned before, this generation of young people and millennials is projected to not live as long as other generations (and actually maybe not outlive their parents). The substance abuse, anxiety, and depression amongst this age group (all possible problems) are skyrocketing. A pain point is that if you are reading this book you are likely a well-intentioned parent/society member who does not need any more guilt to interfere with their self-love. The person who needs that message is not reading this book ☹ We will have to think of other things to get the parenting information to promote self-love out.

Remember how we said in the first part of the book that if your parent is a real jerk then you can actively choose to sever that attachment (no contact). Our kids have the option to sever with us. It is also an option for other toxic relationships you/they might find yourself in. However, when you are a parent you cannot just drop out, or actively exclude them, or leave them to fend for themselves without knowing you are doing considerable harm.

Do you see the hierarchical nature of this relationship? I hope you are sitting down and not getting too angry, but I really believe, even if you kid's a real jerk, you cannot just walk away. All kids are here because of their parents. You had them. You are responsible for the good parts and bad parts of them, until they can take the reins. You might need assistance or help working through this relationship; that is the right answer. You can NOT dismiss them or your parental role/responsibility, no matter the trauma or issue. If you are not up to the task you can find resources or a substitute.

You are in charge of your children's psyches for their life, especially in their early years. How well you do your job impacts them positively/negatively throughout the rest of their lives (or until they make peace with their pasts, which as we can see in this book can be overwhelming!). Please let's all do our jobs and get the parenting right. I really don't think there is any greater legacy to our world than decent parenting skills! If it is hard for you, get the skills and help you need to make it happen whatever that takes. You took lessons to learn to drive, you watched videos to learn how to cook something new. If this parenting thing is not intuitive for you, or if you feel in any way negative about it, or bad at it, please seek out assistance, so you can do better. This is not a child problem. Bad parenting is a parent problem and we all need to do this better (for our kids and our world).

Terry Real said - "we all deserve parenting. It is a birthright, and the job of the person bringing us into the world." Once again from Terry, "we hold ourselves how we were held, BUT we can do it differently as we relate to ourselves AND as we relate to our children." Think back on the behaviors your mom modeled (or didn't because you were neglected/ignored/abused). We need to think of how you are now relating to yourself, what you are modeling, and how you are relating to your children. Remember though, the past is the past - we are starting from right now and you can do things differently. All the things up to this point right now were the important lessons you and your children needed to bring their gifts of service to the world. So thank the lessons and let's do a little unblending (that was then and this is now) and inner bonding with yourself now. Inner bonding to grow your conscious self-love!

Almost every bad parenting mistake (abuse, neglect, abandonment) can manifest in the child as a form of self-hate. It could manifest as resilience, but that is less likely. Plus, other things outside of parenting (social media, peers, school) may manifest as self-hate. So we have a lot of things tipping to the bad side of the scale. It is also unlikely a child under 18 will come to this realization on their own and decide, hey wait, I need to be responsible for practicing conscious self-love. Moreover, even small parenting mistakes (not listening, projecting your needs on to the child, comparing them with siblings or others) can manifest in the child as a form of self-hate under certain conditions. Children are very egocentric and think everything is about them. It is an adaptation we are born with for survival! Even the non-direct instances of abuse, neglect, or abandonment, such as a parent's fight, divorce, fight with your child's teacher/coach, phone call with yelling, will likely be internalized by your child as having more than something to do with them. Even if you didn't intend for that to happen or didn't want it to happen, it happened. If you are not relating to yourself with love and compassion, they are watching your do this, and most likely you are not relating to them with those things and they are just not learning them.

My very good friend (who is an excellent mother) called me with bad news. Her lovely 17-year-old daughter confided in her the night before she was thinking about ending her life by suicide. She just couldn't take it anymore. My friend and I cried. We had talked about the depression and anxiety for all the kids in that age group right now and it is just so sad. We all need to do something. It is hard when it hits home like this. I listened as my friend cried for a good 20 minutes. We just didn't understand what happened. We kept coming back to her daughter had it so good, how can she be depressed. Like we were just seeing the issue from our perspective and saying things like, gosh "if I had it that good back then I'd be so happy. If anyone should have been depressed it was us." We were not seeing her perspective at all and having a little egocentric why me discussion. I kept circling us back to the compassion piece (especially that third part of the compassion definition). It was essential for us to have compassion for the young girl and stop thinking about ourselves here. Seeing the situation from the child's eyes is what needs to happen here. There were some stressors in both the mom's and the daughter's lives this year. My friend took her daughter to a therapist that day.

When a child says the word suicide you go that day to a psychiatrist or Emergency Room. You ask them if they have a plan and if you think they do you go to the Emergency Room. You have them promise they will give you time to get the help they need, and display HOPE that you will be able to help them resolve the issue causing their pain. Under no circumstance do you deny their pain or try to talk them out of their pain. The next day my friend texted a picture of the girl's journal from the day before. The date was at the top. The heading was, Reasons Why I Hate Myself. There were three things about her appearance and then "anxious all the time."

If you want to argue with me about the importance of helping your children love themselves - I am ready. The consequences of self-hate on our world are devastating all aspects and institutions of society. I believe that is what is wrong with our children right now. What are we going to do about it now? The first thing - instead of thinking back to all the missteps you might've done (that is where you went, isn't it?), just hold yourself in a nice moment of self-kindness. Take a deep breath and fill your body with your beautiful loving kindness.

You are making such a wonderful effort to take good care of yourself and your loved ones. Please hold yourself warmly and with loving positive regard. That you are discovering this message now is a gift of a lifetime. It had to be this way, or you wouldn't see this valuable lesson for you and the world. Thank you for making the choices you did to get us to now see this for what it is; a helpful lesson for you. Thank it and please put it down now.

We can tell the story and then let it go. Let it go. Read this and see how it feels. Ron Kochevar noted, "…this may sound a little harsh, but enough with re-healing the same wounds because you don't want to let go of the story." Reading that sort of triggered me and really encouraged me to unblend what was then and what is now and move on myself. How did it make you feel? If you are trying to let it go and you just simply cannot then you might need additional concentrated trauma work. I will have resources listed for this at the back of the book. For now let's move on.

The mechanisms for pain and self-hate. Children are constantly watching their moms and dads and siblings. They hear the things we say on the phone (but only our one side!), they hear us deny compliments (little gifts from others), they hear us berate ourselves (oh mommy is so stupid/fat/clumsy) and overhear almost all conversations. They are like little detectives; especially the exquisitely sensitive ones. They are on a mission to get to the bottom of things.

When someone paid your mom a compliment did she say, "thank you, oh that makes me feel so good," or deflect it and say back to them - "no, you look great?" Do you wonder what your kid is thinking when they hear their mom refuse a compliment? What if a mom blatantly called herself gross or complained about her appearance, or relationship? What if she said she is dumb, can't dance, or is bad at math? I am not saying we can't recognize our strengths and weaknesses, I am saying your kids and your soul is always listening to your words. They are like gold to them.

What about moms who won't accept compliments directed at their kids (in front of them)? I have heard people compliment a mom for something about the child - and she refuses it ☹ This upsets me so much and I see it frequently. Mom 1: *"Your Johnny is so talented, he was wonderful in the play lead."* Mom 2: *"Oh, well he worked hard, he had to. He is not great at singing."* I appreciate your humility? but oh my goodness, enough.

If you call yourself names saying you are ugly, your children will likely do the same. If you allow others to take advantage and harm you, your children will likely allow that as well. If you make choices because you don't like yourself, your children will too. Although it is almost impossible to get it right consistently, what we can do is model self-love, love them, help them make decisions consistent with self-love. We can provide context to challenging things (including our parenting decisions), unconditional positive acceptance, and loving guidance (that is never over- or under-mothering). You can admit to your children you don't know all the answers, you can say sorry, I was wrong about that (even things from 15 years ago). You can say, *"this is really not about you - more about me and my childhood, but I don't want you to go to that event." "I trust you, but I don't trust that situation, or the dad who is chaperoning."* You can say *"there is nothing you could do that would make me love you less, you are amazing, I believe in you, I am here for you, I support your decisions, I am invested in you. I honor you! I adore you and all parts of you."* There are many things to say to help your children. Please seek out advice on parenting. A great place to start will be Dr. Shefali Tsabary. If you Google her and watch some videos you will see ☺

Finally, the motivation for your behaviors as a parent (and when you think about your parent's behaviors) will be obvious to your child even if you don't think they are. You might want to consider loving YOURSELF some more, so you can move around in your parenting relationship authentically and behave with self-love. This will allow you to have unconditional love for your child, and will in turn be much more likely how they "turn out."

Teach kids to celebrate the right stuff. The bleeding hearts for the wrong cause get vocal when all the children are getting participation trophies (instead of just giving trophies to the winners.)   Have you heard this? They think - *oh no, all these kids are going to grow up feeling winners.* Oh the horror. That guy is mad because we are *"teaching kids to be soft and that they can all win."* Yes, that is exactly what we should be teaching our kids. Teaching them to compete with their friends causes broken knee caps of figure skaters, cheerleaders moms killing other cheerleaders, bullying, murders on Facebook, killing over boyfriends/girlfriends. Screaming at your 6-year-old in the T-Ball stands to knock some lights out, or losing your mind because an umpire calls your kid out, or paying thousands of dollars for voice lessons for your teen so she can be the star of the school play each year - are indeed not what we should be teaching our kids. These instead are some examples of ridiculousness from ignorant parents. Of course, all children will learn they won't win. Of course, all children will learn to compare themselves with their peers on social media (which is a series of fantasy posts-to make people feel better about themselves, that again does the exact opposite). Why make it harder? Let's teach the kids the right stuff!

I believe the awards and accolades should be given out for participating in life, for showing up, being creative, trying new things, putting yourself out there. The trophy should not be for the 1% of the race "winners" in a race about nothing. Who is fastest? Who gives a fuck? I mean if your kid does, okay. But how many things did you do when you were young because you wanted to do them? How many kids are doing sports because they want to? Beauty pageants? Even spelling bees? So often these kids are fulfilling the parents unrealized dreams. Of course taking them to activities you as the parent are interested in is better than paying them no attention at all, but I am not giving you your parenting trophy yet.

By rewarding the life participation piece we are not showing them they are weak, can't stand to lose, or not to have high standards. We are showing them the real reward and trophy IS for participating in life! Being engaged in life! Creating something they like! Getting off of the couch! Connecting with others - in healthy ways! Showing up! As I mentioned before, there will only be one winner (sports, CEO, Grammy winner, valedictorian). Most of the time it won't be you or your kid (you know - I mean you should know this). When we reward only the top 1% (or less) of our society and expect our kids to be in that miniscule percentage we set them up for failure. We can understand how ridiculous that is and what a mistake in parenting! Do you see how that makes people cheat, take steroids, harm their bodies, harm other's bodies, steal? Why create such unrealistic and unhealthy expectations (that are not even about the important things in life!) to foster their self-hate and lack of self-acceptance. Isn't that insane?! Life is all about participating. That is the joy, participating in the present moment. It is not the 5 minutes on the podium where you receive your award. Have you ever won an award? It is great for literally 5 minutes. Telling your child that the meaning of life is that 5-minute episode is dumb and a parenting mistake. If we make life about the 1% of winning times, then 99% of our kids, 99% of the time are going to be "losers" and feeling it. How could they not be depressed and anxious?

When you can, point out the things your child is doing right! Give them an affirmation when things are tough (e.g., I am worthy of good friendships). Covey your acceptance. Love them for who they are even when they had a hard day, don't just chime in and point out what they did wrong, or berate the other kid. See them, hear them. You can point out truths when you need to (e.g., *maybe your delivery was the problem, but that is okay, it is hard to get that right every time, what could you do differently next time?*). Be an encourager, be a servant to help them love and accept themselves. Be slow to judge and practice compassion. Help them feel good about themselves and foster their good decision making. You can ask questions to help guide them to acknowledge what they are good at, or what they like. Then display confidence that they will make the right decision, so they feel like you trust them and they can trust themselves too. Of course believe in their ability to succeed, of course support THEIR dreams, but let's not be ridiculous.

Your loving guidance is not about making decisions for them, it is helping them feel good about themselves so they can make good decisions and feel empowered. Once they are grown they will be making their decisions and you will be happier if they are confident decision makers (as will they)! They answer to God and themselves ultimately, not you (or at least not after they left your house AND we need to get them to that point).

Siblings. We as parents contribute to problems by comparing them to their siblings (who they most likely loved before we interfered by doing that!). This makes children feel like others are better, envy their sibling, and hate themselves. Even if your kid just incorrectly assumes you like the sibling better they will take on some activity to get your attention. If you go out of your way to tell them their sibling is better (imbalanced compassion toward the kids; participating in making fun of one child with the other child; spending visibly more time care-taking one of the siblings; actually verbalizing - *why can't you be more like your brother, or you know Johnny does it this way*). If they think they can beat the sibling they may become competitive. Competitive about all things in life- especially about bids for other's attention. I often wonder why someone would date a married person. I think they do it to compete with an incumbent to see if they can win an attention bid. Back to children, if they can't win the attention, or beat the sibling, they may get depressed. If they can't think they can beat the sibling in the first place (because they are younger) they may drop way way out of the competition (and do bad things) to get your attention.

Let's please stop giving attention for the things WE want for our kids (outside of the idea of being happy, healthy, and participating in life), and this insane idea of "winning." Stop comparing, stop striving to have the kids live out YOUR missed t-ball fantasy. Be with them where they are. Love THEM. Teach them to love and accept themselves now *as is*. Nothing to fix, nothing to improve on. The main thing the kid wants from you is your attention, acceptance, validation, and love. Wouldn't it be nice to give them those things without conditions! That what is needed if we want a happy and healthy society.

Should you chime in and solve problems in the sibling relationship? The rule when I was knee deep in reading the parenting resources was- you let them handle it unless one would get hurt. Those resources meant physically, because we didn't know about the negative effects of emotional abuse. Well, may I tell you that you have permission (and encouragement) to step in at the very early stage of emotional abuse and torment (yes, cruel words in addition to punches). Even off handed comments about a body part, lack of intelligence, being clumsy, from the revered sib can be harmful. It is not healthy for a child to hear their big brother or cute little sister tell them they are a piece of shit. That is very damaging and the children just don't know how to process it. It definitely gets internalized as a hit to self-love and possibly a catalyst for self-hate.

Sometimes you are trying to be funny and when one sibling sort of picks on another (or makes fun of him) we laugh or chime in to also be funny. I found that children do not understand these bids for humor when they are about them, or sarcasm when it is about them, or when you are trying to act cool. It is not funny and they just end up thinking there is something wrong with them. I had to turn in my comedian wanna-be hat for my better-at-the-parenting job hat.

Sure, encourage their ideas and behaviors. Quit projecting your pain and your goals on to your kid! Just sit with them. It is their life, about them, NOT you. Ask them what they want and then help them tend their garden. You are the daily visitor who brings the tools they ask for.

Listen to the children (and make eye contact: look like you are listening). I don't know where it is written we shouldn't listen to children. We can and should ask them about what they want and need. I was at a friend's house and a preacher was on the television in the background. The preacher just got done saying how we should listen to others and I was like, Oh good! Then he started making fun of parents for listening to their kids! He was chastising a mom he saw in a parking lot who asked her kid why she didn't want to get in the car. He made fun of her!! He used a sweet, mocking voice. The crowd laughed. He said, *sometimes you tell the child to just get in the car. You know what is good for them!* I pointed out the hypocrisy in that 3-minute talk.

I imagined having a conversation with this preacher lunatic where I said, hey, um, you just said we need to do more listening. Are you saying we don't have to listen to children though? At what age do we get to be heard? I thought life began in utero, preacher? Do you think Jesus woulda said, *get in the car kid*, or would he have just asked, why don't you want to get in the car? What is wrong with asking your kid what is wrong and listening for a change? Why do you think you know better and can keep preaching what everyone should do? What is this an 80s movie?

This exact same thing happened in front of me outside of a store (so I am now betting it is pretty common where the kid doesn't want to get in the car - who knows why? You know who knows, the kid. Ask him). A dear woman was trying to get her squirmy 2-year-old into her minivan. In the past I would skulk by uncomfortable parenting moments in public, now I always stop and see if I can help. I always open by being on the mom's side. This "mom" was actually the grandmom. She was a lovely lady and just had back surgery, couldn't get this squirm bundle into the car and she couldn't bend over. Surprisingly, she was being so nice about it! I complimented her and asked if I could help. She said yes! I got down and looked in this kids eyes for a few seconds. It was about 6 long seconds of eye contact where I saw his eyeballs and communicated love during it. I did that by having my smiling eyes (I smile when I look at someone) on. He immediately stopped whaling. With my smile still on I said, *Hi. I am helping your grand mom, you know it is time for you to leave and she would like you to get in the car. Why don't you want to get in the car?* I just waited still making eye contact trying to be calm and friendly. He thought about it. I gave him the time. Finally he said, I didn't know! I said, oh, I understand! Then I said, well your grand mom's back hurts and she can't bend down but she needs you to get in the van. He said, oh. I said, would you like me to help you to get in the van. He said, Yes! I lifted him up and put him in his car seat. The grandmom couldn't believe it. I guess she had been out there more than 30 minutes with him. I don't know how she didn't lose her patience, but she didn't. I told the kid he was a champ and thanked him for helping his grandmother like that. He smiled. Tantrum over. Self-hate session thwarted. Under five minutes spent. Priceless. The preacher can ask you to laugh at me, or you can stand up for what you know is the right thing to do when it comes to taking care of your children. Your main job - in this life.

If I hear a parent tell their kid one more time...."you know what you should do...." I am going off the deep end. Let me tell YOU what you should do. Shut up. You listen to your beautiful gardener. Let them tell you how you can be of assistance to them. That is your job. It is not the other way around.

The first step in fixing this mess is to regain your (the parent's) self-love, so your kid gets sprung from fixing you, and gets to live their own life. I don't know if we were all ready to hear that just now and I am sorry about it. please consider it. Spread the word. Thank you for having such a brave and open mind!

I am here to teach you how to love yourself, forgive yourself, clear away resentment, live a life where you are happy and engaged, release your special gifts to this world. You are here to teach your kids the same. You do this by being a good role model of your conscious self-love. You do this by being aware of this amazing opportunity to beautify the life of another human being. Honestly, what could be more important?

What about Single Parent Households? There are things that can go right and wrong in single parent homes. I remember when contemplating divorcing my husband of 10 years (my high school boyfriend, the father of my two boys, the guy I was with since 6 months after my dad died) after the second time he cheated on me with a long drawn out intimate and physical relationship with another brand-new work person. I did a lot of research on the effects of divorce on children. There were pros at the time. The household stress would diminish, the kids wouldn't be subject to the constant fighting, bickering, and harsh stares (from both of us!). Sometimes I would cringe at the "lessons" he was teaching my children with his unconscious parenting and unexplored subconscious father or mother wounds that were certainly making my children feel shame, blame, and unworthy. It is hard to be a good parent or father when those issues are still hanging around. Still, I didn't want them to think this is what a healthy marriage (or parenting) would look like, or that this is what they could expect from a relationship.

I know we are all on our own sovereign journey, but what happens when you are living with someone on a journey from hell and they are starting to hurt you and your kids! From my end I thought that man was so flawed I personally didn't want him to even be around the boys, and especially right after the second affair when I was finally standing up for myself-and he was MEAN to me right in front of the kids. Who wants their kids growing up watching someone verbally or emotionally abusing them? Who wants to see a grown man so frustrated that he starts to emotionally abuse his kids? As we are learning, this is hugely damaging! The boys loved me and their dad (despite his abuse of them). Watching their hero berate and emotionally torture their mother was a confusing and painful reminder of the lack of love in the world and for them. What to do in this situation?

Providing context to stop subconscious story development. Many many women come to me with this exact same situation. It is heartbreaking. It is not a decision for anyone to make but the person living through the turmoil. One thing I recommend that I have heard is helpful is to provide context to the children about the damaging words. If we intervene when the words are going in, they may not be seen as traumatic and indicted into the subconscious as such. It is our perception of an experience that makes it traumatic. You can diffuse damaging words from fathers or others in real time for your children by **providing context** about verbal or emotional abuse (*"that is not true what daddy just said, everyone makes mistakes; when people are angry they call you names, but that is not the right way. Even when you are angry you can treat people with kindness and respect. your dad was wrong to do that*).

Providing context is NOT about retelling stories of him cheating on you, or blaming him for the demise of your relationship. Providing context is when you diffuse verbal and emotional abuse aimed at your child (or you in front of your children) to explain the truth with love, kindness, and compassion. Providing context to a child stops a trauma story from entering his or her subconscious mind!

Single parent homes require one parent doing double duty of providing/giving to the children. It is really challenging to get this right. The best way to make sure, is for you to practice conscious self-love, treat your ex with compassion, and even pray/hope for their self-love growth. You can also understand how most every interactive behavior between you to (or eye roll, or actual out loud fight) can be difficult for children. You must also practice your self-care behaviors and reward yourself when you can, so you can muster good and authentic care for your other charges.

Then there are two add ons that can make the situation even more challenging to process. Here is Add On #1: The mom has no compassion for the dad, the kid, or herself because the mom is so accustomed to beating up herself and then just projects all of that harshness and bitterness onto the kids (her ex's children). In this scenario there is very little recognition that the child would be hurting and it is mostly about the mom's challenges (imbalanced compassion to the selfish side). Add On #2 presents when the mom has too much compassion for the kids, recognizes this colossal challenge and feels so guilty for causing them this calamity (practicing compassion steps 1 and 2, but not the most important one-number 3 where she realizes and understand that we, all of us, are human, and it is only possible to be imperfect; impossible to not make mistakes, and when we make a mistake we are to love and forgive ourselves). Based on her daily berating of herself for ruining her kid's lives she indulges the kid in the name of imbalanced compassion and we have an entitlement problem on our hands.

It is hard for kids to be on either end of these parent scenarios (preoccupied parent, lack of compassion parent, or the guilty parent). The magic elixir for all three manifestations is the Awareness of what is happening (the projection), catching yourself while doing it (sit down, unzip your heart, get your unconditional love to you and your kid), and instead relate to you, him, and the situation with compassion.

For me, the last hardest lotus petal for me to shine up was self-compassion. For sure I was not practicing compassion for others and I was judging. I was doing this because I didn't have self-love and without that, I am afraid self-compassion is a no show. I decided to actively try and develop these two things because I was sick of chastising myself for my "poor" decisions and felling like I messed up. For me I had to untangle a subconscious pattern of doing something wrong. Sadly the call to action came because I saw my youngest son taking it on. I don't know if I modeled it and he adopted it, or if I conditioned his environment with my words to him about him needing "to fix" himself and his stuff (that there was always more fixing to do). It hurt my heart to figure it out and now write about it because it was certainly not what I intended to do. I didn't know about the two steps to break the abuse cycle (to be better than my mom; but also resurrect my conscious self-love). To give him that legacy of inner critic to criticize and hate himself and others required a lot of undoing. It is even harder for our kids because in this day and age hating yourself can manifest with much more problematic consequences (i.e., when you hate yourself you do drugs, cut yourself, want to punish yourself).

My other problem was I didn't recognize that growing up without a dad around can be traumatic for a boy. I was so sure I protected my son from trauma of obvious bad stuff, that I didn't understand or do anything about gender role trauma which can occur just because males lack appropriate male figures during their child development and become confused about male role expectations. I kept thinking how I was protecting him from trauma, but I didn't. The consequences of **gender role trauma for males** can be destructive and devastating. I wonder how many young, sensitive, and bright men that we lost to drugs, suicide, gang violence were trying to cope with and figure out their **gender role trauma**. If I could go back in time I think I would be sensitive to this fact. Instead of protecting my children from this man I thought so flawed, I could have provided a better context for them to process things differently. I could have listened more and been more sensitive. I didn't trust men at that time, so I didn't find a male substitute for them. I had heard stories of molestation by uncles, boy scout leaders, sports programs, church people, and others abusing boys. It was on my mind and I am sure projected out as well. I thought I was do doing my due diligence of protecting my sons.

Young men need to learn how to be a man from other men. If you are not a man, or don't know one, then pray for a good male way shower to step in, or better yet, you go and find a male helpful (who will not abuse them or who is not one drugs/alcoholic) for your sons. If there is still no man around **provide context** and give resources (books, article/ video links) as that will be extremely valuable. Chris D'Elia the comedian provided his listeners with a helpful podcast and phone number to text him (I am guessing his fans are mostly young men). What a gift from this decent role model/way shower. When my son would get depressed I would ask him if he listed to Chris lately, or I would sit with him and ask him to play us his current podcast. Never give up - even when it gets hard. The key to not giving up is to take your moments to practice conscious self-love, especially the self-compassion piece. Doing this for even a little while will get your head right for kinder and more helpful interacting.

Finally, we know from research that good decision-making capabilities and patterns of thinking (made possible by the prefrontal cortex) don't really show up until the age of 25. Before that children (yes, even up to 25) are making decisions with their limbic systems (based on emotions and social factors). This is why influencing their peer group decisions (and monitoring peer interactions) is crucial. This is also why social media is a real destructive force for our young iGen right now. We think these kids are arrogant and entitled, but they are traumatized, confused, and need our assistance to get to 25. Plus when children have ADHD (which all kids seem to have been diagnosed with these days) experts say their thought processes, decision making capability, and behavior is really 3 years younger than their actual age. Put that in your pipe and smoke it! To say these kids and this generation needs our assistance is the understatement of the year. Get ready to be on call to 25-28 if you want to get this right.

I dare say my lack of conscious self-love (and insistence to try and get love from external sources) led me to be distracted. My lack of taking care of myself because I didn't feel I deserved love, led me to not pick up on these crucial things, or provide better care to my kids (although as you can feel that was NEVER my intent). Still, to blame ourselves and feel guilty is not the answer. We are NOT to give up hope. We NEED to get back in the parenting game (yes until 25 in some cases), AND to practice your self-compassion (which you will do when you practice conscious self-love) so you can do your very very best without feeling depleted, deflated, or regretful. My lack of practice of conscious self-love was the reason for most of these problems in the first place.

Although my awareness was painful for me in the moment and for a bit of time, it was essential to undo - to help that precious soul I was charged with taking care of. The other option would be for him to make the decision for himself (his awareness of patterns and his conditioning); and that would be okay, but likely not possible until much later in his life. I feel proud and happy I started the process by sharing my news and making repairs in real time! I am glad I owned my mess and made a conscious decision to stop making messes! I did this by making my subconscious, conscious. For some, this insight about you stepping out of your story skin may be enough to do it! For some, this awareness might be step one and then integrating it (working on shaking it off, so you can step out of it) might be step two. For some, you might need assistance with step one if there is buried info. For others, you might need assistance with step two. I can recommend that the time you take to work on the story redo/release (repatterning) be done when you have time. The process will take how long it takes, but take breaks. There is no reason to have it on your mind 24/7. I remember being in that mode and it was kind of a dark time. Remember though, that is not the point of this lesson to create more suffering. The point is to get conscious. To see the truth of the matter that I wasn't loving myself, or that I was even deserving of my love. My life got better when I planned time in my day to work on it and then let it go for the day. You can still wake up each day happy and plan for joy and love and good things and at 3 pm work on your repatterning, then have a nice dinner later :)

What about the really hard stuff? Remember how I said if your parent's didn't practice compassion toward themselves (which is very common) and they were beating themselves up for small and large mistakes and trying to be perfect, I am pretty sure you are doing the same thing. Well, when you think you are a piece of shit you need to escape from that. If children believe they are constantly messing up and that their parents think they are a piece of shit - they need to escape from that. Even if you don't go out of your way to tell your kid he/she is a piece of shit, if you think you are - you will project that, and your kid will think THEY are a piece of shit. Feeling like you are constantly messing up (because of too high of expectations/standards) is painful! We can see why people would want to escape from that pain. I really believe compassion for our mistakes and other's mistakes (parents help your children) is the answer. Self-compassion requires you grow in conscious self-love. If you really want to help your child or another human, the first and most important action to take is to start practicing conscious self-love, along with its self-compassion, especially for the third step about just being human! I want to open with that before I bring down the hammer. I am not saying you caused what is wrong with your kid! I am saying you are not responsible for the problem, but you are still responsible to/for your child (yes, even though she is on her own journey).

One of my kids, my brother's kids, my friend's kids, my neighbor kids struggles with anxiety, depression, substance use/abuse, suicidal thoughts and/or addiction. Can you read that sentence and not relate? Of course you can. Is it going to be helpful for me/you to be wrought with guilt OR ignorance, no; that would lead me to act with enabling behaviors and/or denial. That is NOT helpful.

Could we say my lack of self-love, self-compassion, and self-care, and my perfectionism (and my modeling of this) contributed to this scenario. Of course. It is helpful to have this awareness and to make reparations. Yes. It actually must be done. Finding the balance between needing to be drug czar or warden (because your child lies about drugs and even threatens to kill themselves) or you might miss something, and allowing them to grow and learn is no easy feat. The reparations aren't in the form of more money for drugs, too much freedom, or us giving up, or us ditching them until they go to rehab. The reparations are about you giving yourself more love, acceptance, and compassion AND then doing this for your children. This will in turn change your role from family drug czar and police commissioner to a parent (in charge of providing love and validation to your child) who understands everyone makes mistakes. Really feel that and express it. Even if you are angry, scared, frustrated, or pissed off. .

What if you said something like, *I am reading this book about self-love and I feel so bad some of my lack of self-love or unconscious parenting behaviors might have contributed to how you feel about yourself. I am so sorry. I love you with all my heart and will forever. I am here to support you and I want to make changes starting today. Right now this means I completely accept you and have compassion for this struggle. I realize how hard it must be. I would like to help you. What would my help look like to you? (listen with eye contact) How can I help? (listen with eye contact).* Communicate your caring and love. You might be surprised what you find out! What if your kid says they want more money for drugs, or to just go out with the kid who is the bad influence. You can say something like…*Since you have the addiction/depression/suicide thoughts now and your idea of what is helpful may not be the best for your health (or helpful to others) I have the right to decide if I will do what you are requesting and what I can do for you and we can talk about it). I am respecting and loving myself more. I just want that so much for you too, honey.*

Obviously it is much harder to recover from addiction than to not start using. People who practice conscious self-love take care of their bodies and know they deserve their and other's love. The exact opposite is true for people who use substances and are considering harming themselves. This is no easy feat to address though. For your child or you! Living with a child with addiction, mental illness, or a problem that requires your concern and worry on a daily basis is overwhelming, disruptive, and a constant reminder of pain. I know. Living with adults with addiction or a personality disorder is also not easy. Nothing about it is easy. How can you give your child (or your other adult) AND YOU love during such a challenging situation? Awareness, compassion (for both of you - and balanced!), forgiveness, good messages about conscious self-love, good messages acknowledging mistakes are a part of human nature AND we can stop beating ourselves up about them. The belief and HOPE that things will get better AND that you are a way shower of those two important things and you are moving forward with conscious self-love for yourself and to teach you kid. Show you care. Never give up on this kid or yourself. You can do it!

For me, I loaded on the context. I admitted I didn't know what to do (to myself and my kids). So I told them I was going to find some resources and get assistance. I gave them so many books. I know they read a lot of them! I enlisted almost all the people in my resources section (subconscious repairs) for my sons. Family Constellations therapy, regular therapy, spiritual therapy, karma clearing, resonance repatterning. I told them it is good to get help, and made sure they knew they were not crazy, messed up, or a family embarrassment (who gives a shit what anybody thinks - that is not the main concern here). Give your kid (and you) permission to take care of themselves and permission to dream/believe in a brighter future, just right around the corner - even though it doesn't seem like that right now - no matter what happened in the past.

Most importantly display your deep care for this precious life in front of you. *I love you and care about you! No matter what! Check out this book, I want you to go talk to a professional because I am worried about you, I am here to help you, I want you to be happy. Hang in there! I know I am on your case all the time, but I am trying to help. My version of helping may not seem helpful to you, what would help look like to you?* Start listening. Sometimes I didn't know what to do. A great piece of advice I received at such a challenging time was, "hang in there, you will be guided about what to do." It was a game changer for me. I made it my mission to get quiet so I could hear and feel my golden guidance for my sons. In the meantime, I listened, stop fixing, offered help on their terms. I visualized a milestone event about 5 years down the road (graduation, their wedding, their child's baptism, a family vacation) and meditated on it. I called that future into reality. I believed, hoped, and prayed. I talked with my sons about good things in their future (not pressure, but things to look forward to - that they liked). I told them I loved them and cared for them every day. Some say we are here to learn about how to let go of attachments. I think some life lessons are about the opposite. It is a miracle and a true gift of spirit to love another person even more than yourself. To care deeply about a loved one or friend is a joy and gift of a lifetime. Let's appreciate the gift, have faith in the future, and stop worrying that they/us are messing things up. Find joy in this relationship, whatever it looks like right now!

Forgive me for bringing down the hammer. Sometimes bringing down the hammer is the most conscious self-love (and other-love) choice to make. If any of the words in this section are resonating with you, I cannot think of a better time to start praying. I will spare you details, but I am certain God pulled me and my loved ones out of many a sticky wicket! Praying also always helped me feel better, make positive outcomes more possible because I was worrying less and through my unwavering faith and belief!

Helping Your Relationship Partners Love Themselves

What do you think is the goal of relationships? I came up with - the goal of relationships is to sit with another person in harmony and enjoyment, where both people are seen and heard and the time spent together is valuable and appreciated. Wow, how many of those relationships do you have going on right now? A fun fact is researchers demonstrated on average women speak 4,000 words per day and men speak 2,000. Once the words are used up people will prefer to not use more. Keep that in mind ☺

It is essential our relationship partners love themselves if we want to have a happy relationship. It is essential all societal members start loving themselves more if we want to live in a safe and happy world. As in the previous section, the first, best, and most important thing you can do for your relationship and the other person - is to love yourself. Once that happens, stuff falls into line!

It is amazing how your partner shapes up and gets really good at things once you start taking care of yourself and loving yourself. ☺ There is a smiley here and I hope you caught the joke that your assessment of him/her shaping up had really nothing even to do about him/her!

When you become self-aware and make personal changes, you will see/feel your relationships improving. You can also enlist relationship assistance. There is a lot of help around, even on the Internet, so you have to be an informed consumer and listen to your inner guidance about what feels right and what doesn't. I think the best help would be where you give love to heal their wounds, or both of your wounds together. I already mentioned Harville Hendrix and IMAGO therapy for relationships. The point of IMAGO therapy is to become aware of your past hurts from your parents, understanding them, then releasing the past hurts, and moving forward with love for the other. What a wonderful gift for you and your partner to (1) show up loving yourself!, and then (2) love them for who they truly are.

One way to show your love is to listen to others. Honor them. Listen to them like their words and feelings matter to you. We can do this via processes called holding space or active listening.

Holding Space for another. When we **hold space** for another - we are metaphorically walking on their path for a moment - with them - whatever is happening for them. We are using our active listening skills and we are not thinking about what to say next, how we should tell them to solve their problem, how we would solve their problem, or thinking wow how do they keep getting into these messes, none of that. There is no judging. There is no fixing. There is no making them feel inadequate (which could happen if we offer too many solutions), AND we are not trying to impact the outcome. Can you remember ever once having a conversation like that? I think as a teacher, counselor, parent, my eyes were always on the problem solving.

I've come to realize I have no business solving another's problem. It might seem like others want advice or to solve for them, but even then, I found when giving advice it puts people in a spot where they might feel compelled to take it, or don't want to take it, but don't know what to say. Do you see how giving advice puts you at the center of this space? I also remember having a problem and asking a friend what she would do, then I'd ask another, and another, until the final person I asked advised me to do what I knew I wanted to do all along - I was just looking for support/confirmation/permission! It is most likely the case we know in our soul (not our ego) how to best solve our problem. We need to peel away the interferences that may be coming from the ego, or some other misinformation. Sometimes we need to talk through the details to see clearly. Sometimes we need to get support that our idea for solving is appropriate. The gift of holding space is where we give our heart to the moment of another's journey with nonjudgmental support and anticipate they will arrive at the problem solving for their highest good (something we cannot really know). An amazing note is, we can also hold space for ourselves! Try it!

We actually reap benefits when holding space for others too! Our vibration rises, it feels good to really help people. We also get better at holding space for ourselves, and are less judgmental with us. When we increase our ability to hold space for ourselves and others we learn to be more present and confident in our experience and expression of feelings/thoughts, and to take action when necessary because we heard ourselves and processed. When we hold space we elevate our consciousness to a different level. We refine our awareness to the subtleties of the energy and words of the person. To do this we must be mindfully in the present moment, our only goal is our deep sincerity.

Practicing present moment awareness, mindfulness, and meditation can get us to a place where we can listen to others (and ourselves) without latching on to intruding thoughts and impulses to problem solve, which will interfere in our honest attempts to hold space. Marianne Williamson has a great strategy for getting started with space holding. She says we can set the intention (even ask God) to fill our minds with thoughts of acceptance and fill our hearts with love. Then we ask for help (set an intention) to be nonjudgmental in our listening, be totally present, seeing the person you are with as innocent, and if there is anything to say at the end of the listening we will get the message from the Divine.

Marianne Williamson says miracles happen in the presence of compassion and nonjudgmental listening - we are the faucet - not the water (the person's words are the water, we are just letting them spill it out). She also says that when we try to fix things for others or give advice (when we really don't know what is best in another's situation) they might miss a lesson from some emotional pain that will ultimately help them greatly and move them to a better place. It would also be imprudent to give clichés or misguided advice based on our limited understanding of what they are expressing.

For Marianne, holding space means bearing witness to another's suffering, giving people permission to feel their feelings, with our eyes on the growth that will come from it, and to stay absolutely convinced that joy awaits them beyond this moment. It is not always easy. You can imagine it would be difficult to bear witness to another's suffering without trying to fix something, or yourself being triggered if you have had a similar situation.

My very good friend called me on her way to work the other day and I could hear how upset she was. She shared about her hard morning on her son's birthday and how her husband was making her feel small, wrong, unappreciated, and now this final straw for her-being a bad example to her beautiful sons. She said she was wondering if she should just leave him. I was surprised, but I absolutely could relate. I could've called up several times in my life with my ex-husband, but during this conversation I stayed **present and listing**. This is **holding space** for another.

I wanted to chime in at several points to say what an asshole he was, or tell her what she should do. I didn't. I stopped those thoughts as they popped in and returned to my active listening for my friend. I understood everything and conveyed my understanding and empathy with sounds. When she was all done venting I waited. I waited a little more and showed I understood and felt her pain with, *oh, honey*.

Then I asked a question about something in the story about how the husband's mom was just over and picking on him in a very critical way. I also know my friend had a narcy dad and was constantly picking on her. I just shared the projection insight and said, oh my, it is like he is doing to you what just happened to him with his mom, but he is not seeing it. Fortunately my friend is brilliant and willing to face her lessons head on. She stopped talking. I knew she was processing this important gem. Then I said, and gosh isn't this so interesting he is treating you like his mom treated him and how your dad treated you! She was quiet again. So was I.

This awareness for this exchange that happened to her today before work on her son's birthday that almost had her calling her marriage quits (certainly it was not just this one incident -this was a pattern and today she had just had enough) was not even about her or her husband. This lovely gal then said, *oh wow, you know I used to run away from my dad and hide in my bedroom and shut him out. Do you think that is why I am thinking of leaving him for this fight today?* I didn't even have to answer this question.

The listening, the few questions, and support, and encouragement, and her willingness to practice compassion for herself and another got her to this increased awareness of projection, mirrors, the past. I shared info on self-love and how even if her hubby is not aware of it, it will be okay for her if she is….. if SHE can practice conscious self-love. I wasn't encouraging her to stay put where she didn't want, but I wasn't encouraging her to blow that asshole off either (which is what my first thought was and if I would've stopped holding space for her - stopped being present with her at that moment I would've have not been helpful and maybe even said that). Instead she left the conversation feeling heard and supported (which is really all she wanted from her husband anyway).

It was nice I did that for her, but it was nicer that I told her how to do it for herself! She left this 30-minute call in such a different place. I was thinking of resources to send her so her hubby can get to a place of conscious, but who knows if he wants that. And just so we all know, it is okay if only one person in the relationship is conscious. Because my dear friend had that insight, she can help him if she wants; but most importantly, her experiences with this unconscious (but kind and a good soul) person will be perceived by her in her new and improved compassion and kindness lens. For today. It is a process okay ☺

This special type of listening (holding space and also called active listening) and "being" with a person will the most wonderful gift! It will help the person get those difficult emotions, thoughts, and that story **out of the head**.

Just listen. We want it out of the head, so it doesn't fester and get adopted into the subconscious for more festering! We want it out of the head, so your lens isn't clouded and you can't see the good things. We want it out of your head so you don't run around looking for confirmation of more shit for you today. Once the thoughts/emotions are out of the head they can be set up for processing (letting go) or problem solving. You will initially want to solve the problem for your friend (basically anyone you are listening to). We are fixers/problem solvers by nature! Your friend does not want you to tell you what to do, they really just want you to listen and agree with them. Your friend's True Self doesn't want you to tell it what to do either. The goal is to listen, so your friend can learn about this situation, maybe it is a lesson, so they can discover something useful for the future.

You listening and encouraging their new awareness and eventual problem solving (after the venting - the venting is important for awareness and shouldn't be skipped!). You listening but not solving fosters a person's need for self-determination (whereby a person practices free choice of decisions, behaviors, etc). The more self-determination, the less acting out, or bids for control/punishment. Even when someone asks me what they should do I turn that right back.... *What do you want to do?* It is not in my or their best interest to solve their problem for them. You can help people figure out what they want to do and empower them to have confidence in their abilities. That is the gift. That is the task for you when confronted with, *what should I do?* It is far easier for you than solving another's problem anyway, which is most of the time impossible. All people must solve their own problems. You also don't want to interfere with anyone's lesson or growth.

The best answer is always to return to a moment of love and attention and compassion for you and this person. Return to listening instead of judging, listing, fixing, worrying. Be there/here right now and honor you - if you are by yourself; or honor or you and this other person/people if you are not alone. Release the thought/feeling about the past or future - as only you can do that. In the **active listening** to the other person in this moment, really hearing them (not vestiges of your ex's patterns), or listening to your soul or higher self in this moment you will get the answer you need about a balanced response and when to take action.

I hope that example was a good one. Here is another. I had nurse friend tell me her 27-year-old son was making her SO angry and she kicked him out of the house. I first thought oh no, I have got to get this nice lady to a compassion place. She said she couldn't stand to watch him drink because it reminded her of her ex-husband (the alcoholic she hated). Still, her 27-year-old son had a job he went to everyday and was drinking on Friday and Saturday but it was too much for her to watch.

In my head I was thinking oh gosh each time she is yelling uncontrollably at her son - she was just really yelling at this image of her ex from the past, far outside of her self-awareness and present moment. This was hard for me because wow I could totally relate, but on the other hand I could practice compassion for her son (but wait not mine? it was a timely and good lesson for me!). Still, I fought the urge to veer out of my present moment to consider my woes and instead stayed with her holding space for her and I fought my urge to ask her if she connected her son and her ex by accident (until she was done venting).

I am sure we can all relate to this big struggle where someone is going to lose here. Is she is going to be awake every weekend night for the next 5 years of her life if she doesn't kick him out, or he is going to hear the words from his mother's mouth- I don't want you here anymore and kick his subconscious self-hate into overdrive maybe resulting in even more self-abuse. Yikes, an unfortunate struggle with seemingly no good outcome. I am all for setting up an environment of peace and joy. I will almost only accept invitations to peaceful things I want to do, watch/listen to joyful things I am interested in. What will we do when our loved one (our child who we charged with loving and guiding) is creating such a disruption in our daily peace.

Not an easy place to be, right, and it is all punctuated by the fact that maybe she was projecting some unresolved ex-husband issue on to her son. I certainly didn't know how to answer this for her, I certainly didn't know what to say and the best thing for me was to hold space for her to get her emotions out of her head! When that was done I could maybe point out the fact that she might (just might) be lumping her son with her husband and she might (just might) be projecting some anger issues onto her son (who I know she adores and was just beating herself up for being mean to him) by asking a clarifying question (not telling her she is doing that though). I could possibly help her see some things outside of her conscious awareness, and I could tell her she was doing the best she could (give her my compassion and kindness). She said, oh that's interesting, I didn't think about that, yeah I might be doing that - lumping him in with my ex. I could see her thinking about this important realization. I knew that at that moment of awareness she would be able to think about this situation from a different perspective (including her son's perspective). Also by me displaying compassion and kindness and encouragement for her she might be more likely to pass that on to herself. The more she relates to herself with love and understanding, the more she will relate to her son in the same way. There sure was a need for balanced compassion here.

In therapy, in helping yourself, in helping your friends there are two priorities. The first is to get the thoughts out of your/their head, venting (via holding space, your awareness, journaling). Next is to help yourself or another see the issue with self-love, acceptance, and self-compassion. Suggest a resource at the end if you know one. Otherwise just be happy you helped with listening and a reframe on how to be kinder to their soul. Always reward yourself for anything positive you do for you, or for another person.

Remember there will be challenges, things to vent! The challenges are gifts to remember to bring yourself and others to a place of internal self-love and self-compassion (that all important third step of self-compassion - it is okay to make mistakes). Without the challenges, your self-love might be egotistical, or not real. When I am particularly challenged I pray for the lesson to reveal itself and for quick resolution. Sometimes that is better than praying something away. If everything is too easy you might miss opportunities for soul growth. On the other hand don't make things harder. Balance.

To get the answers you have to be quiet. No run-away thoughts, emotions, worries, distractions, etc. In the present moment you can ask for guidance, return to peace, provide love and attention and acceptance to you and the other person. Then RELEASE! Release the thing taking you out of the present moment. Try it, you will like it, and you will protect your peace (and still be super helpful and nice to others).

The purpose of relationships. There is a dichotomy implicit in consciousness raising about the purpose of relationships and how we relate to others during transformation. This information stands at odds for me in terms of love. I find it very uncomfortable whenever I see it (trigger) and when I explore it. For me, I feel it interfered with my understanding of love and the purpose of relationships and I worry it might do the same to others.

Remember some people claim there are two emotions love and fear. Fear is the coin of the ego. I am no enlightened master, so my ego sits with us today (albeit quieter than before), and I am irritated about the possible mis-messages (that seem so ego driven) and quite possibly interfering with growth and self-love.

Do you recall I mentioned Harville Hendrix said relating to others and interacting within the context of our relationships is healing? All relationships, whether good or bad for you, have lessons. I believe this is true. I also believe what @Warrenzinger wrote on Instagram, "The people who do the most good in helping you unpack is anyone who causes you pain. The ones that treat you poorly, or do you wrong, those are the people opening your baggage for you; we just need to stop blaming them for what's in the luggage we packed."

So, relationships - all of them, good/bad are helpful, right? Well, this is NOT the message to be gleaned from the available food for thought on the Internet about what we are to do with relationships. I think this might come from very deep spiritual quotes being shared with people (me included) not quite ready for the information and we misinterpret it. It becomes a platitude and without proper context, we are getting a little mixed up.

You cannot go a day on Instagram or Twitter without hearing how evolving means eliminating, especially those *holding us back*. I always read the additional comments from that person's followers on these posts and get sad. One lady said, she's eliminating all people from her life and mind who hinder her from getting where she is going. Contrary to what we actually know, these are the very people to hold her mirror to get her there. See, how this is quite an unfortunate message and looks like it is promoting conscious self-love?

I really don't like missing access points for others and I think we should be more responsible with our platitudes - especially if we are coaches, or other professionals who others are looking to for our guidance; especially spiritual guidance. Dr. Margaret Paul said an interesting thing on her flourishtogether.com website, "when someone tells me they're further along than their partner in growth, I immediately know this isn't true-and they still need to heal." Just by you thinking you are good and your partner is the problem means you are/have the problem.

Vibrational discrimination/prejudice. I know you've read some of these messages about leveling up and leaving others who are not on your level behind. Here is a famous one….. you are like the five people you see most, so pick wisely. I think I am coining these terms - vibrational discrimination/prejudice. Vibrational prejudice is when you see and even feel, when you start to shift in vibration (on your path), and you recognize others are not on your level. You make judgments about them not being as high in vibration as you. The paradox is then revealed. That you are comparing, judging and thinking of eliminating connections (being ruled by your ego) suggests you are not high in vibration! Same here for vibrational discrimination - when you change your behaviors to exclude such people from your life, based on that ego judgment. You think you are leveling up and increasing your vibration, but sorry, this is a huge ego play and you might've leveled down.

My personal misunderstanding of these messages delayed my soul growth journey about two years. I kept thinking, *Okay - who am I going to kick out?* I also though, *wait a second here, I thought the benefit of vibrating higher was to improve relationships?* (I sort of liked my soggy chip relationships thank you.) Maybe I didn't want to change because it meant leaving some of those chips behind (interestingly, when I grew in self-love I learned - I was the soggy chip projecting my soggy chipness on these loved ones. Without these loved ones I wouldn't have had this insight).

I am sure the intent of the platitude is to be helpful. But is it helpful to encourage people leave relationships because you are currently not feeling served by them? I guess is okay if you want to lose certain people and you needed the permission to do so, but it seems to me the platitude is suggesting it is essential to lose some people in order to increase your vibrations.

The path is about you, not your externals. Your externals shine up as you grow, but I don't think we need to sell an intentional and required shedding of people "beneath" you. The idea that another human is beneath you and you are not to surround yourself is your ego talking. Maybe the intent is to help you leave toxic people behind? I am okay with that!, but it doesn't sound like that to me. Is the intent to have you be okay with your alone/quiet time? If so, I am all on board with that too. I didn't take the platitudes to mean that though (or they should've just said that!). The platitude made me feel like there is pressure to want to rise out of our cocoon and to shed the dead weight of other's around us who are not at our new and improved vibrational level.

When I checked in and addressed this common message from my authentic place of conscious self-love, I realized it was not true for me. I became okay with moving forward with all types of relationships. The message should really be to love yourself more.

Change is inevitable, change is good, and of course raise your vibration - by all means! In this process, you are changing you (loving yourself and others more, becoming more accepting of yourself and others more, more forgiving for you and the others, being less judgmental of yourself and others). This is the change we are looking for and it is about you! You are changing YOU, not the externals in your life.

We are grateful for these people, experiences, and lessons, and the beautiful mirror they hold up to help us grow and resolve all our issues. (they are helping us - these slugs even!). We don't have to drop them like they are hot because we grew. We can't control the misleading platitude poster's postings, but if you feel compelled when seeing such content, you might consider commenting your opinion. We can have healthy (and even growth promoting) attachments to people at a lower vibrational level than us! I promise!

We can play tennis with people at all levels - even if the people who are better at it than us are best for training. Still, we don't suddenly get bad at tennis if we play with someone at a lower level. Why would it be the case we need to leave people behind because they are not as good as us - is that even a thing? Also, sometimes you are the trainer and sometimes the trainee (in all things, right?!). Still again, not every single interaction has to be for training. All interactional experiences are important! They are the mirrors for us to see ourselves. We don't want to leave them behind for that matter alone. Also, some connections are just for fun, joy, and activity sharing. Why not?

Anyway, it should always be your decision - no matter what - about who you associate with. There should be no pressure on you to sit with relationships that make you uncomfortable, and similarly NO pressure to leave relationships that make you feel good because you "outgrew" them. If a relationship is making you uncomfortable from the inside (not the outside - because they are not woke yet ☺) then trust yourself and walk away. If people don't want to hang with you anymore because you changed, I guess that is okay, but check in (hold up your mirror) to see if you are exuding anything contributory.

If you do still like the low vibrators (ha), feel free to keep those chumps around lol. What if Jesus or Gandhi, or the other Masters were like *"Oh, well we're outta here because you guys not on our level. See ya. I am hanging with only those on my level."* To each his own, and you do what you want, but please don't fall for this negative coaching "advice." I trust you will know who you want to spend time with. There are no rules in the *consciousness manual* that prohibit high levelers from associating with low levelers. When you love yourself - you stop judging other people by their level anyway! Please people. How selfish and NOT in self-love anyway to just be thinking about who can serve US. Think about, who are we here to serve? I feel like it might be a case of shining up a spiritual growth petal, but us still lacking in conscious self-love to believe that we can't associate with those who didn't level up yet.

And finally, I don't think making fun of the people who are not evolving yet is great either. I follow a shaman on Instagram and he was going on an amazing Shamanic Journey - it sounded so exciting! Right before he left he posted, something I am sure he meant to be funny, but it said, "being "awake" isn't cool. It means having to dumb down 98% of your conversations everyday so you won't sound like a lunatic." I know I am being sensitive here and maybe even triggered, but I felt it was a little elitist. It is really not an *us vs. them* type of proposition. A group with high vibration should know better, so I am addressing my views here.

The answer to vibrational prejudice and discrimination is likely enlightenment, but on the way to that the answer is to practice conscious self-love. When you are practicing conscious self-love you are loving to yourself and others. For whatever reason you were discriminating or feeling others not worthy (a projection of you not being worthy), can be addressed by practicing conscious self-love.

When you embody measured compassion, kindness, and are willing to and make an effort to receive love there is no reason to FEAR that another human can or will bring you down. If anything, your practice of conscious self-love should influence people in the other way. The idea of leaving people behind is based on your ego and your fear. Neither very high in vibration ☺ You know.

Just who am I going to date anyway? If you are waiting to find a conscious partner, you might be waiting for a long time. It is far more common to come across a nice unconscious person than a nice conscious one. Still, you are sick and tired of never dating, right? OR, what if you blew off a good partner because they weren't into the consciousness raising like you. You read some platitudes and thought, oh, I need a better partner.

There is nothing wrong with questioning things of course, but why are you questioning this right now? Is it because you just read you need to leave certain relationships in order to grow? Did you read your soul mate is looking for you too right now, or do you feel you deserve someone on your level? I think that all of these questions are projections of your very own lack of self-love. The way we will correct that is not to find a new and improved version of a new person, but to work on your own self-love. Questions about relationships are more about the projections of our issues rather than the other person.

ALSO remember in relationships that we have connections and they serve as a mirror for us to grow. We need to be IN this relationship for this growth. Maybe now you are recognizing this dichotomy or imbalance. This lesson is FOR YOU to grow in your own self-love. This is not a sign for you to move on or find someone who loves you more or even someone more on your level. This is a sign to ponder more about your very own self-love and your feelings of worthiness of love. If you are constantly looking for someone better or different, it may be a mirrored reflection of your lack of internal love/acceptance feelings. We are not going to find better love outside until we get grow inside in our self-love…just something to consider.

To be honest, based on the amount of coaches and YouTube videos about relationships with people who are avoidant or insecure (mostly from abandonment and other issues in childhood!) I would intuit very few people are considered "securely attached." The possibility that you are with a perfect person with no flaws anyway is pretty slim. The first reason for this is there are no "perfect" people. And second, until you are practicing conscious self-love you are sending those "near perfect" people away because you are just not attracted to them. We keep picking people who match our vibration. Until you love yourself, you will keep picking people who also don't love you. Once you start growing in your self-love you can see before your eyes how your partner relates to you differently.

The goal is to love ourselves to the point where we do not need to rely on others for our love supply. We can focus on their behaviors and decide what to accept, what not accept, and what can you learn about yourself in this relationship. Remember, if you still carry your childhood abandonment issues, you select mates to mirror your thoughts about yourself. It is okay, that is all normal and part of the learning experience. Once you get comfortable with yourself inside, you don't need outside reassurance. You can focus on the behaviors of a person and communicate what you like and don't like.

Once we get more people on the conscious self-love train then we will find more securely attached people and we will actively choose to be with them! Before that, you might as well do yourself a favor, step back and realize almost nothing you are seeing in your partner is about them and nothing they are saying about you is about you per se - other than it is presenting a mirror and opportunity for you both to work on your issues. When your partner says he/she doesn't love you - what they are really saying is they don't love themselves. When your partner criticizes you about something - it is really a projection of some inadequacy they are seeing in themselves.

It is important to pay attention to constructive criticism so you can grow; however, most people are just spewing their projections about their own lack of self-love that you need to identify the source. Really look at the situation, try to parcel out what is about you if anything. Remember your love for yourself is going to need to come from the inside out. There is just no other way.

The Instagram post I felt compelled to discuss in an actual manuscript was from yesterday. I know this is our current mode of operandi even for those on the path to enlightenment. Just today I received an offer for a DailyOM course about leaving relationships that are not serving us and how to do it. I LOVE Daily Om by the way. I sign up for a few Daily Om courses each year and highly recommend them. This group charges as little as $15 for a course and you get excellent information. I am sure I am missing the point of this course from yesterday, but maybe not.

I actually took a class about writing down the qualities we wanted in a mate. It was helpful to get familiar with my likes and dislikes. I was probably not able to verbally express them until then, but for me I wouldn't find a person with such qualities until I grew in self-love and worthiness. I needed to realize that I did deserve my own love and other's love first. I don't know if the listing of perfect mate qualities will work until we smooth out our subconscious feelings of lack of love.

Moreover, those items on your list of the perfect mate are really a projection of how you want to be and what you want to do. They are completely about you. If you want to be as "happy" as the course satisfaction guarantee, then we don't go on a mission - seeking out the "perfect" person; this is a fantasy and it does not exist. You need to hear your relationship stirs/questions/midlife crises and develop your self-love. You be the person on your own list and then see what happens. ☺

Once you are clear on that and full of love and approval for yourself, you don't need love from others to repair you. You can seek love just for the fun experiences. You can go about your business serving others -because you are feeling your love and are satisfied that you don't need anyone else to take care of that - you did it all by yourself. We are most likely not here to get served by our relationships anyway. We are here to serve. Understand that your relationship discomfort is not coming from you needing a new and improved leveled up partner. Your relationship discomfort is coming from your lack of self-love and self-growth.

Don't mistake what is happening as a sign you need to move away from people. You need to move away from the old way YOU were relating with yourself and even others. Once you get clear on your self-love and you discover what behaviors you like and dislike in yourself and another human, then you can move away from a relationship if your needs are not being met. I think that is correct. I desire respect, kindness, a similar energy level (energy level is important and people often overlook this!) and another person who is high in self-love. That list is short because when you are with someone high in self-love there is a whole slew of extras to enjoy! When asked to develop a list of attributes of a desired partner, people usually note the petal attributes, but I don't even need to write them down. If you are high in self-love, I know the petals you have are in good, desirable shape!

Also, if you leave a relationship in a struggle stage without processing the anger and hurt you will likely draw in the exact same relationship with a different person. Moving on with peace in your mind and heart is the way to stop the merry go round of bad relationships. Fix what you need to in a relationship and most of it will be about you. Look at the mirror your challenging partner is holding up. What is the message from inside your soul you are sending out that is being reflected back to you. The benefit of not pulling an Irish Goodbye is that you get to work out the pain (insight for what your partner is triggering - where that stems from and how to fix it) and grow in understanding and self-love! Then your next relationship then will reflect your new way of relating to you.

We need things in this world to be a little less difficult right now. People need more tools. There is too much suicide, drug abuse, self-medicating, and violence, period. I know the importance of lessons and karma, and yes I get it, but I just think the lessons can be a little softer so people have more time to process them, or process them more gently. Time is of the essence here and the stakes are so much higher than they were - in the 1980s. Supporting community and connection (with all people - not only those on your level - and really not judging anyone's level anyway) being there for others, helping others by loving yourself and helping others love themselves should be promoted. More love, more friendship - not less. This idea that your growth requires shedding relationships and accepting that loss (unless toxic!) really should cease. Misinformed platitudes are works of the ego in sheep's clothing - stop it.

Loneliness versus being comfortable being alone. I also see a lot of sensitive souls sitting home more and being upset about this. In the beginning of my journey I sat home because I didn't trust men, women, or myself to be a good picker of mates or even experiences. It seemed I was uncomfortable in almost every situation outside of my house! I didn't even like to watch the news. I believed the discomfort was from the world being so icky and me finally understanding it. I thought oh well, I am just above all of this ick. But the discomfort was a great gift to help me see the externals weren't at odds, but my internals were. My lesson wasn't to hibernate more and stay out of life's experiences, it was, *"Hey girl let's work on your conscious self-love and self-worth and start living!"*

In reality (and before I started being uncomfortable on the outside) I did and very much like being alone. Now, it is not a matter of me thinking well, I could go here, but ick, no thanks (as it was before). It is a conscious choice. If you find yourself turning down invitations because your insides are telling you your time is better spent alone with yourself exploration or research, great! - please do that. If you are turning down invitations because your friends don't do yoga, or are not on your level, or you are worried they won't like the new you- then I don't love that. It might be the same behavioral outcome, but the motivation/intention for it and your perceptions about you and the world makes all the difference.

There is a problem with you perceiving yourself to be lonely. I just read being lonely is worse than smoking 15 cigarettes a day! If you are lonely and not engaging in life's experiences because you leveled up and no one else you knew did than sitting at home is not the right answer. Deepak Chopra noted, "Sometimes being alone can seem unappealing, boring, or even scary. But the art of spending time with yourself is one that you can hone in on and come to love."

You might not have things in common with your high school friends who have not evolved. You eschew invitations and feel those friends are beneath you now. As a result you might be missing some fun shared experiences (which again is okay, unless it is not - only you will know that answer) even if all they do is reminisce about the past. Your past, as un-evolved as might have been, is still a part of you. The lessons and experiences you learned back then are is precious. Indeed it is the self-awareness about these very experiences that is likely offering your valuable insights right now - it is your lesson, your friend!

This is the key to growth, not the avoidance of those people or memories. You might not want to attend the annual summer cabin booze fest where everyone just talks about everyone, (this is good that you are acknowledging your sensitivity and doing only things that are enjoyable for you!) but you might attend a ladies luncheon with the group, or engage one or two for a smaller get together. Remember we picked our families, and even communities to be born into. I have to think there is something important (some kind of lesson maybe?) we were supposed to glean from where we chose to incarnate (immediate families and childhood friends). Right? Let's take these experiences and relationships and make sense of them now as we are all grown up and have the right to do so (we did all along). We have the information and context to help us and we are no longer egocentric. The bottom line is - it is likely all relationships are important and have growth opportunities for both people.

Maybe we are here to serve others. I am sorry to bring this up, but the truth is, why are you even thinking about yourself and who is good for you? We are working on your self-love that is true, but self-love is about kindness toward yourself, not a self-absorption or ego centrism that everything is about you.

We already noted most all of another's behavior toward you is about them and NOT of you. So there's that. Then there is a self-absorbed thinking of only your side in the relationship - where you are NOT picking up the effects of what you are putting down.

Granted, when you are practicing conscious self-love - what you are putting down will be kindness, compassion, and consideration; but as we noted, so few are there yet. What are your thoughts about your impact on others? Is it mostly just a projection of what you are feeling/thinking inside? Can you not hang around them because you don't trust them (or you don't trust yourself), or can you not hang around them because they are lacking in some way? This kind of self-absorbed projection is not going to get you very far (unless you need to muster courage to leave an abusive, disrespectful relationship).

It could also be the case in this particular relationship you are being called to be a catalyst/model for your "good guy" and long-time friends who have not yet evolved. We can't just go around looking for all the high vibrating people for our "tribe." If so, I think we are going to be pretty lonely (and maybe question our growth and possibly stop for a while). I hate missing these access points!

We might also miss out on some decent experiences that could foster our and other's vibrations further. I am all for finding your tribe, I am just encouraging you to not overlook potential tribe mates (especially those from your youth that are not toxic) just because they haven't evolved yet. We are all equal and the same. You can learn valuable things about people AND yourself by continuing relationships. Experience is the key to life and growth! That is why we are here. It may also be that you are the tribe leader. ☺ I am also NOT saying you need to make it your mission to recruit people for your tribe and get them to raise consciousness (and actually that would be imposing your will on others - which is not ideal) but you can lead by your example of joy, peace, and good will.

Finally, Harville Hendrix says you can give yourself the love that heals, but it is easier to recognize what that is in the context of your relationships. It is my opinion (and truth for me) that loving yourself will change your vibration, but you don't have to lose relationships. You might inspire others to grow too, but again, this is not your job. Their journey unfolds as it does. You serve only as a model, not a boss or motivational speaker for the consciousness crew.

Magical thinking - seeking. Some other things were present at the outset of my spiritual journey - magical thinking (11:11) and seeking.

I think lots of these messages zero in on our ego to get us distracted. I think the posted platitudes play right in too. Right away I felt like I needed to find a different, more fitting job, a different more fitting partner, a different more fitting friend group. I knew there was something off, and I wanted to fix it. Well, here is a fresh insight you might have not heard yet.... what needed to change was me, not these other things. These stirrings that I believed I deserved a better job, a better partner, better friends - were all brought on by about a lack of conscious self-love and my unexplored subconscious messages spilling out.

I was projecting my lack of love onto all my external fillers - all of them, all at once! The discomfort I was feeling was a lesson - it is time to grow, but I misunderstood the target of growth. It wasn't to take place outside myself by replacing my surroundings - it was inside me - and right near my heart. No petal shining of a new job, husband, or friend was going to fix this.

I was taking all the beautiful instructional sentiments (really mostly platitudes) about seeking (in texts, Instagram, anywhere). I recall being in a small argument with my "good guy" and being on Instagram. I saw the Rumi quote, "What you are Seeking is Seeking You." I recall thinking oh, this fight AND this post right at this very moment - is a sign that my good guy is NOT really my soul mate, but my soul mate IS out there and I need to go looking for him pronto! I am a little embarrassed to even share that, but hopefully it is not as odd as it sounds as I typed it, and maybe will resonate with someone. There is nothing wrong with platitudes and a little encouragement in the form of a one-line sentence can really brighten your day, but if you are using these bits of information without going deeper (into it or you) you can easily get distracted by shiny outside petal things, or even fall completely off track. Did anyone else ever engage in that magical thinking, or spinning everything into deep and meaningful messages when looking for signs? I think we need to be careful and lay down some ground rules about Seeking and how God/the universe (however you refer to it) shares with us.

I must first start by telling you I am certain now the "seeking" is not something you are looking for outside of yourself. It is NOT a new partner, a new location, a new job, a new book, new church, new medicine, alternate healing modality, the perfect training course, or even the perfect guru. What do you think the one thing is you should be seeking?

That's right, your own love and self-acceptance - your truth within!! The perfect guru is to be found inside you! I would have also accepted you are seeking God (but you already have his love and have since before you are born AND because you and God are one) and we need to get you to see your role, worth, and value. That is the true purpose of your very life!! Learning who you are and why you are here. There is NO WAY someone else can tell you what that is (even if they have access to your Akashic Records ☺). You are in control. It is just going to have to be you.

If you are questioning or confused about literally any relationship right now - I firmly believe it is about you and not them. Your stir is your call to relate to yourself differently. Until you answer this call, all relationships will be confusing and you will have questions. Things like, well gee, he is super nice, but he isn't spiritual, or evolved, and he doesn't have a lot of money; my friends are kind and we have fun together and many shared experiences, but they don't do yoga or even know what Namaste means...... then we are at a signpost for YOUR internal growth - not external changes

Who Can We Trust in Raising Consciousness

Many people are seeking the truth: what to eat, how to think, was that a sign? Based on the amount of training manuals and differing opinions of experts I have no idea how we are not running in circles. Oh, wait ☺ When I accessed my consciousness curriculum hard core I tried very hard to find the right information; to be an informed seeker. To get to a place of conscious self-love we must see through some of the illusions and misinformation in our society so that we can make loving choices for ourselves and others.

You might've heard about spiritual journeys/awakening, soul growth, becoming conscious, awake, or woke. I think these are all different terms for the same thing. You may be happy with these ideas, or you may not think they are essential. I think it depends on your life path, which is certainly different for everyone. If you are to raise your consciousness in this life (I don't think that everybody is and that's okay), you may be feeling some stirrings at first but then discontent later if you are not exploring and making sense of the situation.

I don't think you have to be on a spiritual journey to cultivate your conscious self-love, but for me, the two became linked because part of my soul work is showing others about love and peace. For most people, the two paths (path of self-love and the path of spiritual growth) might be separate! I don't believe you must be on a spiritual journey to grow in your self-love; but I do believe you must grow your self-love if you want to grow in your spiritual awakening. I think the people on the spiritual path who do not possess self-love are bound to be spinning at this very moment.

I began my spiritual/consciousness raising about three years before my understanding of conscious self-love. I shined up a lot of my parts and I was looking good on the outside, but there was still much seeking and misunderstanding. This was because, for me, what needed to happen to tie everything together was to practice conscious self-love. For me, it was the magical mystery missing piece to all I had been working on for all that time, but still doing a little spinning myself. I wasn't listing to my soul and was focusing too much on external sources for my repairs and growth.

We must learn to hear and then use our internal truth as our guidance system. Of course we need teachers along the way, but even those with so much more experience still do not know our inside, our truth. We can follow them for a bit, but what needs to happen is a discovery of your truth within.

I am not even sure there are any universal truths at this point. We all come with our very own plan and curriculum to unfold. We cannot all respond in the same way. We all come with our genome (karma if you believe) and different family line experiences. We must realize the experiences we are having now (even seemingly similar experiences across people) are just not the same. This means that a standardized response or certain training way may not be effective for your type of lesson.

There are a few things to be recognized as constants: a love for others (and self), that we are here to serve, there is usually duality (two sides to things) and the two sides are needed to help us learn, and the importance of learning forgiveness. The world will be a much better place if people practice kindness, compassion (self-compassion), and gratitude too. The opposite of love is fear. People have great discussions about the role of the Ego and whether it is a friend or foe. How exactly do we handle our ego on our soul's love journey?

Let's start with something easy to see - some dichotomies (duality). I just watched a Netflix special on the hugely important and hugely researched and hugely positive evidenced facts of eliminating meat from your diet. As the research was being presented to me, I was saying, *yes, yes, Oh my Goodness, yes.* At the end I had made my shopping list and was looking up recipes. As I was frantically making my new diet plan, Netflix started another documentary and I didn't initially pay attention because I was so into my new recipes; however, this next documentary was on the hugely important and hugely researched and hugely positive evidenced facts of eating mostly meat for your diet. I got so mad I tossed my notes/diet plan and was just totally confused. I feel that any and every major trend right now has both sides to their research. I think only meditation is safe with no side effects lol.

People are wasting time arguing, trying to prove their ways. Way showers are showing up in all places! The problem is - the way is different for all people and there is no one size fits all model or curriculum. You need to turn within and feel what resonates with you. Trust yourself (through loving yourself) to do what feels correct as long as it does. Only you know the truth and your truth is within you!! If someone told me this a few years ago I would've been annoyed and kept looking for some absolute truths to follow. This was a time of low self-love for me.

Who can you trust? The answer to this question is YOU. I am sharing this to help you see the importance and value of loving and trusting yourself. So many great things happened for me with my self-love growth including trusting myself. Everything became so much less confusing and I began to answer my own questions and trust my answers within. The words in this book are meant to help you heal, but in all honesty, only you can be your healer. A therapist or coach or partner can help you, but it really does start and end with you. Only you can unpack your journey. As you are reading this book, the information comes from my research and experiences. My current ending points on these issues that resonate with me. As with all information you consume, please read with your critical eye and accept what resonates (feels right and after exploring within you still feels right) with you; and disregard what does not. I am not claiming to be an expert. Anyone who claims themselves an expert - should not be taken too seriously anyway. They would likely have too much ego to see clearly.

I believe the most important strategy to heal yourself and help others, is to start practicing conscious self-love. Nhat Hanh (A-Z Quotes) said, "The moment you understand the importance of loving yourself, you will stop hurting others." This is the way we will change the world. Every day you practice conscious self-love and give out your love and peace you make every single person you interact with better. What an important and positive journey you are on. Thank you for letting me sit with you during this part! Keep up the great work!

Resources

Please check out these resources I found helpful. Please email me for more information at: **drjillblackwell@gmail.com** and **consciousself-love.com**

Resources for Peace

- All the books and everything by Dr. Joe Dispenza https://drjoedispenza.com/,
- A free meditation by Dr. Dispenza https://www.youtube.com/watch?v=VidbmBHK08k
- Deepak Chopra (website) https://www.deepakchopra.com/
- The app: Insight Timer
- The book: *A Course in Miracles (ACIM)* by Helen Schuman
- ACIM website: https://acimi.com/a-course-in-miracles/text/chapter-1/atonement-and-miracles
- The book: *Be Here Now* by Ram Dass
- The book: *The Power of Now* by Eckhart Tolle
- The book: *The Four Agreements* by Don Miguel Ruiz
- The book: *The Way of Rest* by Jeff Foster
- The book: *Real Magic* by Wayne Dyer

Resources for Self-Compassion and Kindness

- Kristen Neff (website) https://self-compassion.org/
- The book: *The Power of Kindness: The Unexpected Benefits of Leading a Compassionate Life* by Piero Ferrucci
- The book: *How Can I Help?* By Ram Dass & Paul Gorman

Resources for Self-Care

- Instagram Account of Anita Moorjani (@anitamoorjani).
- All books by Cheryl Richardson, especially *The Art of Extreme Self-Care*

Resources and Affirmations for Body Healing

- Marissa Peer https://marisapeer.com/
- A wonderful healing tool by Marissa https://www.youtube.com/watch?v=egbiGhAiN8E
- Everything by Louise Hay https://www.louisehay.com/
- The Healing Spectrums with Thomas Gates. Video about how to do self-treatment https://www.youtube.com/watch?v=dyPxB4q9-Mg
- Thomas Gates' website https://thomasgates.com/

Resources about Parenting

- Instagram Account of Dr. Shefali Tsabary (@doctorshefali).
- The book: *Giving the Love that Heals* by Dr. Harville Hendrix and Dr. Helen LaKelly Hunt https://harvilleandhelen.com/
- The book: Love: A Story about Who You Truly Are by Anita Moorjani
- The book: *Conscious Parenting* by Dr. Shefali Tsabary https://drshefali.com/
- The book: *The Five Love Languages of Children* by Dr. Gary Chapman and Ross Campbell (also for adolescents and adults!)
- The website and programs of Artie Wu https://presidelife.com/
- The book: *The Care and Feeding of Indigo Children* by Doreen Virtue
- Danu Morigan https://www.daughtersofnarcissisticmothers.com/danu-morrigan-about-me/
- The book: *The New Peoplemaking* by Virginia Satir
- The book: Everyday Blessings by Myla and Jon Kabat-Zinn
- The book: The Awakened Family: How to Raise Empowered, Resilient, and Conscious Children by Dr. Shefali Tsabary

Resources for Relationships

- Imago Therapy https://imagorelationships.org/
- Dr. Margaret Paul Relationship Course https://www.flourishtogether.com/
- The book: **Inner Bonding** by Margaret Paul (and all her other books!)

Resources about Life and the Universe

- The book: A Message of Hope from the Angels by Lorna Byrne
- The book: *The Gentle Way I and II*: by Tom Moore
- Marianne Williamson (obviously) https://marianne.com/
- The book: *Ask and It Is Given* by Ester and Jerry Hicks
- The book: *The Astonishing Power of Emotions* by Ester and Jerry Hicks
- The book: *12 Rules for Life* by Dr. Jordan B. Petersen
- H. Hendrix/Helen LaKelly Hunt: https://harvilleandhelen.com/
- DailyOM (offers classes and messages daily) https://www.dailyom.com/
- The book: *Dying to be Me* by Anita Moorjani
- The Heal Documentary by Kelly Noonan Gores

Resources for Emotions and Thoughts (anxiety and the feelings!)

- The book: *Senses of the Soul: Emotional Therapy for Strength, Healing, and Guidance* by GuruMeherKhalsa
- Master John Douglas's 3-minute emotional repair meditations https://www.youtube.com/watch?v=P793vlr9bi0
- Client Centered Therapy Information: https://positivepsychology.com/client-centered-therapy/
- Christy Whitman *Watch Your Words* program https://www.youtube.com/watch?v=Ck0Esnd9lzQ
- The book: *Feeling good: The New Mood Therapy* by Dr. David Burns

Resources for Prayers and Encouragement

- The book: *Praying for your addicted Loved* One by Sharron Cosby
- The book: *Illuminata: A Return to Prayer* by Marianne Williamson
- The book: *The Prayer Coin* by Elisa Morgan
- The book: *When Someone You Love Suffers from Depression or Mental Illness* by Cecil Murphy
- The book: *When Someone You Love Abuses Drugs or Alcohol* by Cecil Murphy
- The book: *The Care and Feeding of Indigo Children* by Doreen Virtue
- The book: *The Power of Eight* by Lynne McTaggert

Resources for Subconscious Repairs/Other Helpers :)

- Master John Douglas: https://masterangels.org/ See book by Dr. Richard Sarnat describing the Medical Miracles: Medical Insights Gained from Observations of Angelic Reformation (Book One)
- Inner Bonding Self-Healing Process - Drs. Paul & Chopick https://www.innerbonding.com/
- Victoria Benoit, M.C   https://www.extraordinaryoutcomes.com/
- Dr. Lisa Janelle https://theshiftnetwork.com/
- The Dear Mother Meera https://mothermeerafoundationusa.org/
- Thomas Gates.   https://thomasgates.com/
- Michael Golzmane: Here is his website http://www.clearandconnect.com/ Try any of the AMAZING and free videos he has on YouTube they WILL change your life :) https://www.youtube.com/watch?v=WuAXGdrBTCs (for health and debt karma) https://www.youtube.com/watch?v=IXOEw9-YWFg (for stress and anxiety)

Conscious Self-Love Promoting Activities Index

Strategy for Triggers Activity…………………………………………….42

I Love My Parts Activity……………………………………………..…..47

Self-Awareness Activity……………………………………………...90

What Do YOU Want to Do Activity…………………....…………….…96

Greeting the Feelings Activity……………….............……………….121

Process the Feelings Activity…………………………..……………..125

Managing Expectations Activity……...…………………………….…132

  Catch and Release Thoughts/Emotions Activity……....……………..165

  Catch and Refute Thoughts/Emotions Activity……....………………170

Worry Buster Activity………………………..……………………….173

Banana Breath Activity…………..…………………..……………….186

Hammock Breath Activity…………………………………………….186

Swing Breath Activity……………………..………………………….186

Body Fix-It Breath Activity……………………….….....……………188

Judge Busters Activity…………………………..…….……………..197

Practice Choice Questions with Self Activity…………………..…….203

Practice Choice Questions with Others Activity………………..……204

  Likes/Dislikes/OhHellNo List Activity……………………..…… …..204

Unzip your Heart Activity………………………………………….….205

Open Your Heart Chakra Activity…………………………………….205

Conscious Self-Love Promoting Activities Index (continued)

Mirror Work Activity…………………………………………..…………..206

Picture Work Activity…………………………………………….…………207

Love Letter Activity……………………………………………….………..207

Loving Kindness Activity……..………………………..…………………..207

Start with No Activity……………………………….…………….………..214

Scale of Gratitude Activity……………………………………..…………..215

Happy Place Activity……………………………...…………………….…..216

Gratitude List Activity………………………………..……………..………217

Gratitude Mediation Activity……………………………...…………….…..218

Forgiveness List Activities………………………………..………….……..221

Subconscious Redo Visualization Activity……...…………………..……..229

20 Pleasures Activity…………..……………………………………….…..237

BIBLIOGRAPHY

A Course in Miracles. (1992, 2007). The Foundation for Inner Peace, 448 Ignacio Blvd. Bld. #306, Novato, CA 94949

Byrne, L. (2018). Angels at My Fingertips: The Sequel to Angels in My Hair: How Angels and our Loved Ones Help Guide Us. Coronet Books

Burns, David. (2008). Feeling Good: The New Mood Therapy. Avon Books

Chopick, E. & Paul, M. (2015). The Healing Your Aloneness Workbook: The 6-Step Inner Bonding Process for Healing Yourself and Your Relationships. Echo Point Books and Media

Chopra, Deepak. (2018). You are the Universe: Discovering Your Cosmic Self and Why it Matters. Harmony

Chopra, Deepak. (2019). Metahuman: Unleashing Your Infinite Potential. Harmony

Dalai Lama. (n.d.). AZQuotes.com. Retrieved January 25, 2020, from AZQuotes.com. Web site: https://azquotes.com/quote/575840

Dass, R.& Dass, R. (2014). Polishing the Mirror: How to Live from Your Spiritual Heart. Sounds True

Dass, R. (1971). Be Here Now. Harmony.

Dispenza, J. (2014). You are the Placebo: Making Your Mind Matter. Hay House (and accompanying meditations!)

Hay Louise. (1984). Heal Your Body. Hay House

Hay, Louise. (1984). You Can Heal Your Life. Hay House

Hellinger, Bert. (2001). Love's Own Truths: Bonding and Balancing in Close Relationships. Zeig, Tucker & Theisen

Hellinger, Bert. (2011). Laws of Healing: Getting well, staying well. Hellinger Publications

Hellinger, Bert (2014). Looking Into the Souls of Children: The Hellinger Pedagogy in Action. Hellinger Publications

Hendrix, H., & LaKelly Hunt, Helen. (1998). Giving The Love That Heals. Atria Books

Hicks, Esther & Jerry. (2001). The Astonishing Power of Emotions: Let Your Feelings Be Your Guide. Hay House

Lipton, Bruce. (2016). The Biology of Belief 10th Anniversary Edition: Unleashing the Power of Consciousness, Matter & Miracles. Hay House

Moorjani, A. (2014). Dying To Be Me: My Journey from Cancer, to Near Death, to True Healing. Hay House

Moorjani, A. (2017). Love: A story about who you truly are. Nick of Time Printing

Moorjani, A. (@anitamoorjani). (2019, December 30). If you are going to relax in a bathtub for an hour post.

Nhat Hanh. (n.d.). AZQuotes.com. Retrieved December 25, 2020 from AZQuotes.com. Web site: https://azquotes.com/author/6211-Nhat_Hanh

Pearl. A. (2009). Bert Hellinger Speaks on Forgiveness. (https://www.annieblockpearl.com/bert-hellinger-speaks-on-forgiveness/

Paul, Margaret. (1992). Inner Bonding: Becoming a Loving Adult to Your Inner Child. Harper One

Paul, Margaret (2019). The Inner Bonding Workbook: Six Steps to Healing Yourself and Connecting with Your Divine Guidance. Reveal Press

Peer, Marisa (2018). I Am Enough: Mark Your Mirror And Change Your Life

Real, Terrence. (2002). How Can I Get Through to You? Closing the Intimacy Gap Between Men and Women. Scribner

Real, Terrence. (2008). The New Rules of Marriage: What you Need to Know to Make Love Work. Ballantine Books

Richardson, Cheryl. (2009). The Art of Extreme Self-Care. Hay House

Ruiz, D.M. (1997). The Four Agreements: A Practical Guide to Personal Freedom (A Toltec Wisdom Book). Amber-Allen Publishing

Tsabary, S. (@doctorshefali). (2020, January 3). The One Toxic Person You May Need to Let Go Of

Tsabary, S. (2010). The Conscious Parent: Transforming Ourselves, Empowering Our Children Paperback. Namaste Publishing

Tsabary, S. (2017). The Awakened Family: How to Raise Empowered, Resilient, and Conscious Children. Penguin Books

Weil, Andrew. (2013). Spontaneous Happiness: A New Path to Emotional Well-Being. Little, Brown Spark

Whitman, Christy. (2015). The Art of Having It All: A Woman's Guide To Unlimited Abundance. Micro

Dr. Blackwell, PhD, LPC is an award-winning professor of psychology and licensed clinical practitioner with a unique talent in taking another's perspective and promoting feelings of personal adequacy and empowerment. She provides counsel in a kind, compassionate, and growth promoting manner. Dr. Jill is trained in the Healing Spectrums Method and is a Practical Meditation Teacher. Dr. Blackwell received both her PhD and a Master of Arts Degree from DePaul University. Dr. Blackwell published two popular audio CDs: *Stress Management 101: Imagery Exercises to Promote Sleep, Creativity, and Overall Health and Stress Management; and Stress Management 202: Imagery Exercises to Promote Relaxation, Coping, and Overall Health*; and three books. Her book, *The Dissertation Strategy - Instruction Manual* was voted #1 of the list of 46 Best PhD Degree Books of All Time by Book Authority. Check out: **www.consciousself-love.com**

Made in the USA
Monee, IL
02 February 2020